WARNING SIGNS

How to Protect Your Kids from Becoming Victims or Perpetrators of Violence and Aggression

BRIAN D. JOHNSON, PHD, AND LAURIE D. BERDAHL, MD

CHICAGO REVIEW PRESS

Copyright © 2016 by Brian D. Johnson and Laurie D. Berdahl
All rights reserved
Published by Chicago Review Press Incorporated
814 North Franklin Street
Chicago, Illinois 60610
ISBN 978-1-61373-042-3

Library of Congress Cataloging-in-Publication Data

Names: Johnson, Brian D., 1962 October 3– | Berdahl, Laurie D., author.
Title: Warning signs : how to protect your kids from becoming victims or
    perpetrators of violence and aggression / Brian D. Johnson, PhD, and
    Laurie D. Berdahl, MD.
Description: Chicago, IL : Chicago Review Press, 2016. | Includes
    bibliographical references and index. | Description based on print version
    record and CIP data provided by publisher; resource not viewed.
Identifiers: LCCN 2016000338 (print) | LCCN 2015048726 (ebook) | ISBN
    9781613730430 (pdf) | ISBN 9781613730454 (epub) | ISBN 9781613730447
    (Kindle) | ISBN 9781613730423 (paperback)
Subjects: LCSH: Parenting. | Parent and child. | Family life education. |
  BISAC: FAMILY & RELATIONSHIPS / General. | PSYCHOLOGY /
    Developmental /
    Child. | PSYCHOLOGY / Developmental / Adolescent.
Classification: LCC HQ755.8 (print) | LCC HQ755.8 .J643 2016 (ebook) | DDC
    649/.1—dc23
LC record available at http://lccn.loc.gov/2016000338

Cover design: John Yates at Stealworks
Interior design: PerfecType, Nashville, TN
Interior layout: NordCompo

Printed in the United States of America
5 4 3 2 1

For the millions of victimized youth and the people trying to help them, and for those working to protect children from violence and aggression

Contents

Introduction

Charlotte was a free spirit who jumped, skipped, and ran to the beat of her own drum. She was boldness, she was mischief, and she was love. Her crazy antics made us laugh daily. Her insight and curiosity amazed us. We miss her singing loudly with the car radio, hearing her feet always at a run, never at a walk, down the hallway in our home. . . . She was and continues to be our brightest star in the sky.

—Parents of six-year-old Charlotte Helen Bacon,
a first grader who was murdered at Sandy Hook
Elementary School in Newtown, Connecticut

Young Charlotte was one of twenty-six children and adults killed at Sandy Hook Elementary in December 2012, and her parents are among many forced to wrestle with their anguish after living through the nightmare. While our nation struggles to understand the heinous acts of Adam Lanza in Newtown and numerous young mass shooters since, many parents are asking, "What is going on, and what can be done about it? How can we protect our children?"

Some parents worry that a troubled youth they know could harm people, and others have to accept that their child did the unthinkable. Perhaps wanting to warn the public, Adam's father, Peter Lanza, said, "I want people to be afraid of the fact that this could happen to them."

Are events like Newtown usually preceded by warning signs that could have been acted upon to prevent tragedy? What factors lead young people to commit senseless acts of violence and are there warning signs for those? Research points to many underlying risk factors, and yes, there are often warning signs before young people harm themselves or others. You'll learn about these warning signs as you read this book.

When a young person commits an atrocity, many of us want to think that he or she had a mental illness and there was nothing anyone could have done to predict the event, because it makes disturbing scenarios more palatable. This would indicate that there's not much we can do—but fortunately, that's usually not the case. This book discusses warning signs relating to mental and emotional health, including those shown by Adam Lanza, but you'll learn about other more significant risk factors for aggressive and violent behaviors, which, when recognized, can prompt productive, early intervention.

While we frequently hear news of events that we fear most, such as children being shot in schools or abducted, relatively few children will be victims of these. However, most American kids and young (or emerging) adults ages eighteen to twenty-four are victims or perpetrators of other forms of aggression and violence, with far-reaching consequences.

Aggression is attempting to inflict or inflicting physical or psychological harm to someone by physical, verbal, or situational means, or dominating someone by using power. Examples are taunting, manipulating, threatening, stealing, cheating, humiliating, excluding, and inducing fear. Many of these behaviors are part of bullying and relational aggression, which affect up to 30% of our children. We'll show you how to help your children survive and even thrive in the midst of it.

More severe forms of physical aggression—such as physical assault with or without a weapon, threats with a weapon, vandalism, rape, murder, and child and animal abuse—are considered violence. Cutting and suicide are forms of violence against oneself. Compared to any other age group, adolescents are the most frequent victims of violence.

How many youth are victimized? Here are some statistics for you. According to a 2013 study in *JAMA (Journal of the American Medical Association) Pediatrics*, more than 40% of kids up to age seventeen were physically assaulted at least once in the prior year. During that same period, almost 60% were exposed to violence, crime, or abuse as victims or witnesses, and about 25% were victimized by robbery, theft, or vandalism. In 2013, almost six hundred thousand young people up to age twenty-four were treated for physical assault injuries, and more than two hundred thousand of these people were younger than eighteen.

A hundred years ago, infectious diseases were top causes of death in children. Today, children are slain by murder much more often than disease, and are murdered disproportionately more often than adults. While homicide isn't a top ten cause of death in adults over age forty-five, it's the third leading cause for one- to four-year-olds. In 2013, more than fifty-two hundred children and young adults were murdered and almost nine hundred were younger than fifteen years old.

Reports indicate that of the one in five females who are raped in the United States, more than 40% are under the age of eighteen when first raped and more than 12% are under age eleven. More than 27% of male rape victims were ten years old or younger when first raped. Sexual assault and dating violence harm even higher numbers of youth. Most sexual violence goes unreported.

Suicide is the ultimate violence against oneself, and can sometimes follow cruelty by other kids. Audrie Pott, a bright, lovely fifteen-year-old girl, took her own life after fellow students shared pictures of her being sexually assaulted by three sixteen-year-old boys whom she considered friends. The boys and other students tormented and humiliated her before she hanged herself. In 2013, 17% of high school students seriously considered killing themselves, and 8% attempted it. More than fifty-two hundred teens and young adults died by suicide that year. We'll provide preventive measures against suicide as well as sexual assault, rape, social media perils, and bullying.

Deplorably, millions of children begin their lives as victims of domestic violence, abuse, and neglect at home. According to a joint report by the Children's Bureau and the US Department of Health and Human Services, an estimated 679,000 American children were neglected or abused at the hands of caretakers in 2013, while the study published in *JAMA Pediatrics* estimated that one in four children are victims of maltreatment at some time during childhood. Associated costs are estimated at $124 billion each year. More than fifteen hundred children died from abuse or neglect in 2013, most under the age of three. Millions are also victimized by domestic or family violence, witnessing parents violently mistreating another parent, romantic partner, child, or other family member. Many also endure being bullied by a sibling. Children who experience maltreatment and home violence are at increased risk of being victimized in other ways and of becoming aggressive and violent.

As many youth are victimized, many also perpetrate aggression and violence. Cynthia Alvarez was found guilty of murder in her mother's strangulation death and in the death of her stepfather, who was killed with a baseball bat and knife; the killings occurred after Alvarez, then fifteen years old, lay in wait for her mother to come home. Alvarez testified that she and her sixteen-year-old boyfriend, who was also charged, went shopping for Halloween party supplies in the vehicle in which her dead mother's body lay. The Bureau of Justice Statistics indicates that children killing parents is a fast-growing type of homicide. Although it's fortunate that aggression against parents rarely goes that far, research shows that up to 17% of adolescents physically assault their parents.

Rates of violent crimes committed by male youths are lower than in the 1990s, but violent crime by girls—particularly assault—is increasing at alarming rates. It's important to note that many youth crimes such as theft go unreported, and that detrimental, insidious forms of relational aggression aren't included in crime statistics.

What causes some kids to seriously harm people while others wouldn't think of it? And how can we help kids protect themselves? This book is about the many risk factors for becoming victims or perpetrators of violence and aggression. These include dangerous friendships, social isolation or rejection, sexualization, drug and alcohol use, harmful media exposure, access to weapons, mental illness, ineffective parenting, home violence, and perilous thoughts and emotions like entitlement, rage, and hate. All these common threats to our youth constitute increasing challenges for parents.

Parents today may fear their children's reactions to interventions or face entitled attitudes and aggressive manipulation. During a therapy session, a single mother described telling her sixteen-year-old son that she didn't want him to go to an unsupervised party. Her son screamed, "Lady, you just don't get it, do you? I know my rights and will do what I want—back off!" He then approached, glared into her eyes, and slammed the door as he stormed out. She found herself walking on eggshells, trying not to "set him off," and he often talked her out of setting limits or rules. We'll discuss thoughts and emotions that lead to self-destructive or aggressive behaviors and how to defuse them. Suggestions for teaching problem solving, anger management, empathy, coping, and other protective shields are given.

The good news is that research and clinical experience point to a multitude of things that parents can do to protect and guide their children. Our personal experiences and hunger for solutions to societal violence led us to this writing project. This is the first book of practical parenting advice that provides parents with warning signs and risk factors so they can help prevent their children from becoming victims and perpetrators. This book discusses how to strengthen children for the challenges of growing up in today's aggressive and violent world.

Risk factors are things that make someone more susceptible to a condition (for example, smoking, obesity, and hypertension are risk factors for heart attacks). Warning signs are things that suggest an imminent threat (for heart attacks, they include squeezing chest pain, difficulty breathing, and arm or neck pain). As with heart attacks, there are risk factors and warning signs for violence that, if recognized and reported, can be acted upon to prevent tragedy.

Chapters are organized to address parenting practices, types of aggression and violence, and risk and protective factors. Throughout, we'll provide preventive measures and warning signs illustrated by news and personal stories that can aid decisions to act. You'll find ways to help kids heed your advice to recognize and deal with danger and talk about violent events. Because it can be hard to decide what to say to kids, or how to say it, we will provide suggestions in *finding the words* sidebars. We will also provide advice on approaching other parents when concerned about them or their children.

Our suggestions are based on research and clinical and personal experiences. Data are from reputable sources such as the Centers for Disease Control and Prevention (CDC), National Crime Prevention Council, American Psychological Association, American Academy of Pediatrics, National Institutes of Health and Mental Health, World Health Organization, National Gang Center, US Departments of Justice, Secret Service, and Federal Bureau of Investigation.

We think you'll find that our combined credentials and experience provide a unique set of vantage points on managing risks to your young, adolescent, and emerging adult children. As a husband-wife team of professionals, we have more than forty years of combined experience working with parents and children. Brian is a child psychologist, university professor, and parenting researcher and expert, and Laurie is a retired board-certified obstetrician-gynecologist and a writer and speaker on parenting and adolescent health.

But we're not just professionals—we're parents! We feel fortunate to have raised two strong, caring children together in the face of today's unprecedented parenting challenges. By using our evidence-based suggestions, you can reduce your child's chances of having emotional and behavioral problems and of becoming victims or perpetrators while making your life much easier and happier.

In this book, you'll also read about ways that aggression and violence can be prevented and mitigated nationally. We believe that parents, united in priorities and actions, possess the highest capacity to create powerful solutions that would benefit our families and our country.

1

Disconnected and Troubled Home Lives Linked to Danger

He was there for you, and he was the best listener I ever met. I realize now that that was because he didn't want to talk, and he was hiding.

—Sue Klebold about her son Dylan, one of two
Columbine High School mass murderers

Close parent-child relationships are one of the bulwarks against suicide, homicide, and other violent behaviors. On April 20, 1999, seventeen-year-old Dylan Klebold and eighteen-year-old Eric Harris murdered twelve of their classmates and a teacher before taking their own lives. After the heartbreak of pivotal events, parents who may have thought they had good relationships with their kids find out they weren't good enough. For the Klebolds, in what must be agonizing retrospect, one-way communication didn't reflect closeness with Dylan or insight into his life. The investigation revealed evidence of depression and rage in Dylan in the months leading up to the horrific event, as well as significant time spent with a very disturbed friend, Eric.

Events such as these spark questions about how parenting may raise the risk of violent behavior, or how it can be powerful enough to prevent it. Although parents can't predict or prevent all the ills that befall children, qualities of parenting and home life can reduce the risk that children will be affected by aggression and violence. This chapter will illuminate these parenting and home-life factors.

A good summary of how aspects of parenting can diminish youth aggression is found in the *Handbook of Child Psychology*. In it, experts state, "A variety of family interventions designed to improve parents' discipline strategies, the quality of parent-child relationships, and parents' monitoring and supervision of children have proven efficacious in reducing aggressive behavior."

A low-quality parent-child relationship is, in fact, strongly predictive of antisocial and violent behavior, delinquency (repetitive antisocial or criminal behavior in a minor who parents can't control), and adult criminality. Juvenile delinquents are aggressive, often lying and manipulating people. Affectionate, supportive connections with kids, monitoring their activities, and using certain research-backed discipline methods all greatly decrease the chances they'll be aggressive or violent. Luckily, these same parenting elements also protect children from victimization.

After exploring warning signs of parent-child connections needing improvement, we'll discuss types of discipline and monitoring that can cause trouble or protect. Then we'll review troubled home lives that make kids much more likely to be victims as well as perpetrators. While you read, you'll notice that we mention links between parenting elements and other risk and protective factors for violence and aggression (such as mental health, peers, and substance abuse) that will be explored later.

Some readers may skim or even skip this chapter, anxious to get to the methods for protecting their children from specific situations. But without the research-backed foundations here, using all the forthcoming knowledge may be ineffective. For example, even if you've learned the warning signs for youth violence and tell your son that you'd like to hear about his troubles, without a close connection he might not tell you. Even though you've followed advice on aggression prevention, without a history of *inductive discipline* (see page 13), your child will be less likely to resist a friend's idea to make some quick bucks by stealing. And even when you do everything else well, it can still be hard to know what your children are struggling with and doing with friends, so you'll need to know how to monitor them adequately. In other words, if you don't know and act on the warning signs related to connections, discipline, and monitoring, you could follow suggestions on various realms of danger in this book and still have little or no influence on your children's actions and what happens to them.

Warning Signs of Disconnection Between You and Your Child

A close parent-child connection is a key foundation for being a strong influence in your children's lives. Strong relationships protect kids against becoming victims by promoting mental health while reducing risk factors such as drug and alcohol abuse and delinquent peer influence. They help kids cope with the common stressors of growing up today, a likely boost to protection from becoming violent or aggressive.

A close connection starts early—as infants and toddlers, children need sensitive responses to their needs. This promotes attachment, a beginning to your relationship that protects against behavioral and emotional problems.

What are some hallmarks of good parent-child relationships from preschool through adolescence? You both show affection, regard, and acceptance toward one another; you're involved and interested in their lives; your kids trust you'll be there when needed to help with problems and do what's best for them; you have mostly positive interactions; you both care about what happens to each other; and you're comfortable and enjoy being together. If you can't say these things are true, it's a warning sign that you don't know your child well enough. Along with the following other warning signs, it means that you most likely have, or will soon have, relationship problems—and that's dangerous.

Not Talking Together Often or Having Trouble Doing So

Pleasant conversations are the simplest way to connect and are an essential element of close relationships. Frequent short, friendly chats help you get to know kids as they change, make you seem interested and approachable, and increase chances for important lifesaving conversations. Difficulty talking together indicates disconnection and is a warning sign that your relationship needs work. You'll know you both need help communicating if:

- You have trouble knowing what to say.
- You mostly talk about solving problems instead of lighthearted, enjoyable topics.
- One or both of you feels uncomfortable when together.
- You don't know each other's likes, dislikes, fears, and friends.
- Your conversations generally turn into arguments or teasing.

Here are proven ideas for getting kids to talk and to build your relationship:

- With older kids, minimize asking questions, because this tends to feel like an interrogation and may shut them down. Just start by commenting about something funny or happy until they say something.
- Talk about their interests more often than yours.
- Don't tease them.
- Kids need more time to respond, so leave pauses.
- Occasionally repeat back a version of what they said without interrupting so they know you're listening.
- Look for opportunities to talk about feelings by noticing when they're expressed and when they're not directly expressed (think about their situations and ask yourself what you would feel like if it happened to you, and then start discussing that feeling).

Not surprisingly, there's a new impediment to communication: frequent separate media use. Now children and parents can be home together yet very isolated. You can help by making rules that limit media use and keep you connected.

Unrealistic Expectations of Children

Negative emotions or disregard for children often begins when parents expect things that kids aren't old enough or developed enough to do, or do well consistently. Parents can misinterpret failure to meet expectations as intentional misbehavior, meanness, or even rejection. This can make children lose trust and affection for a parent while promoting emotional and behavioral problems and damaging relationships. Understanding whether expectations for childhood abilities and achievement are realistic is therefore crucial to maintaining a close connection, and having unrealistic expectations is a warning sign that your relationship will suffer.

It's common to have unrealistic expectations for behavior during early childhood. An example is misunderstanding the emotional communication normally used by infants and toddlers to get attention and needs met. Because they're too young to regulate their emotions and haven't developed verbal skills, crying, screaming, whining, and fussing are normal. Toddlers often say no and disobey by choice as part of a healthy developmental stage of gaining independence, not to make parents mad. Some parents are unable to tolerate this, heightening the chance of abuse. When parents overreact with anger or punish small children for normal developmental behaviors, it erodes the connection and the child's future behavior.

Another cause of harmful overreactions that erode early parent-child relationships is unrealistic expectations for children's ability to obey parents. One- and two-year-olds aren't developed enough to follow commands consistently or to follow a discipline plan. By the time kids are three or four, they can do what we ask only about *half* of the time. On average, well-adjusted children aged five to seven can be expected to follow our requests about 70% of the time.

Unrealistically high expectations of a school-age child's performance in school and in activities like sports can lead to depression, anxiety, low self-esteem, and rebellion. Thus, you can harm your child by expecting more than he or she can reasonably (or wants to) achieve or by emphasizing performance over the quality of your connection.

About grades, we feel compelled to comment further. Although good-enough grades and school engagement are protective factors against criminal activity and victimization, focusing on achievement scores and grades can discount the higher protective value of student character and life skills. Grade pressure also increases cheating, depression, and anxiety while lowering another protective factor: involvement in extracurricular activities. Cheaters are often aggressive (they steal, lie, and manipulate) to get ahead.

Parents often seem falsely reassured by good grades, leading them to ignore problems like disconnection, drug use, entitled attitudes, and truancy as long as grades stay high. Klebold and Harris were honor roll students. When children grow up with emotional problems, bad habits, and dangerous character traits, good grades can end up worthless in the big picture.

It can be difficult to know what to expect a child to be able to do and by what age. Interested readers can find an extensive list of realistic expectations for behavior and skills for children of all ages in our prior book, 7 *Skills for Parenting Success*.

Overreactions and Uncontrolled Anger

Healthy emotional expression is an important part of close connections. When a child isn't allowed to express emotions, or a parent takes charged emotions personally, it can damage their relationship and increase aggressive behavior. Encouraging kids to express emotions helps them deal with stress nonaggressively and promotes mental health. Although small children can't, older kids gradually learn to express emotions well by watching adults around them. You can help by looking for signs of distress and helping them describe and talk about their feelings. We'll discuss handling uncontrolled youth anger in chapter 3. For now, let's talk about uncontrolled emotions in parents.

Luckily, it's good for parents to show how they feel about how things are going, because it aids coping, and it's beneficial for youth to see how their actions can hurt our feelings as part of developing empathy. Plus, too much bottled-up, unexpressed anger can create other problems—depression, substance use, and child abuse. But it's how we express emotion that matters.

Expressing uncontrolled anger toward children is a warning sign that disconnection has happened or will happen. What does this look like? Yelling, belittling or making fun of people, putting them down, being sarcastic, using profanity, throwing things, physically threatening (slamming doors, pumping fists) or harming others, or destroying objects. Also, if you find yourself thinking that you overreacted, your anger was probably unhealthy.

When you've had enough and feel like lashing out, take a breath and share feelings with calm but direct speech by saying, "I feel . . . when you . . . " Be specific about what your kids did that hurt or was wrong and what they need to do about it. Get an apology, but keep in mind that apologies mean very little when behavior doesn't change; actions speak louder than words.

To stay calm, try asking yourself what you were thinking about the situation that made you upset. You see, what we *think* leads to how we *act* and *feel*; our reactions and feelings don't just pop out of nowhere—they come from what we are thinking about. And sometimes what we think about a child's behavior isn't true. For example, if you feel your blood boiling when you think that your son never does what you ask, check if this is true (it probably isn't). If you feel teary when you think your daughter is misbehaving because she doesn't care about you, ask yourself what evidence you have for that thought. Is she just mad or misbehaving, both of which don't have anything to do with caring about you?

Inaccurate negative thoughts about our kids can cause us to over-react with anger, feel depressed, or even hesitate when we need to act to protect our children. Overreacting to children's behaviors erodes our relationships and teaches them to overreact. So try making it a habit to check your thoughts about your child's behavior before reacting. If you find yourself regularly crying while sharing hurt feelings or still have uncontrolled anger, it's a warning sign that you need professional advice.

Exaggerations also defeat relationships by causing kids to lose trust in our ability to fairly judge them and the situation at hand. Exaggerations are used to make something seem extreme and persuade people to act, but because they usually don't reflect reality, listeners may tune out. All-or-none statements and ones containing the words *always*, *never*, *every*, *none*, *all*, *any*, and *worst* are examples: "You're the worst . . . " (certainly someone in the world does something even more poorly), and "She never does anything without me asking" (surely she has picked up her clothes from the floor because she needed them). Your relationships will benefit from avoiding exaggerations and helping children recognize and avoid using them as they grow older.

Unhealthy Responses to Conflict

Conflict is normal in every family, but when it doesn't regularly get resolved equitably and nonaggressively, it erodes relationships, causes emotional distress, and teaches children to approach conflicts aggressively. Research clearly shows that parents arguing in front of kids is a significant stressor that impairs social and emotional development and undermines kids' ability to resolve problems. If it happens, make sure your kids know it isn't their fault.

Using *nonaggressive conflict resolution* in the family has the added benefit of teaching kids how to do it. Children need to learn to resolve conflicts with others nonaggressively so they won't get taken advantage of or get depressed or violent. Doing this face-to-face is best, but you can do this talking on the phone or even by text if it feels more comfortable. Here are some basics of nonaggressive conflict resolution:

- Start by saying, "You seem upset about this. Let's talk it out to find a solution or a way to make it better," or "Are you upset at me (are we OK)? Let's talk."
- Allow everyone to calmly explain their views, and apologize for parts played in the conflict (that lowers other people's defensiveness).
- Use statements that begin with "I think . . . " and "I feel . . . " Thoughts and feelings are part of the person expressing them,

so they're hard to argue or get upset with. Show empathy: "I feel bad that your feelings got hurt."
- Make compromises where everyone gets a little of what they want.
- Don't allow disrespect or teasing.
- Escalation of anger means that talking should cease until everyone regains composure.

When doing this with your kids, saying, "I feel upset when you talk to me that way" will more likely keep communication going as compared to saying, "You make me mad when you talk to me that way," since your child can't argue that you don't feel upset. Saying, "I think you might change your mind later," or "I feel afraid when you do that," instead of, "Listen to me because I know better" helps kids understand your feelings, thoughts, and needs.

Also, model nonaggressive conflict resolution skills with coparents or other adults: let your kids observe you talking calmly about problems and coming up with mutually agreed-upon solutions.

Unproductive View of Parental Love

You may have heard this said about parenting: "All you need to do is love them." But this enticing, simplistic view appears inadequate in today's complex, aggressive, and violent world. Besides, love can be expressed and interpreted differently by parents and kids. What some parents consider loving behavior can come across to children as rejection (like when parents practice tough love).

Giving children optional items that parents wanted but couldn't have when growing up can feel like a loving gesture, and seems to be a common parental desire. Parents also often find themselves giving material gifts out of guilt (because of losing their tempers, not making it to a child's game, or being away too much). Although making children happy with gifts can feel good initially, it can promote spoiled attitudes that erode relationships. It also feeds entitlement, a risk factor for being aggressive or violent. Entitlement is when children have an exaggerated, unrealistic sense of self-importance and thus expect to get special treatment and pretty much whatever they want, regardless of the situation. Associating material gifts with love doesn't build healthy relationships, but connecting gifts of attention and caring to the concept of love does. The fondest memories of childhood usually involve pleasant experiences with parents—not gifts.

Here's a view of love that we believe bolsters connections with children and discourages aggressive habits. As you're able, love your children by promoting self-reliance and providing opportunities to obtain the best things in life: fulfilling family and friend relationships, education, emotional and physical health, spiritual connections, and having fun. To us, love means showing affection, interest, compassion, and support while also trying to do what it takes for children to grow up as caring, emotionally strong adults. Love means guarding their safety as best we can and promoting healthy maturity by saying no even when it makes them mad.

But we strongly believe, and evidence supports, that giving this type of love often isn't enough to produce kids who are self-protective and nonaggressive. It takes specific skills, which we'll give you in this book, to counteract all the detrimental influences from the modern world.

The more of the warning signs that describe you and your children, the weaker your relationship likely is, but it's almost never too late to improve it. You'll want to start by managing your time so there's more to spend on fun activities together and improving your communication. Then work to minimize each warning sign. If needed, get more specific advice from our suggested reading list or resources, or from a mental health professional.

Warning Signs of Discipline and Monitoring Leading to Trouble

A son of a minister was convicted of the murder of his mother and attempted murder of his father after they took away the *Halo 3* game he bought against their wishes. Daniel Petric was sixteen years old when he used his father's gun to shoot both parents. He appeared obsessed with the game, playing for hours at a time at friends' homes because his father forbade it.

Although factors leading to extreme events like these are complex, they illustrate problematic breakdowns in discipline and relationships. In addition to the quality of your connection, how you discipline strongly affects whether your children are aggressive, or instead, exhibit moral and prosocial behaviors. Prosocial behaviors are actions intended to help others rather than oneself, such as aiding, comforting, cooperating, and showing compassion for others. Discipline methods can strengthen (or erode) your connection while protecting (or weakening) emotional strength and ability to resist dangerous influences.

Good relationships lead kids to want to please you and to perceive discipline as reflecting concern instead of control or anger, thereby increasing acceptance of discipline. It also helps to tell kids that you discipline because you care about them.

Here are research-backed discipline features that prevent aggression and promote protective emotional health and connections:

- Firmly set limits while allowing for child input and flexibility for circumstances and advancing age.
- Explain good reasons for limits and enforce them with consequences that aren't harsh (see page 12).
- Allow children to gradually gain autonomy (that is, make their own decisions and express individual tastes as safety allows).
- Monitor your kids' activities and friendships.

Now let's move on to warning signs that your discipline strategy may limit your children's ability to protect themselves or promote aggression and violent behaviors.

Setting Too Many Limits or Too Few

Why do some children learn kindness while others learn aggression? One major factor is how parents set and enforce limits. Think of limits as rules on behaviors that you either desire (good things like kindness or empathy) or forbid (bad things like bullying or stealing). Setting limits can fix and prevent behavior problems but can also develop a child's self-control and character. In the book *Character Matters*, psychologist Thomas Lickona describes how parents can directly teach moral behavior. Michele Borba also describes the use of moral discipline to teach children right from wrong in her book *Building Moral Intelligence*. Limit-setting can be started around age three, but often takes a while to work well, given the learning curve for parents and kids.

Although kids need limits to learn how to behave well, trouble occurs when parents set too many or unnecessarily rigid rules, or ones too difficult to follow. When kids (especially adolescents) think they have too many or rigid rules, they may believe that parents care more about control than about their needs and desires. This can lead to depression, anxiety, rebellion, and disconnection. When limits are too hard to follow (because of circumstances, being unclear, or not being developed enough), kids have anxiety about failing and more trouble making good decisions.

Therefore, a pearl of protective discipline is to set only limits that there are good reasons for and that children can understand. When you only set necessary limits, you have fewer to enforce, which increases your consistency. Inconsistent discipline is a significant factor behind antisocial and delinquent behaviors. (For interested readers, we developed a novel limit-testing tool to help parents decide which limits to set and practical ways to enforce them in our previous book, *7 Skills for Parenting Success*.)

Here are warning signs that you need to set fewer limits:

- You give frequent commands throughout the day.
- You're often upset because your kids don't do things well enough.
- You emphasize obedience more than your relationship.
- Your child is rebelling.
- You're finding it difficult to enforce rules because there are so dang many.

A warning sign that you're setting an unnecessary limit is that you can't explain good reasons for it to your children (other than saying, "because I said so").

On the flip side, kids who don't get enough limits, or get limits that aren't enforced, often sense that no one cares and more often act aggressively and engage in perilous behaviors. Parents can set limits that develop character, morality, and social integration—all protective factors against aggression. Examples are showing kindness, respect, and concern for others; not bullying; accepting responsibility for mistakes instead of blaming others; respecting other people's possessions; and honesty.

Setting rules on prosocial, nonaggressive behaviors is part of something called *inductive discipline*. A hallmark feature is how you enforce limits: instead of using authority or power, help children see how their actions affect others. Ask how they think another person felt when they did something hurtful, or express disappointment by saying that you never expected to see that kind of behavior from them. This helps your children develop empathy. Also, if you want your kids to disapprove of things, it really helps if they hear it from you, along with your reasoning. Explaining reasons for limits is part of effective inductive discipline.

Here are warning signs that you probably need to set *more* or *firmer* limits: your child isn't gradually getting more responsible and caring like other kids that age, or has behavior problems. It's also important to prevent boredom, because it's linked to hazardous behaviors like drug use and crime. Kids need to stay busy with homework, extracurricular activities, chores, or other work, but also need playtime with others.

By the way, there's a common reason for limits not being set or enforced: children complaining or arguing about them. It's important to have open communication in which you listen to their side, explain your good reasons for limits, and compromise when safety allows. However, if arguments continue to the point of not being able to enforce limits you feel are necessary, it's a warning sign that you need help with discipline.

Also, not setting limits to avoid angry tirades encourages kids to lash out to get out of complying. If this works, it can become a repetitive tactic to get parents to back off and may escalate to violence to get results. When tirades result in kids getting what they want, they gain control over parents, as Janet Sasson Edgette points out in her book *Stop Negotiating with Your Teen*. Kids who use it successfully will most likely grow up using similar tactics in future relationships or conflicts. If fear or running out of energy to deal with your child's angry or violent reactions is preventing you from taking needed action, it's a warning sign that you need urgent professional help.

Not Monitoring Closely Enough

Friends reported that Harris and Klebold had experimented with explosives for more than a year prior to their rampage. In Eric's bedroom, police found a shotgun, shells, a bomb, *The Anarchist Cookbook*, which contained recipes for explosives, and a journal he kept for detailing his plans.

When children aren't monitored enough, they're more likely to affiliate with deviant peers and become aggressive and antisocial. Yes, hindsight is 20/20, but examining histories of violent youth illuminate how parents can monitor their activities with foresight. Monitoring is an essential part of preventing victimization as well.

Monitoring solitary, home, school, and peer activities can help parents identify concerning situations. Stories of children affected by violence illustrate the importance of knowing what children are struggling with and what they're doing, where, and with whom. One way to do this is active surveillance (watching and listening) and seeking information from other parents and kids. This is a constant necessity with small children to ensure their safety.

But it's natural for parents to believe that teenagers don't need much supervision. And teens often reframe supervision as mistrust, leading parents to back off. But the rights and responsibilities of parents to monitor still apply because of teens' natural tendency to engage in risk taking due to underdeveloped decision making and emotional control. Monitoring is critical in the context of today's outside influences like peers and media that can otherwise affect childhood outcomes more than parents.

Keep in mind that research has shown that the best way for parents to know what is happening in their teenagers' lives is for teens to spontaneously tell parents. Perceiving a close, loving relationship makes youth more likely to let parents in on hazardous situations and be open to guidance. Also, even when kids don't say exactly what's up, connectedness leads to good talks that reveal clues to what is really happening to them.

It's especially important to check their activities when you suspect something may be wrong. Warning signs of needing to actively investigate activities include these: your child seems more aloof, isolated, upset, or just not herself; she's spending a lot of time with a new friend and you aren't sure what they do together; or someone else expresses a concern to you.

First, talk to your child for clues and say why you're worried. If still concerned, check through your home and your child's bedroom, car, and social media for evidence of hazardous activity. You don't need to forewarn, but it's best if your child is with you when you search: you could say, "I'm going to help you clean your room. Let's go do it together and get it over with." If you suspect dangerous activities with other kids, find out where the group is going and check on them. Although your child may react negatively, this won't matter if your actions save him or her or someone else from trouble.

Inadequately Reacting to Serious Problems or Warning Signs of Imminent Violence

When you monitor and find evidence of serious behavior problems (such as substance use, alcohol abuse, violent writings, criminal or gang activities, bullying behaviors, anger management problems, or recurrent violent behavior) you must intervene to protect your child and others. These can be early signs of impending violence. Covering up problems to protect personal or family reputation won't help your child and can endanger others.

As suggested in the informative book *Staying Alive: How to Act Fast and Survive Deadly Encounters*, here are warning signs of imminent violence. These mean a youth or young adult is at high risk of being a grave danger to self or others now or in the very near future:

- Serious physical fighting with peers or family.
- Severe destruction of property.
- Severe rage for seemingly minor reasons.
- Talking about suicide or having a suicide plan.
- Possession of weapons.
- Communicating (in writing, online, or verbally) a detailed plan to attack a place or people.

We think readers will agree that parents and other adults have a duty to take action to prevent further harm or tragedy when these warning signs occur. In particular, if the last two warning signs are both present, immediately notify authorities and other people who may be harmed. See chapter 3 for more information on warning signs for suicide and when to take action.

In 2012, a mother turned her twenty-year-old son in to police because she feared what he would do with the assault weapons and four hundred rounds of ammo he bought. It was discovered that he was planning a massacre at a screening of the movie *The Twilight Saga: Breaking Dawn, Part 2*. This heroic mother did what she had to do to protect the community from her own child and thus saved many lives.

Limiting chances for teens to be together without enough supervision will reduce risks for victimization or perpetration. But sometimes, you may worry that other parents don't share your view of the need for limits or supervision. You might fear that your kids are engaging in unsafe behavior at another parent's home. The sidebar on page 17 suggests ways to discuss monitoring connected to media, substance use, and dating violence with other parents, and can be adapted for discussing other concerns.

Finding the Words

• •

When you worry that your child may not be monitored closely enough at someone else's home or is engaging in behaviors you forbid there, it can be uncomfortable to bring it up with other parents. Try expressing concerns about your own child instead of what their child is allowed to do, or how much these parents are or aren't monitoring. For example:

- *We're afraid Matt might be drinking (or using drugs). We told him we won't allow it, and we were hoping when he's over there that you'll let us know if you see anything suspicious.*
- *Tyron's been playing violent games too much, so we'd like to ask if it would be OK if you didn't let him play games at your house.*
- *We're worried that Tina's boyfriend isn't being good to her. Can you please make sure they aren't together over there? And if he shows up, we'll come over and get her. We don't want to be a bother, but it's really important to us. Thanks.*

It's better to risk embarrassment or discomfort than for your child to be harmed.

Using Intrusion, Psychological Control, or Overprotection

As opposed to inadequate monitoring, excessive and unnecessary monitoring—intrusiveness—can lead teens to think that parents want to control them or are interfering without good reason. This can backfire and result in increased rule breaking as well as two risk factors for becoming victims: depression and low self-esteem. Think of being intrusive as intruding into their lives in unnecessary and harmful ways.

You can avoid intrusion by not monitoring or setting rules in ways that infringe on gaining autonomy. This would mean avoiding restrictions on clothing, friends, and activities when there's no safety concern but instead allowing your children to make those kinds of choices. Also, don't invade privacy when you don't have legitimate concerns (don't ask detailed questions about an event or activity, or listen in on conversations).

Psychological control means taking advantage of your kids' psychological and emotional needs to get them to do things. Examples are using guilt and withdrawing affection and attention (or threatening to do so) in order to try to change behavior. This increases delinquency, aggression, depression, and anxiety in kids.

Another type of monitoring—hovering or overprotectiveness—promotes immaturity, entitlement, and anxiety about failure while inhibiting self-sufficiency. It also can increase vulnerability to being bullied. Parents who hover pay extremely close attention to children, assisting even when not needed, and are involved in their children's decisions in an overcontrolling, intrusive way. They watch and intervene to prevent failure and discomfort.

Does any of this sound like what you're doing? Using psychological control, intrusion, or overprotection are warning signs that you need to change how you monitor in order to protect your children.

Using Harsh Punishment

How you punish also greatly affects your kids' ability to protect themselves from aggression and violence. Before we discuss harsh punishment, let's briefly review mild punishments, which are part of an effective discipline plan. Mild punishments withdraw privileges or take away possessions for a short time and are a good way to discourage misbehavior. But, just so you know, one common discipline mistake is using more punishments than rewards. Kids learn how to behave much better and for longer when they're rewarded (get something good after they behave well). Rewards also motivate good behavior when you're not around. In contrast, using frequent punishments is linked to aggressive behavior.

Using harsh punishment is the most detrimental practice in discipline. Touching or threatening to touch a child in a negative way (hold down, yank, push, or hit) is harsh punishment. Yelling or swearing, insulting with put-downs or sarcasm ("You're an idiot," "Thanks for messing up again"), teasing about behavior, giving the cold shoulder, throwing things, withholding meals, and threatening to leave are all harsh punishments and they are usually unplanned.

The bottom line is this: if you use harsh punishments today, your kids will have more problems tomorrow. These punishments weaken your connections. Harshness teaches kids that it's fine to hurt someone when upset or to get what one wants, but it doesn't teach good behavior. Harshly punished kids have more troubles with substance abuse, deviant friends, and violent behaviors. They also suffer more relationship and emotional problems. If someone is using harsh punishment in your home, it's a warning sign that your family needs help.

Spanking

Many parents use spanking (hitting a child on the bottom, arms, or legs with an open hand) for discipline. Even though it can stop bad behaviors, research shows that spanking doesn't help children behave better in the future like other discipline methods and its effects are temporary.

Plus, research now shows that spanking increases aggressive behavior and delinquency while diminishing connectedness (both children and parents experience bad feelings from it). A large 2010 study published in the journal *Pediatrics* showed that mothers who spank children at age three have more aggressive children at age five, regardless of how aggressive they were at younger ages and other risk factors that could account for the difference. In addition to being more likely to be aggressive and have poorer mental health as youths, spanked children are more likely to become criminals as adults. Spanked children are more likely to abuse their own kids or spouses. Spanking meets the definition of violence and recent research shows that bad outcomes can apply across races.

Spanking is a common precursor to physical child abuse: what starts as spanking can end up as abuse when parental anger increases along with the force of blows. Parents who physically abuse their children often think they are simply "spanking" when their actions have gone too far. Over time, more force is needed to make an impression. Also consider these issues:

1. Spanking can spark anger in children, causing more misbehavior.
2. Are you still going to spank your kids when they're preteens or teens? If kids don't learn to respond to nonphysical discipline when they're young, it likely won't work when they are too big to spank.
3. Children learn to do what parents do. Spanking teaches that it's OK (or even good) to hit and hurt loved ones to solve problems and show feelings.

Many experts now view spanking as harsh punishment and spanking with an object to be child abuse. Twenty-four modern nations have abolished spanking. Given the prevalence of aggression and violence in our society, and the increased aggression and mental illness associated with spanking, it seems very wise to stop using it and to discourage its use by other parents.

Troubled Home Lives Linked with Becoming Victims and Perpetrators

Things happen behind closed doors in homes that traumatize children and greatly raise their risk of growing up to be perpetrators or victims of aggression or violence. These aspects of home life endanger both parents and children and are warning signs that help and intervention are needed.

Domestic Violence

Mom is sweet to me. She made me an after-school snack and we talked about what I brought for show-and-tell—oh, oh, Dad is home early. Mom tells me to go upstairs. He is yelling stuff I don't understand and Mom says please don't. I sneak downstairs as his fist slams into her face. She falls back and dishes smash. Why does this keep happening? He says he loves her. Maybe that's love when you're grown up.

The stories from a five-year-old boy seen in clinic echo millions of children who suffer the effects of domestic violence, also called *intimate partner violence*. Tragically, more than 6% of children in the United States witnessed a parent physically assault another parent (or parental partner) in 2011, according to research in *JAMA Pediatrics*, and 28% of teens (aged fourteen to seventeen) reported witnessing an interparental assault in their lifetimes. All the kinds of family violence found in this study were unacceptably high: 34% of teens reported witnessing assaults involving kids, parents, or other family members at some point in childhood.

Domestic violence involves perpetrators engaging in physical and sexual assault, robbery, emotional and psychological abuse, and intimidation and threats to control partners. Each year, at least ten million men and women are victims of physical domestic violence and many more don't report it. In their lifetimes, one in five American women and one in seven men will experience severe physical violence at the hands of an intimate partner. A common victim is a young woman aged eighteen to twenty-four.

Witnessing intimate partner violence is a common way that children are victimized. Research shows that child witnesses are more likely to have problems with aggression and violence and to have psychological repercussions (like depression, anxiety, posttraumatic stress disorder, and low self-esteem) and social problems, such as trouble making friends. Living with domestic violence makes youth significantly more likely to be abused (suffer additional victimization) and to abuse others, including parents. Growing up with domestic violence compounds the chance of being involved with it as adults—and so the cycle continues.

If violence is happening in your home, it's a serious warning sign that you'll have trouble with your children and your children will have trouble. It needs to be stopped now for everyone's sake. Domestic violence costs American taxpayers more than $8 billion each year. Exorbitant costs and evidence linking exposure with victimization and perpetration means that perpetrators need to be stopped and treated. Although it usually happens behind closed doors, it needs to become all of our business.

Child Abuse and Neglect

The father of seven-year-old Evan Ramsey fired weapons in a newspaper office and then held the publisher hostage for refusing to print his letter blaming politicians for a fire in his home. Evan's father went to jail and his alcoholic mother moved in with a series of violent, abusive boyfriends. Due to neglect, Evan was placed in more than ten foster homes in two years. In one, he was reportedly physically and sexually abused. A month after his father was released from prison, then sixteen-year-old Evan, depressed and suicidal, shot and killed the principal of his school and a student and wounded two others. Although he had planned to commit suicide, he couldn't pull the trigger in the end.

The most common way that parents victimize their children is by neglecting them. Parents are guilty of neglect if they purposely don't give the physical, medical, educational, or emotional care their children need, even though assistance to fulfill those needs was available, resulting in harm or danger of being harmed. Although it doesn't always happen, studies show neglected kids are more likely to become aggressive and develop antisocial traits or personality disorders.

Physical abuse is purposefully hurting a child, or doing something that could harm a child, including discipline that leaves a mark lasting twenty-four hours or requiring medical care, as well as restraining or requiring a child to perform physically demanding acts. Emotional abuse (frequent negative attention or severe emotional neglect) is equally or more damaging. Involving a child in any sexual activity is sexual abuse, including exposing him or her to pornography or adult sexual activity. Sexual abuse is a cruel, selfish, immoral act that is unbelievably common. Adding to their agony, many abused children must also endure neglect, multiple types of abuse, and witnessing domestic violence.

James Garbarino, the author of *Lost Boys*, demystifies the link between abuse and aggression as well as internalized problems. Children who are physically abused are more likely to behave violently and commit crimes. Abused and neglected kids develop many precursors of aggression toward themselves and others: substance and alcohol abuse, low academic achievement, and delinquency. They're more likely to suffer lifelong anxiety, impulsive behaviors, depression, and relationship difficulties. Girls who are sexually abused are more likely to be raped in adulthood. Abused kids are more likely to abuse their own children, continuing a malicious cycle.

Here in the United States, we have the worst record of child abuse and neglect among Western nations—in 2013, there were an estimated 679,000 child victims of neglect or abuse, and an estimated 1,520 deaths. The costs associated with child abuse and neglect, from health and social services to criminal justice, are estimated by the Centers for Disease Control and Prevention (CDC) to be $124 billion each year.

Child abuse and neglect's unacceptably high prevalence and impact make them immense risk factors for societal aggression and violence. Their overwhelming nature and commonality make them seem unsolvable and can paralyze us into inaction. But there are things that parents and concerned citizens can do to help. We think many readers will agree that being a parent is the most difficult job there is and many need assistance.

What can we parents do collectively? First, we can make neglect and abuse of children our business: aside from caring about helpless innocent children being harmed, affected children become our problem when they harm themselves or others. We can contribute our time and money to support organizations that fund or provide prevention and intervention services.

Second, it really helps to gently approach parents of children who may be at risk: parents who roughly handle or use harsh, disapproving language with a child. But be careful not to say anything critical because the parent may take that out on the child later. Simply let the parent know that someone is paying attention by saying something positive and supportive such as, "Boy, raising kids is hard work. Mine sure were (are), but I'm so glad I have them." Then say something good about the child: "Your daughter seems to have good willpower—that's a good thing for a girl. I'm happy my daughter's that way because she can take care of herself," "Your child seems so sweet," or "Your little boy has good energy—that's a good thing to have as kids get older." If you know the parent, you can gently mention what works for you or offer to watch the child for a while to give the parent a break.

Third, report suspected abuse or neglect to your county child protective services agency, or county or state abuse reporting hotline. You can do this anonymously and it greatly helps affected children.

Abuse and neglect inhibit formation and maintenance of close parent-child relationships. When these connections aren't possible, finding a support system for kids early is monumentally important. You can ask for help from relatives, trusted friends, mentoring organizations, and youth groups at places of worship.

Living in Violent Communities

Living in high-crime neighborhoods increases childhood victimization and perpetration. Impoverished, overcrowded neighborhoods with high unemployment and lack of community facilities have higher rates of juvenile violence and crime. Drug availability in neighborhoods also strongly predicts violence. But research suggests that the nature of these neighborhoods doesn't directly increase antisocial behavior in youth— a combination of parenting and peer influence can either amplify or shrink a neighborhood's bad influence.

What are some things that parents in violent neighborhoods can do to protect their kids? First, consistent monitoring and enforcing rules strongly protect against victimization as well as violent perpetration. Second, teaching kids "street savvy," or ways to recognize and avoid dangerous situations where victimization could occur, is helpful. Third, there's evidence that access to safe and successful schools, social and recreational programs, and employment reduce juvenile delinquency, crime, and violence; supporting schools, youth programs, and employment opportunities can benefit us all.

Warning Signs That Parents May Still Have Trouble

Now that you know the warning signs of disconnection and troublesome discipline and home lives, we'd like to prepare you for reasons that tragedy can still strike families who felt they didn't need help or who did the right thing by seeking advice.

Deciding Not to Follow Advice

Parents may not get professional advice, or get it and then decide not to follow it, because they're tired of trying or may not think they need to because things aren't that bad—yet. Parents may believe their situations are somehow different, negating the need for change, or their own needs take priority over children's needs. This can also happen when parents can't afford (or don't think they can afford) professional help. Yet, just like in the field of medicine, preventive care is much cheaper and more beneficial than dealing with the aftermath of violence. Adam Lanza was evaluated for mental health problems but there's evidence that his mother reinforced his disagreement of his diagnoses and refusal of treatment.

Wanting People to Think You're a Good Parent

You may act as if things are OK when they're not because you want people to think you're doing a good job with your children. While this is a common, natural inclination, and it's hard to get negative feedback, parenting (like other jobs) benefits from willingness to learn and change. Peter Lanza reported that he thought his wife Nancy's pride kept her from asking for help with Adam because she didn't want people to think there was a problem.

Defending Your Child's or Your Own Reputation

After a Denver-area middle school boy brought an incendiary device to school, legal charges were filed. When his parents were interviewed, they expressed concern about how a legal record would damage their son's reputation, just because he made a mistake. To us, these parents were, perhaps unknowingly, endangering their son and others by focusing more on their son's reputation than his behavior.

Should Parents Be Held Responsible for Their Children's Actions?

We'd like to address the intriguing question of whether parents should be held legally or financially responsible for their children's aggressive or violent actions. When parents are held accountable in court for their children's acts, they're more likely to be involved in their children's lives and encourage good behavior. To this end, city ordinances around the United States require parents to be legally charged or pay restitution (via fines, damaged property repair, or community service) when their kids commit crimes. Some ordinances allow parents to avoid paying restitution by attending parenting classes.

While holding parents accountable in court may be helpful, it seems vastly more effective and logical to intervene before crimes are committed by helping parents do their difficult job more effectively when their kids are young. According to the US Department of Justice, we had about fifty-five thousand troubled youth who'd been convicted of a crime deemed worthy of residential or juvenile detention center placement (juvie) on any given day in 2013, and incarceration alone costs up to $150,000 each, per year. Community and residential home center rehabilitative treatment yield much better results at lower cost compared to detention centers, leading experts to strongly recommend juvenile justice reform. We can't afford to ignore the evidence that early intervention prevents significant tolls on our society from aggression and violence.

Parents and Home Lives Do Matter

Research consistently shows that quality parent-child relationships, monitoring, and effective, nonharsh discipline strongly predict children's future mental health and behaviors. Victimization at home and exposure to real-life violence are common and raise the risk for more aggression and violence. All the crucial risk and protective factors for youth aggression and violence are controllable—by parents and the public. We believe it does take a village for children to turn out as self-protective, mentally healthy, nonaggressive adults.

In the coming chapters, we'll cover things that make our parenting jobs harder than ever and endanger our children. We are our children's first line of defense. There is strength in asking for help and advice—most of us need it from time to time.

2

Perilous Thoughts and Emotions and Their Solutions

You girls have never been attracted to me.... It's an injustice, a crime because I don't know what you don't see in me, I'm the perfect guy and yet you throw yourselves at all these obnoxious men instead of me, the supreme gentleman. I will punish all of you for it. [Laughs.]

—Elliot Rodger on video recorded prior to his shooting rampage near the University of California, Santa Barbara

As a professor, Brian is often asked by students to make exceptions to university policies. One day, a student wanting to add a class he was teaching, even though the class was full and prerequisites weren't met, came to his office to appeal the denial. After receiving an explanation of why he couldn't add the class, the student became angry, stood up, and approaching in a threatening manner, said, "Who above your head do I need to go to in order to get into this class?" Flabbergasted, Brian thought to himself, "Ah, I don't know . . . God?" but calmly explained that there was no one at the university who would approve the exceptions.

Across the country, educators have witnessed an increase in entitlement and use of manipulation by students to get what they want. Entitlement and anger management are two troublesome problems that can preclude acting in a self-preserving, productive manner while promoting aggressive behavior. In his video, Elliot Rodger showed signs of both these problems.

This chapter explores these and other thoughts and emotions that are linked to aggressive or violent behavior and victimization. We'll explain how to prevent, identify, and mitigate dangerous thoughts such as entitlement and hostile attributions, as well as how to promote coping and resilient thinking to strengthen children for life. We'll give you strategies for managing rage, preventing hate, and instilling empathy, and discuss how to recognize dangerous levels of social isolation.

First, we need to comment on how young brains are very different from those of adults. Starting at about age eleven and continuing into the midtwenties, new neuron growth and reconnection occurs. One area that undergoes development in adolescence and young adulthood is the prefrontal (also referred to as frontal) cortex. This area of the brain controls executive functioning, including problem solving, decision making, impulse or urge control, personality, emotional stability, short-term memory, and planning ahead. Certain aspects of intelligence can be affected by prefrontal cortex function, but it doesn't appear that being smart helps this area mature any faster or better.

This remodeling period is when crucial learning occurs to allow good intellectual, emotional, and social functioning, and is also when the brain is very susceptible to exposures that can damage these functions, such as isolation, drugs, alcohol, violent media, and antisocial peers. In addition, dysfunctional beliefs and emotions often develop during brain remodeling. Parents and mentors can help adolescents remodel their brains for good function by modifying experiences, controlling exposures, and addressing perilous thoughts and emotions. Let's begin our exploration of dysfunctional beliefs by discussing entitlement.

The Dangers of Entitlement

Entitlement involves an inflated sense of self-worth in which one expects special treatment and to get what one wants, regardless of the situation. This is opposed to feeling deserving of reward because of good character or work. A sense of entitlement (which acts as if to say, "When I want something, I expect people to give it to me" and can say, "I am not to be challenged") increases the chance of lashing out aggressively when criticized, wronged, or upset. It's associated with perpetrating crimes such as theft, burglary, assault, and rape. Criminologists theorize that this way of thinking serves to rationalize or justify illegal behavior. Thus, it appears to be an especially significant factor in aggression. Another related way of thinking linked to committing crimes is failure to accept responsibility for one's actions while blaming others for bad outcomes.

It's important to understand how entitlement differs from healthy, protective levels of self-esteem, so we'll discuss this next as well as the pitfalls of low self-esteem and how narcissism is related to entitlement.

Self-Esteem: Aggression Versus Protection Against Being Victimized

Inflated self-esteem can manifest as entitlement, and entitled youth may use aggression to support their self-aggrandized views and to maintain a superior view of themselves in the eyes of others.

But there's another way that self-esteem can be connected to aggression: low or unstable self-esteem can cause youth to loathe themselves and perseverate over personal failures. They then may compensate for it with aggression, as if to say, "I am superior." With threats to their fragile ego such as rejection, they may act violently to prove their importance. Hence, both low and inflated levels of self-esteem can be linked to aggression.

Self-esteem differs from entitlement in that it stems from feeling valued by other people. As opposed to entitlement, children with healthy levels of self-esteem think and act in a self-protective way while caring about others. Protective levels of self-esteem help youth feel and desire to stay connected to family and society. It helps them resist bad influences while not allowing others to endanger, abuse, or take advantage of them. Having a reasonable level of self-esteem buffers risk factors and thus protects children from becoming victims and perpetrators. Low self-esteem, however, makes children vulnerable to perpetrators, bad influences, and self-harm.

You can promote protective levels of self-esteem by praising children's good personal qualities and saying something when they make good choices. General compliments also help: "I missed you today," "I'm so glad I have you," "What a nice kid you are," "I love you so much," and "I like hanging out with you." Helping to build healthy self-esteem also likely protects against a particularly dangerous form of entitlement that we'll discuss next.

Aggrieved Entitlement

Entitlement mixed with uncontrolled anger can have devastating results. An analysis of thirty mass school shootings that ended in perpetrators' suicides was published in 2010. It revealed that nearly all perpetrators felt peers had treated them cruelly or in demeaning ways. For instance, the Columbine High School shooters complained that they were routinely teased and called "gay." At the beginning of the shootings, a group of girls reportedly asked them, "Why are you doing this?" Harris and Klebold replied, "This is payback. We've dreamed of doing this for years. This is for all the shit you put us through. This is what you deserve."

Feeling mistreated, wronged, and cast out is unfortunately common in adolescents. So what turns a hurt, angry boy into a mass murderer? The authors of the mass school shootings study concluded it was the combination of feeling aggrieved (being wronged by the world) and entitled to get back what they lost: their masculinity. The term *aggrieved entitlement* was used to describe an emotional state that inspires males to seek violent revenge for being humiliated by threats to their masculinity and a sense of being entitled to make things "right" by making others suffer too. In this way, shooters felt their actions were justified. The authors also discussed how boys are socialized to assert their manhood and use violence when it's threatened, often thinking it will elevate their masculinity.

We suspect that aggrieved entitlement may also apply to Elliot Rodger's rampage. Reportedly upset that girls were sleeping with "ugly, rich guys" and not him, and still brooding that a girl didn't like him in middle school, the twenty-two-year-old shot or stabbed roommates, college students, and strangers, killing six and wounding thirteen before killing himself. Emerging research suggests aggrieved entitlement is associated with lashing out violently when feeling wronged by other types of losses such as jobs or relationships, or by perceived assaults on egos.

Entitlement and Narcissism

Where is the line between entitlement and narcissism? Entitlement is one element of narcissism, which is a pervasive pattern not only of entitlement but also grandiosity, need for admiration or worship, and lack of empathy. It involves exploitation of others (taking advantage of or controlling) for personal gain, belief in being special or unique, preoccupation with fantasies of achieving unlimited success and power, and arrogance. Narcissists feel entitled to admiration and respect and get aggressive when they don't get it. In his book *Character Disturbance*, George Simon describes how aggressive personalities share elements of narcissism such as entitled attitudes and exploitation of others.

Entitlement in childhood can precede narcissism in adulthood. But researchers also describe narcissism in youth as extreme entitlement or an egotistical view of extraordinary self-worth that justifies exploiting others for personal gain, and that preoccupation with looking out for themselves combined with low empathy appears to underlie the development of narcissism. Because some of these traits are seen in mild forms in normal teens, narcissistic personality disorder is usually diagnosed after age eighteen.

Multiple studies have linked overindulgent parenting to narcissism. There's also evidence that parental coldness, psychological control, and excessive or inconsistent control increase the risk.

Warning Signs of Entitlement

Now that we've discussed healthy, protective self-esteem versus unhealthy levels linked to aggression and violence, here are warning signs of entitlement. Keep in mind there's a normal amount of selfishness in children, especially when young, which does not indicate entitlement. Adolescents are naturally somewhat self-centered, so what you want to look for is when self-centered thoughts and behaviors appear to go overboard. Here are some warning signs of entitlement:

- Expecting good grades or other things desired, even when not putting in the work.
- Expecting special treatment in school or work.
- Expecting you or others to do things for him or her.
- Believing he or she has a right to get what other people have.
- Acting like his or her own needs are more important than other people's; acting greedy.
- Acting competitive more than cooperative.
- Showing low empathy and ability to see things from someone else's perspective.
- Showing little respect for romantic partners.
- Responding to criticism aggressively.
- Using aggression, including manipulation, to get what he or she wants.

Entitlement can lead youth to manipulate people—including parents—to fulfill desires. By manipulation, we mean controlling others by influencing their actions and emotions to get what one wants. It's an aggressive act. Warning signs of possible manipulation are when youth use fear, guilt, repetitive lies or arguments, or angry tirades, or pit parents against each other to get their way. When manipulation works with parents, kids may not learn other ways to resolve conflict and stress so they continue using it with teachers, peers, partners, or coworkers. Manipulation takes knowledge and planning that isn't yet possible in preteens.

A great example of teenage entitlement came to us from a friend. A loving father's ex-wife convinced their two girls that he should pay nearly all their expenses as opposed to specifications in the divorce settlement. He received this letter from the girls after he questioned the necessity of expenses such as new cars and electronics. Here is an excerpt.

I don't really get why you can't grasp how expensive we are . . . or see how worth it we are! I'm sorry but you have two absolutely incredible daughters. The thing is that you don't get that we are 20 and 18 and quite mature and extremely grown up, extremely intelligent and understanding . . . we are kind and wise and beyond our years.

Please don't think that we are greedy. Mom wants to give everything to ensure a comfortable and easy and healthy life for us, you don't see things that way, you think we should work more, do with less. But I know that deep down you recognize that there is a real issue that lies in your priorities. I really don't expect less than you crying after reading this, believe me it hurts me to say such truths. But at this point, there's nothing more I can do to help you.

Pray a lot as we do for you every day, and maybe consider some BIG changes you really need to make. Changes that might allow you to love yourself for the first time in what seems like a long time. Changes that will bring you true joy, true self forgiveness, and an end to bitter memories and guilt.

Wow. This father, who had in the past been apologetic and obliging, responded appropriately by telling his girls that he wouldn't be able to respond until they speak to him respectfully. Their relationship greatly improved and his daughters are now maturing into responsible, loving adults.

Keys to Preventing or Defusing Entitlement

To prevent or defuse entitlement, avoid certain types of praise and doing specific things for children. Here are our recommendations:

- Avoid giving exaggerated compliments or saying things indicating kids don't need to work to succeed: "You're the best at . . . " and "You don't need to . . . (practice, work, or study) like other kids do."
- Don't tell your kids they're very intelligent. This can discourage work and effort and lead them to think they can't learn from adults but can use their intelligence to argue their way out of things or manipulate you.
- Avoid spoiling your kids by giving most of the material items and privileges they want. This may lead them to grow up expecting to get things quickly and with little effort. Instead, consider kids' needs versus wants and have them earn privileges and desired items. Delay gifts for special occasions so they don't expect to get things right when they want them.
- When kids repeatedly put their desires above someone else's, call it what it is: "You're acting selfish and that's not OK."
- Be careful not to help kids get out of following rules, schedules, responsibilities, and policies.
- Avoid seeking exceptions or special treatment on their behalf from bosses, teachers, and coaches.
- Try not to take responsibility for things your kids should be responsible for, and discuss their roles in failures when they blame others.
- Ensure your kids don't feel neglected: children who are deprived of nurturing and love can feel entitled to things that other people have and show little empathy for others.

Also, to prevent entitlement, make sure that you have seen your children consider and respect other people's perspectives on issues and defer to the needs of others many times—it's not all about them. If you don't see considerate behavior, set rules and consequences to train them to do these things.

Anger Turned to Rage Breeds Violence

Anger is a normal emotion that can motivate people to make necessary changes. For example, when being treated badly by a friend or romantic partner, feeling angry can help one reject excuses or attributing blame to oneself. Expressing anger can protect victims from turning anger inward as depression, a risk factor for being hurt again.

In contrast, rage (or what psychologists may call *intermittent explosive disorder* when it's a repetitive pattern) is an intense and often sudden uncontrolled fit of anger shown by verbal or physical aggression. The magnitude of aggression expressed is grossly out of proportion to the situation. Anger can turn into rage that can lead to violence.

We shared signs of uncontrolled anger on page 30. The inability to regulate anger in youth is linked to depression and suicide. Uncontrolled, aggressive, or violent anger—rage—can lead to failed relationships or jobs and being bullied, raising the risk of violent behavior.

Research points to multiple origins of anger problems in youth including individual (temperament, poor social skills), family (harsh discipline, low support of the child), school (lower grades), and peers (associating with aggressive or angry peers, peer rejection). Common triggers for anger include kids not getting what they want or what others get (which occurs more often when spoiled or entitled), mistreatment by family or bullies, excessive pressure to perform, family conflict, and loss of friends. People who become violent because of anger often don't know how to talk things out, or don't have people they can express emotions to and get support from. Here we'll share some pearls of teaching anger management and what to do when anger progresses to the aggression of rage.

Anger and Aggression in Toddlers and Preschoolers

It's very important to understand anger and aggression from a developmental viewpoint so that you can tell if your child's anger is normal or problematic. Infants and toddlers (ages one and two) aren't developmentally ready to manage their frustration, so aggressive behaviors are normal (pushing, screaming, hitting, biting, pulling hair, taking things from others, fighting, and throwing things). Aggression is out of their control, shouldn't concern you, and shouldn't be disciplined.

Temper tantrums, meaning anything from short vocal outbursts to kicking and dropping to the floor, are normal and common (and such a joy), peaking around age three and then declining. The most important thing to do is to not pay attention to the child (while ensuring the child's physical safety) until he or she has calmed down. You might be able to identify and avoid triggers that set off emotional outbursts.

Normal early childhood physical aggression to get what one wants peaks around age two or three but then should gradually decline. Verbal aggression becomes more prominent as kids learn to talk, such as yelling or telling peers they won't play unless they get what they want. Early childhood aggression may or may not be associated with anger. If it is, try our recommendations for anger management that follow. Starting at about age three (younger children aren't developmentally ready for discipline plans), use limits and consequences just like you would for any other misbehavior.

If you're seeing repetitive physical or verbal aggression that isn't getting better by age five or six, it's best to get professional help. Failure to help children stop behaving aggressively at this early age can lead to lifelong problems with aggression, bullying, and violence.

Techniques for early anger management training include modeling calmness with your own anger and helping kids talk about emotions. When kids are old enough to understand, you can say something like, "Everyone gets mad, and it feels better when we talk about it. Talking about it helps us figure out what to do about it." Praise talking when they're upset and be empathetic, even when you find it silly or don't plan on giving in to what they want, and address concerns that repetitively underlie anger.

If your preschool child gets aggressive or violent when angry, ask him to say why he's upset instead, emphasizing the benefit to him (he won't get in trouble, it'll help him have friends). If he has trouble talking, or talking doesn't seem to help, practice doing nonaggressive physical things when mad (blowing away anger, counting loudly to ten, or running around the room). Praise trying things even if they don't work: "I'm proud of you for trying that. Keep practicing and if we need to, we'll find something else that works."

You might be able to avoid aggressive outbursts in kids by having them come to you for attention when frustrated. Hugging them for a few seconds may be all they need. It's important that you don't respond to aggression with anger or aggression, and that you praise or give other rewards when you see them play cooperatively with others.

Helping School-Age Kids Learn to Manage Anger

Kids (and adults) with uncontrolled anger often react before they realize what they were thinking about that made them angry. Helping your children figure out thoughts that precede anger helps separate facts from feelings.

When your children are upset, simply ask, "You seem upset. What are you thinking about?" Then listen without judgment. Help them figure out why they're angry by identifying what they were experiencing or thinking about before their emotional reaction. They may be thinking things that aren't true or are exaggerations. They may be angry at you—listen calmly and let them talk. Gently offer your perspective and address dysfunctional thoughts as we discuss later in the chapter. Even when they don't agree with you, saying what you think matters. Ask what you can do to help the situation. This approach helps kids talk about all emotions, including sadness.

Teach your kids that expressing anger in healthy ways means calmly telling others why you're upset. When feeling wronged by someone, being assertive is expressing anger in a nonthreatening and honest manner to support well-being, not selfish desires. Assertiveness doesn't hurt others like aggression does, because it also considers the rights and needs of others while stating one's own opinions or needs. To teach assertiveness, you could say, "When you're assertive, you nicely say how something affects you and what you would like to see happen or how it could work better." Suggest saying, "I feel . . . when you . . .," or "That makes me think . . . " instead of "You are mean" or "You had better quit it." So for example, if a child feels bad when repetitively teased about her accent, she could say, "I feel bad when you do that. Could you please stop?"

Warning Signs of Rage in School-Age Kids

When a seventeen-year-old soccer player got mad at a referee for giving him a warning, he argued with the ref and finally punched him in the face. The teen fled the scene and the referee was taken to the hospital, where he slipped into a coma and died.

Because the brain isn't fully developed, normal children are often moody, overreact, and are unable to recognize other people's emotions as well as adults can. As they age, they should be gradually learning to express emotion appropriately. Those who don't can become dangerous.

Signs of rage include the following:

- Throwing things or destroying property.
- Threatening to physically harm people, possessions, or animals.
- Acting with intent to inflict harm.
- Yelling profanities or disrespectful names.
- Violent writings and communications.
- Reactions way out of proportion for the situation and inability to communicate what he or she wants.

Steps to Manage Rage in School-Age Kids

If parents appropriately don't allow kids to act out their anger physically (such as by hitting someone or throwing things), kids will be forced to do better things like talking it out or walking away. Responding by doing the same thing the kids are doing (swearing, yelling) escalates the problem. Don't let their rage control your actions. Only give in to demands and threats if you feel that you or someone else is in physical danger, and seek professional help afterward. Advice for managing rage based on clinical experience and research follows.

Loud, angry, but nonviolent outbursts from older kids and teens are common and not concerning, but you still need to prevent them from becoming repetitive or escalating. First, they need you to hear why they're upset. Resist yelling at your child to stop yelling—this escalates emotions. Calmly and quietly say, "Whoa, what's happened to make you so upset?" or "What's up and how can I help?" You could say, "I could understand you better if you lower your voice a little. Come on, I really want to hear."

If your child is calling you disrespectful names or swearing, say, "I'd like to hear about what's going on and why you're so upset. But first I need you to stop calling me that (or swearing) before we can talk." Then wait patiently, say it once more, and walk away if it doesn't work. Talk later when he or she is calm. If you can figure out what's so upsetting, say, "I can see why that upset you." Validate rather than dismiss your child's feelings. If he or she is able to talk, use praise: "That's really good that you got in control of your emotions. It shows you're growing up."

At the end of the conversation, if your child was calling you disrespectful names, say that you don't deserve and won't allow it and which consequence he or she will get if it happens again (including that you won't be able to listen to him or her when you're called disrespectful names in the future but will walk away instead).

If your angry child becomes violent but isn't damaging property or harming anyone, calmly say, "I'd like to hear why you're upset, but you need to stop kicking the wall/throwing things/hitting/before we can talk." It's appropriate to raise your voice firmly, but don't yell. Repeat this once and then walk away until the behavior stops.

If that doesn't work, say, "I'll take something away (a privilege or possession the child cares about) unless you stop before I count to three." If a different aggressive behavior like yelling begins, say, "Thank you for stopping the kicking, but now you need to lower your voice." If that doesn't work, calmly suggest doing something else, such as, "Please take twenty slow deep breaths and then we'll talk if you're calm," or "Why don't you lie down until you're ready to talk." If the child can't calm down, walk away and check back in a couple minutes and ask, "Are you ready to tell me what you're upset about?"

However, if people or possessions are in danger of being harmed (or are actively being harmed) and aggression doesn't stop with one simple command, go ahead and use gentle physical intervention, but only with the amount needed to stop the dangerous behavior. You may need to remove an object, gently hold extremities of the child, or remove the child to a place of safety, such as another room or car. Terry Hyland and Jerry Davis, authors of *Angry Kids, Frustrated Parents*, provide similar practical advice for these types of situations. When children are too big for gentle physical intervention and people or possessions are being significantly harmed, see the next section on law enforcement involvement.

Once you have the aggressive behavior stopped, and your child is calmer, describe the bad behavior. For example, "Breaking things when you're mad isn't allowed. Tell me what happened." Listen to what he or she says without interruption, judgment, or criticism and then repeat back what you heard.

Explain how your child's reaction affected other people and his or her own well-being: "When you cuss and yell when you're mad, it tunes people out to your concerns and they won't want to be around you," or "When you hit when you're mad, it hurts and scares people so they won't want to be around you (for adolescents, say that someone might call the police)." Then calmly discuss what to do instead next time and give a consequence.

In the future, when your children are angry and talk instead of reacting with anger, praise it immediately. You can set up reward systems where a privilege or item is given for showing no aggression for a length of time corresponding to how often you're seeing the problem (reward after one day of showing no anger if it's a daily problem). Remember that rewards work much better and for much longer than punishments.

You'll want to consider other feelings and thoughts that might be underneath the anger, such as feeling ignored, hurt, scared, embarrassed, or uncomfortable. In *The Explosive Child*, Ross Greene points out that thinking in black-and-white terms is common in kids who explode with anger, and provides helpful advice. You can help kids by pointing out "gray" areas in events (views that lie between the extreme ends of how people feel or think). Kids younger than eight naturally think in black-and-white ways, but as they grow older they should gradually begin to see multiple perspectives of a situation.

If you're dealing with rage in a school-age child on multiple occasions after trying our suggestions, it's a warning sign that you need professional help. Another warning sign of needing help is if your teen or emerging adult uses physical force with you or other family members to get what he wants—even once. Without help, you and your family could be in grave danger. One therapy that has shown good results is called *cognitive behavioral therapy* (CBT), especially when focusing on relaxation techniques, recognizing thoughts that trigger aggression, problem solving, and communication skills.

Another dire situation is when older kids who *can* control their reactions learn that anger and aggression works for them and use them to get what they want. We talked about when kids use angry tirades to manipulate and control parents in chapter 1.

Calling Law Enforcement

When should parents call law enforcement for help? Call if a child is too big (or old) to successfully use gentle physical intervention that we described previously, and his or her behavior constitutes a crime and doesn't cease after you give one direct, calm warning that you'll need to call police for help if the behavior doesn't stop. Such crimes include threatening or committing assault against you or someone else, especially if your child has a weapon, or significant destruction of property. Charges may be filed or a referral might be made to family services. Also call if you have reason to believe that your child may be planning a violent attack.

For other aggressive behavior problems when safety isn't in jeopardy, try calling a coparent, trusted adult friend, or relative for backup. But if you need to do this, it's a sign that you would benefit from seeing a professional.

Hostile Views of People's Actions and Blaming Others

A thought pattern that can feed rage, aggression, and violence is seeing actions by others as hostile or threatening when most people would interpret them neutrally. These thoughts feed self-destructive, antisocial beliefs and behaviors. They can also make rejection by peers more likely, another risk factor for aggression.

Here's an example. Austin was a friendly and successful student working long hours. One day during his lunch break, he was sitting in the food court of a busy university center. Taking a break from eating, he stared off into space, deep in thought, thinking about his life and where it was headed. He was content. Suddenly, his brief break from life's stress was interrupted as a big, burly guy raced toward him and said, "Hey freak, what's your problem? Why are you staring at me and my girlfriend?!"

When youth believe that the world is out to get them, or is a hostile place, it leads to assuming that negative, unexpected, or strange events are purposefully directed toward them, even when they aren't. It leads to feeling and acting like a victim or target, instead of seeing a situation logically and problem solving through it. Viewing bad events as hostile attacks by people or entities is also linked to thinking that violence is a good way to solve problems or promote an agenda.

Other thought patterns linked to rage include having a general negative view of life, and chronically blaming disappointments or failures on other people. Blaming others, who perpetrators think of as unfair or out to get them, is linked to rage and committing violent acts after experiencing a loss. There's yet another emotion and thought pattern linked to violence that we'll discuss next: hate.

Hate

Dylann Roof, a twenty-one-year-old white male, reportedly wanted to start a race war when he shot nine people to death during a Bible study at the Emanuel African Methodist Episcopal Church in Charleston on June 17, 2015. His reply to pleas to stop shooting was reportedly, "No, you've raped our women, and you are taking over the country. . . . I have to do what I have to do." Legal documents state that "prior to leaving the Bible study room he stood over a witness . . . and uttered a racially inflammatory statement." Writings on his website have been described as a "long, hate-filled screed" and "racist manifesto."

Thought patterns underlying rage can also lead to hate. Hate is a learned emotion that some psychologists think may be the most dangerous, since it's one of the underpinnings of terrorism, massacres, and genocides throughout history. Hatred can be thought of as extreme dislike and hostility for people different from oneself and seeing all members of that group as having the same negative characteristics. People are abhorred for what they are, not who they are.

Hate can lead to violent acts called hate crimes. A hate crime is defined by the US Department of Justice as "violence of intolerance and bigotry, intended to hurt and intimidate someone because of their race, ethnicity, national origin, religious, sexual orientation, or disability." The number of these crimes is increasing. More than half of hate crimes are committed against people because of their race, and the next most common victims are chosen because of religion and sexual orientation. Every day, at least eight black people, three white people, three gay people, three Jewish people, and one Latino person become hate crime victims, and every week, a cross is burned. Half of all hate crimes in the United States are committed by young people aged fifteen to twenty-four.

People who commit these crimes often aren't mentally ill but are very disturbed, aggressive, and antisocial. They react to their own crises by finding a scapegoat to blame, finding them in ruminations about their prejudices. Motivations for hate crimes are desires for excitement and display of power, moving from smaller offenses to violence. Perpetrators tend to come from abusive homes where violence is used to solve problems.

What kind of thinking leads to hate? In the book *Prisoners of Hate*, Aaron T. Beck describes the egocentrically biased cognitive distortions that lead one to inappropriately feel like a victim wronged by a group that is imagined to be a dangerous villain or enemy. The intensity of misplaced anger against a category of people prompts hostile aggression involving dehumanization and demonization of the enemy, leading to violent and even homicidal ideas. But rather than enabling people to support their well-being, the overwhelming emotion of hate makes people more vulnerable to becoming violent or to ineffective coping.

Psychologist and author Dr. Robert J. Sternberg, past president of the American Psychological Association, wrote, "Wise people do not hate because they understand things from other people's points of view, including those of people with whom they may have strong disagreements. Teaching people to think wisely, therefore, may be the best way to teach them to reject hate."

Parents play a monumental role in preparing children to productively inhabit this diverse world and in teaching them to "think wisely." The National Crime Prevention Council suggests ways that parents can prevent hate by teaching kids about diversity and tolerance, and we've adapted those here:

- Speak positively about people different from oneself.
- Watch and listen to positive entertainment showing people of diverse backgrounds (cultures, sexual orientations, religious affiliations).
- Show the value of diverse friends and coworkers.
- Create opportunities for kids to interact with people different than themselves.
- Enforce a rule that being different is never an OK reason to tease, reject, or label someone.
- Bring attention to scenarios in movies and real life when people are treated cruelly for being a particular race, gender, or minority group.

- Answer your kids' questions and talk about what makes people different.
- Discuss how America is a nation of immigrants with diverse backgrounds.

Extremism

Can entitled attitudes combined with hate and rage promote the development of extremist views? The possible link is intriguing, and we believe that Dylann Roof is an example of how these combined distortions led to extremism and mass murder.

Extremists tend to see and argue only one perspective—theirs. And unyielding views of issues with little or no respect of different opinions held by the majority of other folks are likely extremist ones. Merriam-Webster defines extremism as belief in and support for ideas that are very far from what most people consider correct or reasonable.

Tending to use aggression and violence to advance their one-sided views and desires, extremists can distort the truth and manipulate, threaten, bully, and hurt people who either don't agree or won't give in to their opinions and wishes. Stretching even further, extremists who become terrorists believe that harming innocent people who have no involvement in the issue is appropriate, justified, and promotes their cause.

Timothy McVeigh was a homegrown terrorist who killed 168 innocent young children and adults and wounded hundreds more by bombing the Alfred P. Murrah federal building in 1995. A member of a right-wing radical survivalist group, he bombed the building because he thought it would punish the government for the siege on a cult in Waco, Texas, and for what he saw as infringement of gun rights. Ironically, McVeigh was already in custody for unlawful handgun possession when law enforcement identified him as the bombing suspect, saving the country from a continued massive manhunt and the possibility of additional atrocities. We lived in Oklahoma City during the attack and remember the generosity and resilience of its people.

Before discussing how to mitigate perilous thoughts and emotions, let's move on to positive thoughts and emotions that protect youth from becoming victims or perpetrators.

Empathy Is Self-Protective and Prevents Aggression

Compassion and kindness comprise the essence of humanity. Empathy is the critical emotional ability to put oneself in other people's shoes to understand their feelings and situations. Children may understand it as having sympathy for people when they experience misfortune. Because low empathy or lack of it is a risk factor for aggression and violence, instilling empathy in our youth is essential. Perhaps unexpectedly, having empathy also protects them from becoming victims.

Empathy for Oneself and Others Is Protective

Antoinette Tuff, a bookkeeper at a Georgia elementary school, calmly talked a twenty-year-old armed with an AK-47-style weapon and five hundred rounds of ammunition into surrendering instead of shooting her or the school children. She artfully used empathy by addressing his situation and need for help, saying she had been suicidal too. "It's going to be all right, sweetie," she told him. "I just want you to know I love you though, OK? And I'm proud of you (for giving up)." This strong, smart woman's use of empathy likely saved countless lives.

This story illustrates how empathy for people protects against becoming victims. But empathy for oneself is also protective, particularly after being harmed. Becoming a victim is linked to relationship problems, suicide, delinquency, committing crimes, depression, anxiety, posttraumatic stress disorder (PTSD), and other serious mental illness. How do victims reduce the risk of these aftereffects? They stay connected to supportive people, realize that other people go through trauma too, and treat themselves well—they're compassionate to themselves.

Self-compassion (empathy for oneself) is a strong component of coping and recovering from adversity. It means not repressing painful feelings but empathizing with and processing them rather than trying to change them. It means being patient and kind to oneself in order to ease suffering, just like one would do for a friend. This helps build resources to recover or be assertive when provoked by perpetrators, making revictimization less likely.

Warning Signs of Lack of Empathy

Here's a good (and frightening) example from Brian's clinic of how a child's lack of empathy led him to harm others.

I once worked with a thirteen-year-old boy and his mother who had been swarmed by a SWAT team pointing guns at them while they were getting into their car to go to school one morning. The boy was pulled out of the car, thrown on the ground, and placed in handcuffs. After several tense hours, he was released. His mother learned that someone had called a crisis hotline claiming to be her son, saying he was going to shoot kids at his school and kill his family. This mother and her children were deeply traumatized by the incident.

Two weeks later, I saw a different boy who was in legal trouble for making a false report. It turned out that he had called in the fake threat, and then rode his bike to the other boy's home and watched the SWAT incident unfold. Having seen how his prank affected an entire family, I was struck by this boy's lack of emotion when talking about what he did. When asked why he did it, he said, "To up my cool factor at school." This story illustrates an appalling lack of empathy in a child and how it led to menacing action.

Young children often don't show empathy, because it develops gradually with increasing age. Here are some warning signs of low empathy in later elementary school–age and older kids:

- Doesn't show sympathy for people or characters who are suffering (doesn't care or feel sorry about someone else's trouble, grief, or misfortune). For example, when someone falls down or gets hurt, the child shows no interest or concern, or laughs as opposed to asking if the person is OK or helping.

- Is usually insensitive to the needs of others (watches someone clearly needing help and does nothing).
- Is inconsiderate or doesn't think about other people's feelings: when someone appears upset, the child ignores it as opposed to asking what is wrong.
- Doesn't compliment others (sincere compliments show ability to notice what other people do and give them positive feedback).
- Doesn't listen to others when they're talking, which indicates lack of interest in other people's ideas, situations, or feelings.

Teaching Empathy

Parents and other adults can teach empathy to kids just like reading, writing, and arithmetic. Be aware that harsh punishments interfere with developing empathy, as does watching trusted adults tolerate bullying. From being sensitively cared for in early childhood to being listened to while venting emotions as emerging adults, kids need our continued warm and kind attentions to develop empathy.

In the book *Born for Love*, the authors artfully explain the early origins of empathy, such as parents soothing crying infants and building deep relational bonds over time. They also describe elements of teaching empathy, such as asking kids how other people and story characters feel about their situations, what they might be thinking (their perspectives), and how one's actions affect other people. It's also important to model helping the less fortunate and promote unstructured, nonmedia play allowing for social interactions.

Modeling empathy by empathizing with your children's situations starting in early childhood is also essential. When your kids have problems, think about what they're going through and how you would feel instead of criticizing their emotions ("I see why you're sad, Honey," rather than "Stop crying about it"). Also, starting at about kindergarten age, let your kids know that kindness is very important and you expect it from them. If you note unkind or aggressive behavior, ask how it made people feel and why it's harmful: "You didn't help that kid who got hit by the ball. How would it feel if you got hurt and no one helped?" Remark when they should've been concerned about someone and what they could have done. Instead of saying, "You're mean," focus on the behavior instead: "Laughing at her is mean." Use consequences to enforce kind behaviors—rewards for showing empathy work much better than punishments for not showing it. Talk about feelings and emotions often.

When a boy with awkward movements and slow speech joined our daughter's seventh-grade class, she felt sad because some kids laughed at him. She told us how she invited the boy to eat lunch with her and it made his day (and hers). We extolled the kind gesture and told her we were more proud of her for this than any grade or sporting feat she could accomplish. Achievements fade, but character endures.

Feeling Different with Nothing to Do: Social Isolation and Boredom

Healthy social interactions beginning in early childhood help children feel connected with family and society. While feeling connected protects people, disconnection—social isolation—is a risk factor for victimization and perpetration of violence. We'll describe concerning levels of isolation, how it exacerbates dysfunctional thinking and may get mislabeled as shyness or uniqueness, and how boredom can lead to negative outcomes. These recommendations apply to kids from about fourth grade on. Friends are less important in early childhood, when primary social interactions occur in classrooms and within the family.

Social Isolation

Social isolation is defined as disengagement from social ties, institutional or community connections, or participation with others. Decades of research have shown that social isolation is associated with mental illness and irrational thoughts because we need to be able to test the reality of our thoughts with others. If we can't, we lose touch with reality and may even develop delusions and paranoia that can lead to becoming victims or violent perpetrators.

Social isolation is a risk factor for youth violence, including suicide, especially when combined with anger or depression. Although not all mass murderers are "loners," perpetrators of school shootings are often found to have been socially isolated. Children already struggle with self-concept and commonly have troubling thoughts about themselves and the world. If a child is too isolated, these dysfunctional thoughts can go unchecked. This may result in beliefs that one is not like other people, but is special or superior to others, or instead, an outcast.

Warning Signs of Concerning Levels of Social Isolation

Some children who are alone much of the time might be OK, but the following raise concern about being too isolated and needing help:

- Relationships are impacted (the child doesn't want to be with friends or family so relationships are damaged).
- Difficulty relating to other people.
- Expressing unusual or bizarre thoughts.
- Being preoccupied with fears and activities that feed the desire to isolate oneself.
- Being isolated as a result of being rejected by peers or victimized.
- Not being involved in clubs or organizations.
- Infrequently interacting socially by text or talk.
- Infrequently getting together with friends or family.

A child who is too isolated may be mislabeled as shy or unique. How can we recognize concerning social isolation versus shyness? We suggest looking at avoidance. Shy or unique kids don't tend to avoid close friends and loved ones and still enjoy those contacts but struggle when they get in large groups or new situations. It's when youth avoid contact more pervasively, with rigid refusal to interact with almost everyone that's concerning. Also, if your child has been rejected by a group of friends, it's time to see what's going on and help your child get connected to supportive friends. Read our tips in chapter 7.

Boredom

Adolescence and young adulthood are times when there's a natural tendency to take risks that may include aggressive and violent acts. Boredom is also linked to risk taking and can be a chronic understimulated state leading to thrill seeking such as drug use and crime. In addition, understimulation can lead to feelings of boredom, which can result in engaging in more socially isolating activities like playing video games, watching TV, or surfing the web. Some kids use boredom as an argument for why they should be allowed to do isolating activities. Excessive video game playing or movie watching in isolation can be more harmful, since no one is there to challenge its appropriateness or reality. When children need something to do, parents may even encourage isolating activities to occupy them. Boredom can result from not having enough tasks—kids need us to give them things to do, like chores and helping others. We can also insist on extracurricular activities or youth group involvement. These activities can get them socially connected to siblings, peers, and community.

When Kids Are Socially Connected to Dangerous People

In October 2014, three girls aged fifteen to seventeen skipped school and boarded a plane with intent to eventually join ISIS fighters in Syria. The girls' parents became aware of their plan after their plane bound for Germany was in the air. US officials had the girls detained and returned when they landed in Frankfurt. Review of their social media accounts found that they had been radicalized, in their Colorado homes, by online ISIS recruiters living throughout the Middle East. Unlike the December 2015 case of the radicalized San Bernardino shooters, this story had a very fortuitous ending.

Not all young victims or perpetrators of violence are isolated but instead are very socially connected—to dangerous people. Perilous social connections can occur when your child associates with other aggressive or disturbed individuals face-to-face. But their influence may be even stronger when youth identify and associate with strangers espousing antisocial views and hate online. We'll provide ways to counteract hazardous relationships later in the book.

Changing Perilous Thinking

We've discussed detrimental, self-defeating ways youth may think and feel that are linked to aggression and violence, such as entitlement, rage and hate, hostile views of actions, blaming others instead of taking personal responsibility, lack of empathy, and boredom. You can help your kids reframe dysfunctional thoughts into more protective beliefs. As you try these suggestions, use the axiom "Actions speak much louder than words" as your guide to progress; kids may conceal beliefs by not saying anything while their actions say much.

What to Try

We can gently challenge dysfunctional thoughts by pointing out inaccuracies, unrealistic aspects, and how these thoughts can harm our kids or others. This process takes several conversations over time.

Finding the Words

To gently challenge dysfunctional thoughts, it's most important to say things using the word *I*, such as *I think . . .* , *I feel . . .* , or *I believe . . .* , because this conveys your feelings and opinions while preventing defensiveness. On the other hand, saying, "That's wrong," or "You shouldn't feel that way," will likely be unpersuasive and off-putting. Talk when something related to your concern surfaces in your child's speech or behavior. Simply state your thoughts and beliefs. You can also use *I worry . . .* and *I wonder . . . . .* For example:

- *I feel worried about you because of the way you're thinking.*
- *I'm sad that you feel that way. Over time I believe (I hope) you'll realize . . . for your sake . . .*

- *I wonder how that belief is going to work for you.*
- *I noticed you said . . . and that's not part of our family's values.*

Gently correct exaggerations that make things seem worse than they are (*You said the word "always," but that isn't really correct, is it?*). Don't tease or humiliate kids for their opinions or feelings. Also, talk through and test the accuracy of their assumptions to help them avoid jumping to conclusions about events or other people's actions. For example, if your child inaccurately sees someone's action as a personal attack: *Let's look at the facts and his perspective, because I think what he did wasn't a personal attack on you but just an accident (or he was just upset).*

Let's look at examples using wordings in the sidebar. Let's say your child repeatedly expects teachers to accept late assignments (a sign of entitlement): "I'm worried that if you expect special treatment now, you'll expect it in other things like sports and jobs. I think you'll find you won't get it, which could make you angry or unhappy as you continue to struggle for it."

If your child states that all members of a race or gender act the same negative way (a risk factor for rage and hate): "I feel sad and disappointed that you feel that way. For your sake, I hope over time you'll realize it isn't true. If not, I feel afraid that you'll learn to hate and hurt people different from you, which can lead to danger."

If your child believes in fistfighting to solve disputes (belief in using violence to solve problems): "I wonder how that belief is going to work for you in life. I think it'll lead to trouble in relationships, school, and jobs, and may even lead you to use weapons someday when fists aren't working. I want better for you, so let's figure out other ways to solve problems."

If your child chronically blames others for disappointments or failures: "I'm worried about the way you're thinking, that others are mostly to blame. If you don't learn to see how you can do things differently and which things are under your control, I worry it'll limit your happiness and success in life by making yourself a chronic victim."

Don't expect your children to say, "Yeah, you're right, I changed my mind." That's unlikely to happen and doesn't need to for your comments to sink in. Even when they don't appear to have changed their minds, what you say can still affect their beliefs and actions. If they continue to behave dangerously, your actions to stop activities based on dysfunctional thoughts will matter more than words you use.

How to Challenge Entitled Thoughts and Attitudes

You can reframe entitled thoughts into prosocial ones and help kids see the benefits by using the steps just described. But you'll also need to know what to do when they bring up their "rights." Entitled kids often believe they have "a right" to do whatever they want, even when it could harm you or them: use drugs and alcohol, ignore curfew, quit school, purchase whatever they want, or disrespect you.

Entitled kids may engage in repetitive arguments, trying to impress you with their knowledge of an activity or issue and convince you to approve. Your knowledge and experience are better bases on which to make decisions; besides, you're responsible for their well-being. Simply say, "You don't have the right to do things that harm you (or us)," or "I'm not going to let you grow up only looking out for yourself, because that'll make you and others around you unhappy. Entitled attitudes will make people not trust or want to be with you. You've got to care about others if you want them to care about you."

How Youth Cope with Adversity

Kids can develop protective thoughts that help them cope with bad events and stress. Methods of coping change as children age, from fussing in early childhood to thinking things through and adapting emotions and behaviors by young adulthood. When young people are resilient, they can bounce back from disappointment, failure, criticism, and other adversity without hurting themselves or others.

People often remark how resilient children are when they seem OK after a traumatic event. But just because a child appears to be all right doesn't mean that he or she won't have negative psychological effects from a traumatic event—kids need resilience and coping skills to thrive. Being able to cope protects a child who has risk factors for violence. Kids with aggression problems may be using it as a coping mechanism.

The good news is that parents can help build resilience and teach coping skills. Entire books have been written about this, so we'll simply list some pearls for you.

Ways to Build Resilience and Ability to Cope in Youth

The *Handbook of Resilience in Children* and recent research reviews of resilience and coping point to the following components that protect children from harmful consequences of adversity:

- Having warm family relationships in which they feel valued, appreciated, listened to, and empathized with. Positive relationships with mentors and others can also work.
- Enduring brief, intermittent, minor stressors. This helps build experience and confidence in their ability to solve problems. We can dampen resilience by solving their problems when they can do it themselves (so we should let them try even when they can't do it as well as we can). But you can help them recognize when something is out their control and be their adviser when they ask for help and when you're worried about safety.
- Learning that it's good to seek help from supportive people.
- Feeling successful at doing one or more things (schoolwork, hobbies, music, sports, or other abilities), but these successes need to come from taking responsibility, making decisions, and learning from mistakes. This may require parents to accept their kids for who they are and help them avoid unrealistic achievement goals.
- Gradually gaining control of actions and emotions.

You can help model good coping skills by using them at home with your own problems. One way is by not blaming others for your problems. When kids blame others for a disappointment, help them see their role and discuss what they could do differently in the future. Feeling like a victim when one isn't can be a lifelong habit that leads people to lash out in anger when disappointed. Also, don't allow children to ruminate over losses. Ruminating (rehashing the distressing aspects of an event over and over) is clearly linked to depression and aggression and sabotages coping.

Problem Solving for Kids

One important element of coping with adversity is being able to solve problems, especially with other people. This involves gathering information, planning, and then acting. The *Handbook of Parent Training* provides a good overview of teaching children how to solve social and other problems. Conflict resolution between family members was covered on page 8, and your kids can also use this for conflicts with friends.

Here are steps to teach problem solving to kids. If they're upset, wait until they've calmed down. Once they have some success, it's important to let them try to solve their problems by themselves, using you as an adviser when needed:

1. Help your child identify the problem. Ask what's wrong and try to understand from the child's perspective by having him or her explain what is happening. Ask about the possible causes so the child can see his or her role in the problem.
2. Ask for possible solutions—what your child thinks might help with the problem. If your child is unable to think of anything, or only thinks of solutions that are harmful, make suggestions.
3. Evaluate the consequences that might come from each possible solution (the pros and cons of each), including how your child

would feel or others would feel about that solution, in order to decide which ones seem best.

4. After deciding on one or more solutions, ask if your child followed his or her plan. This and the next step are probably only appropriate when kids are nine or older, since younger kids have limited ability to follow through on plans.

5. Ask how things went to help your child learn what works and what doesn't work for that type of problem.

There are many forces that can mold the way children think, such as media, peers, and substances. But now you know how to promote thoughts and beliefs that will provide your children with protection against harm while recognizing and squelching risky thoughts and emotions. Enabling social interaction and coping skills, teaching problem solving and empathy, and building self-preserving resilience and self-esteem are also lifetime gifts you can give your children. Like all parenting skills, these things take patience, work, and practice, but your efforts will benefit you, your kids, and all of us.

3

Mental and Emotional Issues Tied to Aggression and Violence

At the root of this dilemma is the way we view mental health in this country. Whether an illness affects your heart, your leg, or your brain, it's still an illness, and there should be no distinction.

—Michelle Obama

What do Buzz Aldrin, Terry Bradshaw, Drew Carey, Winston Churchill, Ernest Hemingway, Abraham Lincoln, Jane Pauley, and Princess Diana have in common? They all experienced mental illness and achieved great success through outstanding accomplishments.

It's estimated that about one in five adults had a mental illness other than a substance use disorder in 2014, and that nearly 50% of all US adults will develop at least one mental disorder during their lifetimes. Mental illness simply reflects altered processes in the brain that harm our emotional, psychological, and social well-being by disturbing how we think, feel, and act. Mental disorders reduce our ability to deal with stress, relate to others, and make choices. As with many physical illnesses, they are caused by biochemical imbalances, exposures, and family history. And like most physical illnesses, mental illness can be managed and treated.

According to a 2013 CDC report, mental and emotional issues are increasing in children. About one in five children living in the United

States experiences a seriously debilitating mental illness, with an estimated annual cost of $247 billion. There are even higher numbers of children with milder forms of mental disorders: about 45% of youth will have a mental illness at some point by age eighteen.

Parents often wonder if their children's issues are "normal." Many mentally healthy children show behaviors that are part of diagnostic criteria for an illness. But when children are diagnosed with a mental disorder, it means their symptoms are significantly impairing the way they learn, behave, handle emotions, or interact with others, reflecting higher frequency, intensity, and pervasiveness of symptoms compared to nonaffected kids.

This chapter will review psychological disorders that first appear or have origins in childhood or young adulthood and factors that increase or reduce risks of aggression and violence. Information and warning signs will help you recognize when your children need help.

Most People with Mental Illnesses Are Not Violent

When Alvaro Castillo was eighteen years old, he had already tried to commit suicide and had been hospitalized for mental illness. Soon after discharge, a social worker tried to get him an urgent psychiatric appointment but there was a six-week backlog and another clinic wouldn't see him. Not long afterward, Castillo shot his father dead and, dressed like the Columbine shooters with whom he was obsessed, drove to his alma mater and opened fire. It may be natural to blame mental illness for Castillo's actions, but we'll begin by emphasizing two very important points.

First, while having certain types of mental illness can raise the risk for becoming violent, the vast majority of children and adults with psychiatric disorders are *not* violent or aggressive. Conversely, the vast majority of violent people don't have a mental illness.

Second, adults with mental illness are significantly more likely to be victims of violence rather than perpetrators. In fact, mentally ill people are up to twenty-three times more likely to be victims of violence than the general population, often due to emotional regulation difficulties. This victimization alone strongly increases the chances of being aggressive and violent. One study showed that having any mental disorder increases the risk of homicidal death fivefold and having a substance use disorder increases it ninefold. When people with mental illness do become violent, two-thirds of episodes occur at home rather than in public.

Research suggests the top ten personal risk factors for perpetrating violence in the general population are as follows, in order from strongest to weakest:

1. Age between eighteen and thirty-four.
2. Male gender.
3. Substance abuse.
4. Low educational achievement.
5. Underemployment; poverty.
6. Entitled, aggressive, or antisocial attitudes that condone hurting others to get what you want; impulsive anger.
7. Deviant friends, relationship problems.
8. History of child abuse or other victimization.
9. Parental criminal activity.
10. Witnessing domestic violence.

Mental illness is around number fourteen on the list. If we were able to magically eliminate mental illness, it's estimated the population prevalence of committing violence would go down only by about 4%.

Factors That Increase or Reduce Risk of Violence in Mental Illness

Some factors appear to increase the risk of violence for people with mental illnesses. These include not receiving appropriate treatment, not staying on medications, active substance abuse, history of violent home backgrounds, social isolation, and history of being victimized (such as by child abuse). As you may recall, people with mental illness have high rates of violent victimization. So the real trigger for violence doesn't appear to be the mental illness as much as these other factors, which are regrettably all too common. Speaking of drug and alcohol abuse, *substance use disorder* is a psychiatric diagnosis clearly associated with victimization and perpetration of violence.

While there are biological and genetic factors in many mental disorders, how people function can often be altered by experiences. Protective and risk factors—which are most often experiences in a child's life—affect the chance of victimization and perpetration. We believe that research shows parenting is the single most important experiential protective factor affecting children's mental, emotional, and behavioral outcomes (and that's why we wrote this book). Now let's take a look at psychological problems in youth.

Types of Childhood Psychological Disorders

Mental health professionals frequently group childhood disorders into one of three broad categories: externalizing (outwardly exhibited symptoms and behaviors), internalizing (processes directed inward), and developmental (affecting development) disorders.

Externalizing Disorders

Children with externalizing disorders act out excessively, are disinhibited, or lack restraint. Their behaviors typically create problems for others.

Attention-deficit/hyperactivity disorder (ADHD) is the most prevalent; it affects about 9% of kids under age eighteen, and boys are affected twice as often. It is characterized by the so-called holy trinity of symptoms: developmentally inappropriate levels of inattention, impulsivity, and hyperactivity that negatively affect social, academic, or occupational functioning. There are essentially three types: predominantly inattentive, predominantly hyperactive-impulsive, and combined. Inattentive symptoms include often being distractible and making careless mistakes, inability to sustain attention, and difficulty organizing tasks or activities. Hyperactive-impulsive behaviors include frequent fidgeting, being on the go as if driven by a motor, running about, and getting out of one's seat when expected to remain seated.

For diagnosis, there should be evidence of problematic symptoms before age twelve, and behaviors should be present in more than one setting. Girls are more likely to have the predominantly inattentive subtype, which is diagnosed later in childhood when kids are described as being daydreamy, spacey, and lethargic.

While ADHD can be linked to aggression, management of symptoms minimizes the risk. Parents often wonder if their child's aggression can be explained by ADHD. In other words, can we tell hyperactive kids apart from aggressive ones? The short answer is, not easily. It can be helpful to consider the impact a child has on adults other than caretakers. Aggressive children are more likely to induce anger, frustration, or fear in teachers or relatives. Also, peers tend to avoid aggressive children, so they often don't have many long-term friendships; kids with ADHD who aren't aggressive are more likely to have long-term friendships.

Oppositional defiant disorder (ODD) affects about 3% of children and is characterized by anger, irritability, and aggression. For diagnosis, these symptoms need to be accompanied by arguing with authority figures, intentionally not doing what is expected, and acts of revenge, and these behaviors need to be present for at least six months and negatively affect others. Kids with ODD often lose tempers, are easily annoyed, deliberately annoy others, and have increased risks of antisocial behavior, substance use, depression, anxiety, and problems in academic and occupational settings. Boys are more likely to have it.

Conduct disorder (CD) is the most serious of the externalizing disorders and is commonly found in juvenile delinquents. Few children with CD receive treatment and so it often progresses into antisocial personality disorder in adulthood. CD affects about 4% of children and those diagnosed before the age of ten often have a worse prognosis. Boys are more likely to have it. Some associated behaviors include frequently initiating physical fights, being physically cruel to people or animals, fire setting, breaking and entering, and skipping school without good reason. Children with CD have risks similar to those with ODD, including aggressive and violent behavior.

There's an interesting relationship among these three externalizing disorders. About half of children with ADHD will eventually be diagnosed with ODD. About half of those with ADHD plus ODD will eventually be diagnosed with CD. Consequently, ODD and CD affect millions of children. Harsh, inconsistent discipline, parental rejection, and lack of parental supervision have been strongly associated with this progression and thus development of criminal activities in youth. Our society would benefit greatly by prioritizing parenting help.

Warning Signs of Externalizing Disorders

Here are some signs that children likely have externalizing disorders and need evaluation:

- Increasing number or severity of diagnostic symptoms just described.
- Impulsivity that leads children to take dangerous risks resulting in more accidents.
- Cruelty to animals—this reflects a concerning lack of empathy and sadistic tendencies. It's common for kids to harm insects and to kill animals when hunting for sport, but when children are intentionally cruel to domesticated animals, or torture any mammal, the time to intervene has come. Mass murderer Jeffrey Dahmer got his start dismembering small animals and we know where that led.
- Fire setting. While many kids are fascinated by flames, most will resist playing with fire outside of appropriate settings. By definition, concerning fire-setting behavior is when a child intends to cause damage. Claiming a fire was "an accident" should only happen once and many fire departments offer programs for kids who have started fires.
- Poop problems. Another interesting warning sign concerns what they do with their feces (poop). Children with externalizing disorders are more likely to relieve themselves inappropriately, like in bathroom sinks, showers, or on floors. They may smear their

feces on walls or mirrors. (Brian once had a child hide some feces on the inside of a toilet paper roll and then put the roll back in the dispenser!) They may intentionally soil themselves, but parents need to be sure their child doesn't have a treatable medical condition called *encopresis*, in which children get so constipated that feces leak into their underwear. This leakage is beyond their control and they mustn't be punished for it.

Internalizing Disorders

Children affected by internalizing disorders often exhibit behaviors that are less disruptive to others but problematic to the child and often overlooked by parents. For this reason, kids are typically older when first diagnosed.

Depression is an internalizing disorder that has been called the "common cold" of mental disorders because it's so, well, common. This doesn't diminish the impact that depression has on the lives of those affected and those around them. Up to 10% of adults are clinically depressed (meaning they have diagnosable depression) at any given point in time, about 20% will become so in their lifetimes, and females are twice as likely to be diagnosed. About 9% of American children up to age seventeen are clinically depressed, up to 20% of teenagers develop major depression, and almost 4% are currently taking an antidepressant. However, in 2013 the CDC reported that almost one in three high school students reported feeling significantly sad or hopeless, indicating a much higher number of undiagnosed cases.

Being unable to adequately express and regulate sadness and anger can lead to depression. This disease involves definite and persistent changes in mood (feeling sad, hopeless, empty, or worthless), lack of interest in previously enjoyable activities, weight changes, sleeping problems, difficulty concentrating, fatigue, and thoughts of death. In children, depression can present differently: extreme irritability can replace sad mood, and agitation and argumentativeness can replace fatigue. Depression can detrimentally affect relationships and academic performance.

Disruptive mood dysregulation disorder is a new psychological diagnosis (like we needed more). It's characterized by frequent, severe, and inappropriate temper outbursts (at least three times a week) inappropriate for age. Affected kids are at elevated risk of aggression and suicide. For diagnosis, mood is persistently irritable or angry between outbursts and symptoms need to be present before age ten. It's an internalizing disorder because follow-up studies show eventual diagnoses of anxiety or depression.

Anxiety and depression commonly co-occur. As with depression, there are different subtypes that are quite common. It's estimated that 25% of thirteen- to eighteen-year-olds have symptoms of an anxiety disorder and 6% have a severe anxiety disorder. Females again are diagnosed about twice as often. Anxiety disorders can be expressed in different ways, from fear of specific animals or activities (phobias) or being away from important people (separation) to panic attacks. All subtypes involve fear, anxiousness, avoidance, and worry. By the way, fear is an emotional response to a real or perceived current threat, whereas anxiety results from anticipating future threats.

While some anxiety is normal and even motivating, it becomes a disorder when it impairs one's social, emotional, academic, or occupational functioning. Individuals often overestimate the danger being posed to them, and as a result, experience physical symptoms like racing heart rate or chest pain. Common illogical thoughts linked to anxiety include, "I'm going to die," "I'm going to lose control," and "I'm going crazy."

Posttraumatic stress disorder (PTSD) is related to anxiety disorders and affects 4% of children. Children with PTSD were either victims of or witnesses to traumatic situations involving actual or threatened death, serious injury, or sexual violence. Individuals with PTSD have intrusive thoughts (harmful thoughts they can't control), persistently avoid things related to the event, and have trouble accurately remembering the event, persistent negative emotions, and increased reactivity.

Being victimized may make youth more aggressive by promoting retaliation. Even when they are not victims, people with depression and anxiety may have reduced ability to accurately assess a threat or respond calmly to provocation, thereby heightening the risk of aggressive or violent responses. Internalizing disorders are also risk factors for suicide.

Bipolar depression generally begins in late adolescence to mid-twenties, but can develop throughout adulthood and affects about 2% of the population. Its presence in children is a subject of debate because symptoms frequently don't meet diagnostic criteria. Bipolar disorders are now considered to be a separate class of mental illness that "bridges" depressive and psychotic disorders. There are two common subtypes. In Bipolar I disorder, mania is the most prominent feature and diagnosis requires at least one distinct manic episode in which the person has abnormal, persistently elevated, expansive, or irritable mood and increased energy or activity level. The manic episode may, but doesn't have to be, followed by a reduction in mania symptoms (called *hypomania*) or the development of depression. In Bipolar II disorder, depression is the most prominent feature and requires meeting criteria for a major depressive episode preceded or followed by elevated mood not necessarily meeting criteria for mania.

Bipolar disorders are a risk factor for violent and aggressive behaviors toward others and oneself. About one in three affected individuals has attempted suicide at some point in his or her life.

Warning Signs of Internalizing Disorders

Warning signs that children may have internalizing behaviors include these:

- Significant or worsening difficulties functioning in daily life.
- Significant moodiness, isolation, irritability, or lack of interest in enjoyable activities. It's important not to discount these as "just being teenagers"; when these cut off interaction with other people, it's a warning sign that intervention is required to prevent harm to self or others.

- Any type of skin cutting or scratching—this is a cry for help that must be met. If your child doesn't want you to see her or his arms or legs, it's time to look.
- Frequently creating drawings or stories with dark content and themes.
- Making statements suggesting negative views of themselves, their world, and their futures.
- Excessive worrying or unreasonable fears.
- Unusual, repetitive, and planned behaviors that interfere with functioning (needs to open and close the back door five times before leaving for school).
- "Accidents" that are potentially life threatening.

Early intervention is associated with not only faster recovery from internalizing disorders but also fewer future episodes. For instance, a child with untreated depression will typically return to baseline functioning in about six months. So yes, a depressed child will get better. But six months is the majority of an academic year, and the damaging recurrent episodes resulting from not getting treatment may last a lifetime.

Developmental Disorders

Developmental disorders are often diagnosed when children are young, usually before the age of five, and frequently co-occur with other disorders.

Children with **intellectual disabilities** have significantly below-average ability to perform age-appropriate self-care, communication, academic, and socialization skills.

Learning disabilities, another type of developmental disorder, are characterized by persistent difficulty learning key academic skills that can't be explained by low intellectual functioning. Intellectual and learning disabilities are both linked with poor academic performance, a risk factor for aggression, victimization, and criminal activity.

Autism spectrum disorders are estimated to affect one in sixty-eight; boys are affected almost five times more often than girls. One, named **Asperger's syndrome**, has received considerable attention because Adam Lanza was reportedly diagnosed with this condition. However, as of 2013, Asperger's is no longer classified as a mental disorder; rather, its symptoms represent a less severely impaired end of the autism spectrum. Autism spectrum disorder is a neurodevelopmental disorder characterized by (1) persistent problems communicating with others; (2) restricted, repetitive patterns of behavior, interests, or activities; (3) obvious symptoms before age five; and (4) significant impairment in social, occupational, or other important areas of current functioning. The severity of this disease is now based on the level of support required by the child on a scale of one to three, with level three indicating the highest need for social communication, behavior, and activity support.

People with autism spectrum disorder frequently have intellectual or learning disabilities, but not always. They can have additional medical, genetic, or mental disorders. Aggression and temper tantrums can be seen in autism spectrum disorder. However, experts agree that people with these disorders rarely commit violent crimes and are no more likely to become violent than someone in the general population.

Children with symptoms of any mental illness need to be seen by a mental health professional. Untreated, these disorders are risk factors for being victims and offenders of violence and aggression, but affected youth are much more likely to be victimized. Why? It may be due to associated substance use, living in violent areas or those without services, putting themselves in riskier situations, closer contact with other mentally ill people, lower ability to recognize dangerous situations or defend themselves, or appearing vulnerable to bullies or predators.

What We've Learned About Adam Lanza

So if people with autism spectrum disorder aren't more likely to commit violent crimes, what happened with Adam Lanza? Before he did the unthinkable, people generally thought Adam was a socially awkward, bright twenty-year-old with Asperger's syndrome. The event sparked many questions about how his mental disorder and life events may have contributed to his crimes.

We've assembled what we believe were important contributory factors that led to a rare violent act in someone diagnosed with autism spectrum disorder. We've used important work by Andrew Solomon in his interview with Adam's father, Peter Lanza, the joint article by the *Hartford Courant* and *Frontline*, and the *Shooting at Sandy Hook Elementary School: Report of the Office of the Child Advocate*. The following are elements of Adam's life that we'll tie to warning signs for violence.

Adam had few friends growing up and was described by his father as being "just a normal little weird kid." Adam reportedly had trouble understanding the emotions of others and was coached by his mother on how to read and interpret people's facial expressions. In fifth grade, he reportedly didn't think much of himself.

Adam's parents' worries increased when he entered middle school, because he stopped engaging in previously enjoyable activities—he now hated birthdays and holidays. He developed an awkward, stiff gait and reportedly had more "episodes," perhaps representing panic attacks, in which he would become too emotional or agitated to engage in specific activities.

At age thirteen, Adam was reportedly diagnosed with Asperger's syndrome. From eighth grade on he was homeschooled because the typical middle school was too overwhelming for him. Problems continued, and at age fourteen his parents took him to the prestigious Yale Child Study Center for another evaluation. The psychiatrist who assessed Adam noted features typical of Asperger's but also ones that were excessive and concerning. Adam had reportedly developed signs of rigid orderliness and fears of being contaminated after touching objects. The psychiatrist saw Adam's mother as practically a prisoner in her own home. Adam had even been requiring her to walk a certain way and not to lean on things, saying it was "improper."

While orderliness and rigidity are features of autism spectrum disorder, these features generally present in a way that controls only the child's life. Affected children are not usually interested in actively controlling the lives of others, such as telling a parent how to walk. Thus, Adam's symptoms were consistent with having a second psychiatric disorder: *obsessive-compulsive disorder* (OCD). The Child Study Center staff was also concerned that Adam's parents were too focused on academic progress instead of his severe social deficits, anxiety, and isolation.

When Adam was sixteen, Nancy's e-mails to Peter describe further deterioration: "He had a horrible night. . . . He cried in the bathroom for 45 minutes and missed his first class." Later she wrote, "I am hoping that he pulls together in time for school this afternoon, but it's doubtful. He has been sitting with his head to one side for over an hour doing nothing."

Warning Signs That Youth with Mental Disorders Are at Risk for Committing Violence

Yes, Adam had odd behaviors, and yes, children with autism spectrum disorders can behave oddly. But in addition to evidence of OCD, there were warning signs of more serious psychological illness that we'll review. Parents may attribute worrisome behaviors to an emotional or mental diagnosis like autism. But in hindsight, many of Adam's behaviors were not remotely characteristic of it.

Adam's case provides us with valuable information to help formulate warning signs of increased concern and need for comprehensive treatment in a child with a mental health diagnosis. These warning signs indicate the need for intervention regardless of diagnosis, and even when violence is not a concern, they indicate the child needs help.

Evidence of severe depression. It's unusual for children with autism spectrum disorder to suddenly develop a dislike for previously enjoyable activities like holidays and birthdays.

Isolation and withdrawal. In early 2012, Nancy said that Adam had agreed to see Peter but nothing came of it. Both Adam's older brother and Peter made multiple attempts to communicate with Adam, but there was no reply. Peter later recognized that "Adam was drifting away." The state's attorney's report noted that people who worked on the Nancy Lanza property couldn't enter the house and were warned to never ring the doorbell. In the months prior to his heinous crimes, Adam reportedly would only communicate with his mother through e-mail despite living together. About a week before the shootings, Nancy reportedly told an acquaintance, "I'm worried I'm losing him," reflecting his withdrawal.

While children with various disorders may not be very interested in social relationships, they don't typically actively isolate themselves from others, especially loved ones. Homeschooling further isolated Adam, gave him control, and further interfered with his learning how to relate to others.

Parents walking on eggshells around their children. Perhaps not knowing or considering the long-term consequences, Nancy reportedly would do whatever she could to ensure that Adam's day was as stress free as possible. She indulged his compulsions and desire for isolation, despite how controlling and hostile he became. "She would build the world around him and cushion it," Peter said. Thus, Adam may have exhibited symptoms of the newly designated disruptive mood dysregulation disorder, which is associated with aggression and suicide.

Catering to children's demands for fear of how they will react is a warning sign that things need to change. Catering to make a good day often creates a miserable year when things progress. Parents of children with or without mental disorders learn quickly what things set off their children; these are known as triggers. Understanding triggers doesn't mean parents should avoid them at all costs, but they should prepare for their child's reactions that follow and help the child regain composure.

Peter's interactions with Adam gradually became very limited, especially after the divorce. Nancy had often asked Peter not to see their son when Adam was having a bad day. Frustrated, Peter reportedly adopted a hands-off approach to parenting so he could avoid confrontations with Nancy and Adam. In hindsight, Peter indicated that Adam was probably cutting him out because he could control Nancy more easily.

It's not uncommon for children to try to manipulate their parents following a divorce. If they can put their parents at odds, they can get pretty much whatever they want. When this happens, children will usually get one parent to side with them, and together they will minimize the influence of the other parent through a process called *triangulation.* When divorced parents can maintain respectful, open communication focused on joint parenting, triangulation is less likely to occur.

Worsening signs of other emotional and mental illness. After Nancy told Peter about one of Adam's breakdowns where he cried for hours and moved most of the furniture out of his room, Peter reportedly replied, "Adam needs to communicate the source of his sorrow. We have less than three months to help him before he is 18." In an interview, Peter stated, "It was crystal clear something was wrong; the social awkwardness, the uncomfortable anxiety, unable to sleep, stress, unable to concentrate, having a hard time learning, the awkward walk, reduced eye contact. You could see the changes occurring." He also acknowledged that it was hard to know if new problems were developing or old ones were getting worse.

The last time Peter saw his son alive was in September 2010. Nancy's e-mails to Peter had been painting increasingly dire situations: "He is despondent and crying a lot and just can't continue. . . . I have been trying to get him to see you and he refuses and every time I've brought the subject up it just makes him worse." But in 2011 Nancy communicated apparent improvements, perhaps indicating her denial of the situation. During this time, Adam stopped returning his father's e-mails.

Violent writings, gaming, and fantasies. In fifth grade, Adam and a friend wrote a story in which a character liked hurting people, especially children, and a granny and son wanted to use taxidermy to mount a murdered boy for their mantelpiece. Two years later, another teacher had concerns about disturbing violence in his writings. After the murders, investigations of Lanza's online and home activities revealed an obsession with mass murder and fascination with guns, war, and serial killers. He even reportedly edited Wikipedia entries on various well-known mass murderers. Inside his mother's home, he played video games for hours at a time, some of which were violent. He developed a spreadsheet of mass murderers with numbers of victims and had cyber-friends with whom he would discuss mass killers. Black trash bags were put over his windows to block out sunlight, furthering his isolation.

Low self-esteem and personal failures. Children with low self-esteem and histories of personal failures are at increased risk for both victimization and perpetration of violence. In his later teens, Adam took classes at a university for high school credit. He apparently had many goals that were beyond his abilities. Nancy related his increasing despair at his inability to understand and learn: "He said he tried to concentrate and couldn't and has been wondering why he is 'such a loser' and if there is anything he can do about it."

Hate and entitlement. In his isolation, Adam's hate for everyone, including himself and his indulgent mother, appeared to grow. A document was found on his computer named "Selfish," which described why women are selfish by nature. It's ironic that he wrote this, given that Nancy appears to have dedicated her life to Adam, and suggests how out of touch with reality he had become.

Nancy was the first person Adam killed. *Matricide*, or the killing of one's mother, is usually committed by overprotected boys wanting to free themselves from dependency on their mothers. It's been reported that when Nancy asked him if he would be sad should anything happen to her, he said no. Nancy was shot four times while sleeping in her bed.

Adam also reportedly discounted his parents' knowledge when they were trying to homeschool him. This may have been another missed warning sign—entitlement. Understandably, Peter and Nancy attributed it to the "the arrogance that Aspies can have," but Adam's arrogance appeared extreme. At one point, he reportedly asserted that he needed to teach himself chemistry. Aggrieved entitlement and lack of empathy are possible reasons for Lanza's actions: because his suffering wasn't relieved, other people deserved to suffer too. Therefore it appears that in Adam's mind, his mother, other people, and he himself needed to die.

Suicidal tendency. Peter Lanza has stated, "I know Adam would have killed me in a heartbeat, if he'd had the chance. I don't question that for a minute. The reason he shot Nancy four times was one for each of us [members of their family]." Killing others and then himself appeared to be a crucial part of Lanza's plan.

Almost all mass shooters in recent years committed a type of suicide. In other words, if they didn't kill themselves or weren't killed by law enforcement, those who were arrested were locked up for life if they didn't get the death penalty. Thus, suicidality is a risk factor for committing mass murder. Adam's self-loathing, despair, and isolation were risk factors for suicide.

Unwillingness or inability to recognize urgent need for treatment. Adam apparently didn't agree with his parents or doctors that he had Asperger's and wasn't open to counseling. A nurse practitioner expressed concern that he refused to take an antidepressant due to side effects and reportedly didn't think anything was wrong with him. If Adam had been forced to see a counselor, the counselor would have needed to form a therapeutic relationship with him in order to be effective. On average it takes three to five sessions to establish this, but for some clients it can take much longer. Among the most difficult people to treat in outpatient settings are young, angry, suspicious, isolated males who don't think anything is wrong with them. Adding social awkwardness with Asperger's, it's quite likely Adam would have frozen in a counseling environment. Perhaps a school counselor or psychologist could have been successful via almost-daily contact with him over an extended period of time, but Adam had been homeschooled.

We believe this indicates Adam needed facility or inpatient treatment. When he was still a teenager, he could have been involuntarily hospitalized for treatment. It becomes much more difficult to force youth to get treatment after age eighteen.

What to Do When You Notice These Warning Signs

When children display these warning signs of worsening mental illness or distress, it calls for lifesaving measures:

- Ensure that your child cannot access firearms or other weapons.
- Obtain psychological evaluation and treatment.
- Increase supervision and monitoring of activities, including electronic and written communications. This involves going into your child's "private spaces," including rooms and cars.

- Tell friends, loved ones, teachers, and others connected to your child about your concerns and ask them to notify you of any concerns.
- If you find evidence of a plan where others could be harmed, call police, and notify pertinent professionals and family members. This is no time to "save face" or avoid embarrassing your child. The more detailed the plan, the greater the urgency.
- Follow suicide precautions discussed later in this chapter.

Shooters and Other Violent Youth Don't "Just Snap"

Many normal-appearing children and young adults have committed violent crimes, leading people to say things like, "He just snapped." But there's very little evidence to support the notion that people suddenly act out in unpredictable, violent rages without warning. Adam Lanza was in control of his actions: he destroyed electronic evidence and left a photo of himself pointing a gun at his own head, suggesting a well-planned massacre.

For most violent perpetrators, "snapping" occurs after a prolonged period of "boiling"; when the ability to cope is overwhelmed, an explosion occurs. Thus, even though predicting who will become violent in the future is relatively difficult, it's much easier to predict and identify who's at high risk for becoming that distressed. By identifying and helping children who are in despair or at risk for despair, we can help avoid future mass shootings—but we won't know for certain how many we prevent, given that they won't happen.

Keep in mind that problematic youth behaviors like those just reviewed need to be addressed regardless of the diagnosis. Now we'll explore the most concerning types of mental illness and links with violence and aggression.

Psychopathy, Psychosis, and Violence

All the above mental illnesses can be associated with being victims and perpetrators, especially when illnesses and exacerbating factors combine, as in Lanza's case. But there are other disorders that by themselves have strong ties to victimization and violent behavior.

Psychopathy

Psychopathy (pronounced sigh-COP-ah-th-ee) is characterized by three separate but overlapping traits: interpersonal deficits (arrogance, deceitfulness, grandiosity); emotional deficits (lack of guilt, or lack of concern or empathy for others); and impulsivity paired with criminal attitudes (sexual promiscuity, embezzlement, or stealing). Because they can be superficially charming, psychopaths often make good first impressions but actually are dishonest and unreliable, using others for personal gain.

Physical aggression and violence is associated with psychopathy, but not all psychopaths act this way. Men are much more likely to be physically aggressive or violent than women. Some psychopaths, however, go on to attain high positions in business, government, or religious organizations.

Antisocial Personality Disorder

The term psychopathy is not a formal psychiatric diagnosis. The closest current diagnosis is *antisocial personality disorder* (ASPD). Like psychopathy, behaviors associated with ASPD generally violate the rights of others and include unlawful behaviors (like theft), aggression or violence (such as assault), deceitfulness (repeated lying, use of aliases, manipulation), impulsivity, irritability, reckless disregard for oneself and others, consistent irresponsibility, and lack of remorse. Antisocial behavior in adolescents usually manifests as delinquency. A formal diagnosis of ASPD shouldn't be made until age eighteen and requires evidence of a conduct disorder prior to age fifteen. About 25% of children with a CD are eventually diagnosed with ASPD.

Up to 3% of the adult population has ASPD, which is more common in males. There are conditions that appear to increase the likelihood of developing it: a childhood behavior disorder such as ADHD or CD; child abuse or neglect; and inconsistent parental involvement and discipline. Some children's families have the money to hire attorneys to make their juvenile's legal history disappear at age eighteen, which makes it harder to document an important diagnostic feature of the disorder: evidence of early legal troubles. So, it's not surprising that ASPD is more commonly diagnosed among impoverished males.

Warning Signs of Psychopathy or ASPD

Here are warning signs of dangerous mental illness that we've described in psychopathy and ASPD or risk of developing them:

- Callous-unemotional traits in response to those in distress.
- Cruelty to domestic animals, such as dogs or cats.
- Difficulty understanding the emotions of others, including non-verbal expressions.
- Illegal behaviors and association with peers who engage in them (especially prior to age ten).
- Regular use of others to get own needs or desires met.
- Sexual promiscuity.
- Substance abuse.
- Often deceitful, irresponsible, and untrustworthy.

Research suggests that *callous-unemotional traits* (lack of guilt, remorse, and empathy, and shallow emotions that limit formation of meaningful relationships) are the most important precursor to adult psychopathy and antisocial personality and so we need to pay attention to these in children and adolescents. There's evidence that parents and peer interactions can affect whether children's symptoms progress to ASPD. Rather than punishments, at-risk kids (just like all kids) appear to benefit from positive parenting practices such as rewards, involvement, and warm relationships.

Psychosis and Schizophrenia

"Insane" and "crazy" are words often used to describe violent people. Technically, these terms have different meanings. "Insane" is typically a legal term implying decreased culpability due to a mental disease or defect, and is used in cognitive insanity pleas. Specific states determine the definition for insanity. "Crazy" is a colloquial term, usually referring to someone who is experiencing symptoms of a psychotic disorder or psychosis.

Psychosis is a group of severe mental disorders characterized by severely impaired reality testing typically shown by psychotic symptoms such as delusions, hallucinations, disorganized speech, or disorganized or catatonic behavior. Delusions are irrational or bizarre thoughts with no basis in reality ("the teacher is reading my mind"). Hallucinations are sensations that don't exist, such as seeing or hearing things that aren't there.

Schizophrenia is the most common reason for psychotic symptoms, but other things like drug intoxication, brain tumors, and depression can also produce them. Onset prior to adolescence is rare and typical onset is between late teens and midthirties. Although schizophrenia is linked to perpetration of violence, patients are much more likely to be victimized. It's a relatively rare condition, affecting less than 1% of the population, and is manageable with medication and supportive, stress-controlled environments. Unacceptably, most patients can't obtain the care they need and many don't take medications because of uncomfortable side effects.

Suicide: Youth Violence Turned Inward

Being suicidal is perhaps the ultimate level of personal distress. More than forty-six hundred young people aged ten to twenty-four commit suicide each year. Most use a firearm (45%), and the next two most common methods are suffocation, such as by hanging or plastic bag (40%), and poisoning (8%).

But many more youth attempt suicide and survive. Surveys of high school students reveal that 16% seriously contemplate taking their own lives and 8% attempt it every year. In 2011, suicide became the second leading cause of death among young people aged twelve to twenty-four.

Risk Factors for Suicide

Although there's no single risk factor that can predict who will commit suicide, the more of the following risk factors present, the greater the risk of suicide:

- Gender. Females are about three times more likely to attempt suicide, but males are about four times more likely to complete suicide.
- Mental illness or substance abuse. Although 95% of people with a mental or substance use disorder will not complete suicide, about 90% of those who complete suicide are affected by mental illness or substance abuse.
- Aggrieved entitlement characteristics.
- Access to means or method to commit suicide, such as firearms or medications.
- Chronic pain and medical conditions (they're linked to feelings of helplessness, hopelessness, and the desire to have control over one's death).
- Family history of suicide, especially of a close relative.
- Impulsiveness. Most suicides appear to be impulsive. Of the more than two thousand people who have jumped off the Golden Gate Bridge, about a dozen have miraculously lived to tell about it. Of those interviewed, all said that the moment they let go of the bridge, they knew they had made a mistake.
- Aggression. Aggressive acts frequently precede suicides. These include verbal conflicts, physical assaults, and even mass murder.
- Previous suicide attempts. About 20% of people who commit suicide have made a prior serious attempt requiring hospitalization. Recentness, method lethality, and low opportunity to be rescued all heighten the risk that the next attempt will result in death. Despite this, most people who attempt suicide don't ultimately die from suicide.
- Stressful life events, such as loss of a loved one, financial losses, legal trouble, domestic violence, child neglect and abuse, and bullying.
- Active substance abuse (drugs or alcohol).
- Other self-injury, like cutting or burning.

Another risk factor is something called *suicide contagion*, which describes the increased risk that youth will commit suicide if they personally know someone who died by suicide or identify with a high-profile celebrity who did. Adolescents appear to be particularly vulnerable to this. Studies show that how the media covers suicide plays a role in contagion. Social media and Internet websites that glorify suicide or provide "how-to" directions increase contagion effects.

Warning Signs for Suicide

Most people who kill themselves had exhibited the following warning signs. These signs are cumulative in significance—the more that are present, the greater the concern. The American Society of Suicidology provides the acronym IS PATH WARM? to identify concerning thoughts, feelings, or actions for suicide:

I Ideation—thinks about death or suicide plans.
S Substance abuse—actively abusing drugs or drinking alcohol.

P Purposelessness—life without direction.
A Anxiety—agitated, unable to sleep or sleeps too much.
T Trapped—feels trapped, desperate, humiliated, or a need to escape an intolerable situation. Many individuals who make serious suicide attempts develop tunnel vision where suicide is seen as their only option.
H Hopelessness—thinks that things will not get better or change.

W Withdrawal—from family, friends, and society.
A Anger—irritable, enraged, or talking about seeking revenge. Acts of aggression and violence often occur before suicide.
R Recklessness—having multiple accidents may actually represent poorly executed suicide attempts.
M Mood Changes—both worsening and sudden unexplained improvement in mood, especially depression.

To this list we would add the following:

• Indicating in writing or verbally that they want to kill themselves, or saying things like, "I wish I were dead" or "Things would be better if I were gone." Many people who attempt suicide have informed others about their intentions.

- Having a detailed plan—the more detailed their plan, the greater the risk.
- Having the means to carry out the plan, such as a firearm in the home or collected pills for an overdose, means the risk is even greater.
- Giving away valued possessions.

What Parents or Others Can Do When Noticing Warning Signs

If children you know are showing these warning signs, it is time to act. Begin by telling them you are concerned for their welfare and describe the signs you see. People often avoid asking if someone is thinking about suicide, for fear that it might put the idea into their heads. You can't make someone more suicidal by asking about it. Plus, most suicidal people report feeling relieved when someone asks because it gives them an opportunity to talk about their problems.

Finding the Words

If you notice warning signs of suicide, simply ask, *Are you thinking about hurting yourself?* Parents may avoid asking this simple question for fear of putting the idea into their child's head, but if someone is suicidal, the idea is already there and the person is usually relieved that someone noticed that something is wrong. If your child says yes, the next question to ask is, *How would you do it?* If your child has a plan, the plan is detailed, and he or she has the means to carry it out, the risk is very high. Regardless of whether or not your child has a specific plan, ask, *What is keeping you from doing it?* Reassuring responses would be global reasons, such as faith in

God or not wanting to hurt family or loved ones. Less reassuring responses are specific and temporary, such as thinking that a romantic relationship will continue or waiting to see if a desired award will be won. Since many mass shootings appear to be perpetrated by people who are suicidal, it's also important to ask, *Are you thinking about hurting someone else?* Again, the more specific the response, the greater the risk. If your child identifies a specific person or group he or she intends to harm and has the means, it's time to notify the authorities and the individuals targeted.

If you're concerned but don't think you can ask your child the suggested questions, or if your child denies having a plan and has no means but displays multiple risk factors for suicide, talk to a mental health professional (school counselor, psychologist). To speak with someone immediately and anonymously, call a suicide hotline such as (1-800) 273-TALK (8255) for information and referral.

If your child describes a plan *and* has access to means to commit suicide, get immediate professional help (not later today or tomorrow) by taking him or her to a hospital emergency room or psychiatric facility that takes inpatients. If there's a delay in getting services, remove means by hiding guns, knives, pills, and other means, and don't leave your child alone. Given that many suicide attempts and completions are committed when an individual is under the influence of alcohol or other drugs, remove access to these substances as well. Once at a treatment facility, the staff will either recommend admission or make an outpatient safety plan with your child. A safety plan lists things that your child agrees to do, including contacting someone on a list, *before* attempting to hurt himself or herself. All good safety plans have at least one contact who will answer at all times (like suicide prevention hotlines or 911).

Of course kids could lie and say they'll follow the plan but won't. But most suicidal people are ambivalent about death—they don't want to die but don't want to keep going on the same way either. Safety plans give them alternatives to hurting themselves. Since most suicide attempts appear to be impulsive, helping them identify alternative solutions to death is very important. Even when youth are released from emergency rooms, it's wise to limit access to methods they could use to hurt themselves. Remove access to substances like alcohol as well. Suicide pacts among teens, while rare, do occur. If your child's friend has talked about or attempted suicide, find out how your child is doing and pay greater attention to warning signs if the friendship is very close.

Preventing Suicide and Other Self-Harm

It greatly helps kids if parents try to discover and understand what kids are stressed out about and help them cope. Relationship angst, popularity, achievement concerns, and bullying are common childhood stressors. While children may be able to emerge unscathed by using their own resources, there are times when parental support and guidance is essential: when children express concern, it needs to be taken seriously even if you think they are exaggerating. Often just listening, providing different perspectives, and helping them generate alternative solutions to problems is all they need. Close relationships, healthy self-esteem, and resilience are protective factors in helping prevent the development of mental disorders.

Parenting Methods Have a Big Impact on Childhood Mental Disorders

Eddie was a rambunctious child. At age nine he was terrorizing the neighborhood by riding his bike on the sidewalks, kicking or running into anyone in his path. By age thirteen he began smoking, drinking alcohol, and experimenting with marijuana. At age fifteen he was arrested for petty theft and vandalism. Most predicted that Eddie was on his way to a life of delinquency and crime, but his parents sought professional help. By the time Eddie was nineteen he was attending a university on a full academic scholarship. Changing his life circumstances likely prevented a conduct disorder from developing.

Parents have considerable influence on mental disorders in their children, both in terms of prevention and helping them function, cope, and recover once disorders occur. Sometimes parents dismiss serious behavior problems as either normal (boys will be boys) or part of a diagnosis (that's just what kids with ADHD do). But denying serious problems that interfere with function leads to inaction when parents really need to act to prevent bad outcomes. If you think your child has any of the common mental disorders described here, you can give your child a fulfilling, joyful life by getting him or her help from a licensed mental health professional. You can also make an important impact by examining and altering your parenting methods accordingly.

A teenage boy was brought to our clinic by his parents, who were seeking a new opinion on their son's troubled behavior. In the past, the boy had been diagnosed with ADHD, depression, and conduct disorder. Now he had been arrested for theft and suspended from school. His parents reported that the multiple medications prescribed over the years had not helped. When questioned, they reported only limited conversations with previous therapists and physicians about their parenting methods. Once we investigated current parenting methods and home environment, we were able to make modifications that significantly improved the child's mood and behavior and the quality of both his and his parents' lives.

While the disorders reviewed here can produce significant problems for children and their families without help, working to obtain and follow professional advice can greatly improve things. Also, untreated mental illness in parents is common and greatly impairs parenting ability. Remember that taking care of yourself helps you take care of your kids.

Treatment of Mental Disorders Benefits Everyone

Research shows that treatment reduces the risk of perpetration of violent acts as well as victimization in those affected by mental disorders. Getting help for yourself or your kids shows you are smart and caring. Preventive mental health care is just as important as preventing heart disease or cancer, and emergency mental health care can be just as lifesaving as emergency surgery.

See professionals with advanced degrees (doctors such as PhD, PsyD, MD, and DO) or master's degrees (MA, MS, MSW) who are licensed by your state. You need to know that people can call themselves psychotherapists without having had any specialized training, so check to make sure they have degrees.

Although early intervention is key, it can be very difficult to find treatment. One reason it's hard to find providers is poor coverage and payment by insurance companies. If you have means, paying yourself without billing insurance will give you the most options. Also, check for university training clinics and counseling centers that work on a sliding scale, where you pay less if you earn less. Social service agencies, mental health centers, and schools may provide services or have recommendations.

The decrease in available psychiatric beds has created a mental health care crisis. When people are considered dangerous to themselves or others, they should be held in a hospital or psychiatric facility for assessment and treatment, for their own and the public's safety. But when no beds are available, this doesn't happen. Between 1955 and 2005, the number of psychiatric beds in the United States shrunk by 95%. Between 2005 and 2010, the number decreased by an additional 14% and has continued to decrease since. It's estimated that we need triple the number of beds we have now to provide minimally adequate treatment in our country. Individuals with mental illness are more likely to be seen in emergency rooms or land in jail than to be treated in specialized facilities.

After family homicides and mass murders, we try to find explanations and make sense of the senseless. We may want to blame mental illness for these events, but there are many other factors more likely responsible that could have been addressed to avert tragedies. There is also a concerning tendency to blame mental health providers for the actions of their patients, which will reduce the number willing to treat high-risk individuals. People might also avoid or delay treatment for mental illness due to the fear that their mental health records will be discovered and negatively affect their lives.

Mental illnesses are very common in parents and their children. They're diseases with biological and environmental foundations just like any medical condition. While we would expect and encourage people to get treatment for heart disease or diabetes, for some reason we feel afraid to let other people know about our common mental health symptoms—this needs to change. We need to prioritize mental health promotion and destigmatize and applaud treatment of mental disease for the benefit of everyone.

4

Harmful Media Influences and How to Deflect the Damage

Because children have high levels of exposure, media have greater access and time to shape young people's attitudes and actions than do parents or teachers, replacing them as educators, role models, and the primary sources of information about the world and how one behaves in it.

—American Academy of Pediatrics' 2009
Policy Statement on Media Violence

A scorned teddy bear named Naughty Bear is driven to seek vengeance by terrorizing bears who didn't invite him to a birthday party. Featuring an array of weapons, objects, and scare tactics, gamers strive to earn points as they inflict physical and psychological harm on Naughty Bear's enemies. Players win the most points for being deviant and maniacal. While there is no blood (murdered bears spill stuffing instead), players get extra points for torturing and bullying other bears to the point that they commit suicide. Creativity in injuring and killing is encouraged and rewarded. You can hurt a bear by slamming a car door on its head, jumping on it, and impaling it with sharp weapons. There's also a narrator who encourages players to be extremely naughty, and players can chat online while playing.

These descriptions from IGN Games, Common Sense Media, and www.parenting.com shed light on the video game *Naughty Bear*, rated T for teens.

While saddened and frightened by the rash of school and other mass shootings, many people wonder if there's a connection between violent media use and violent behavior in youth. You might be surprised that research has shown the correlation between childhood exposure to violent media such as *Naughty Bear* and later violent behavior to be greater than that between bone mass and calcium intake, and nearly as strong as the link between smoking and lung cancer.

That said, almost all children are exposed to violent media, yet very few become mass murderers or school shooters. The more pervasive concern for society is that media exposure during youth promotes other aggressive and violent behaviors. Media violence also traumatizes children, producing prolonged fear, anxiety, and depression, all risk factors for victimization.

This chapter will present evidence on media forms and content to help you make informed choices on monitoring and managing exposure. In addition to violent content, we'll explore drug, alcohol, and sexualized content because it promotes other risk factors for being affected by aggression and violence.

Risky Media Forms and Content

Kids now spend most of their waking hours outside of school exposed to media like television, music, games, and cell phones. According to a recent study by Common Sense Media, this is typically about six hours a day for tweens (ages eight to twelve) and nine hours a day for teens, and doesn't include media use during school or homework. This is cumulatively a staggering amount of time during childhood.

So what's the problem with having such wired kids? First, media time replaces time with worthy role models (such as parents), face-to-face social interactions, real-life experiences, and physical and other activities necessary for healthy development. The more kids see behaviors, the more likely they are to learn, imitate, and adopt them.

Research shows that this applies to what is seen and heard from screens and other media, especially when actions are portrayed realistically or are rewarded. Children under the age of eight may be more vulnerable because they're unable to distinguish reality from fantasy. But the fact that media exposure also clearly affects adolescent and young adult behavior means that this ability doesn't prevent media influence.

Second, this huge dose of media contains increasing amounts and degrees of harmful content, such as meanness, manipulation, aggression, violence, unhealthy relationships, sexualization, profanity, vulgarity, and drug and alcohol use. Studies show that exposure is linked to acting similarly—youth are likely to approve of and do what they see and hear. Thus, actively managing media in your kids' lives is a modern must for protecting them from becoming victims or perpetrators.

Media Violence

"The scientific debate over whether media violence increases aggression and violence is essentially over," asserted Craig Anderson and colleagues in 2003 in *Psychological Science in the Public Interest*. Research consistently shows irrefutable evidence that exposure to aggression and violence in media increases those behaviors in youth. Out of thirty-five hundred studies, all but eighteen showed an association.

Media violence has become frequent, severe, and graphic. Average American kids see two hundred thousand acts of violence on television alone, including assault, rape, and murder, by the time they turn eighteen. Besides violent lessons, media also teach youth aggressive behaviors, such as lying, taunting, manipulating, threatening, cheating, humiliating, bullying, and inducing fear in people.

Seeing violent encounters between characters leads youth to believe that violence is a good way to solve problems with others and to fulfill desires. When violent characters seeking revenge are portrayed as heroes, it encourages young viewers to think that violence is justified to support beliefs and to show feelings. Seeing real-life or entertainment media violence also desensitizes youth, making them less likely to react and help or empathize with victims.

Seeing explicitly violent scenes can also result in intense fear of being harmed that can last for years, causing insomnia, nightmares, and two risk factors for victimization and perpetration: anxiety and depression. Children and adults can have flashbacks of scenes that aren't needed to tell a story but are included to embellish violent aspects of the situation—these scenes are often the only ones they remember. Fearful kids don't do as well in school and activities and more often use drugs.

Keep in mind that kids find different things frightening than adults. Children ages three to seven find scary fantasy and transformation figures, personal violence, war, suffering, accidents, and fires to be very frightening. Older children and teens are most frightened by personal violence or threat of it, and possible threats from disasters, war, and terrorism. Let's look at violent, aggressive, and other content in various media forms that promote risk factors for victimization or perpetration.

Television and Movies

Many movies and network TV shows are now full of portrayals of relationship aggression, cruelty, graphic violence, drug and alcohol use, vulgarity, and profanity. Vulgarity and profanity can be considered aggressive because they make people feel uncomfortable and more vulnerable to manipulation. (By the way, many kids "hear" what is said when words are replaced with bleeps because they've heard the words before.) Reality and other mainstream shows often show people judging and manipulating others while highlighting extreme behavior, relational aggression, and sexual coercion.

There's no reason to believe that ads for movies and TV shows aren't just as damaging: although you may not allow your kids to see a violent crime show, they may view bloody bodies repetitively in commercials. One particularly disturbing recent ad for a prime-time TV show contained a scantily dressed woman hanging from bound wrists in front of a perpetrator armed with a very large bore drill, obviously indicating a threat of torture—it was shown several times during a two hour-period of afternoon network TV.

Along with many experts, we worry that children are learning that violence against others is entertaining—and even exciting and pleasurable. We find it distressing that movies containing torture "sell" due to enough people apparently finding it acceptable or even entertaining. Could media be promoting sadistic traits in our children that can lead to heinous crimes like serial killings by psychopaths? If children learn to do what they see, why would it not promote this behavior?

The Aurora, Colorado, premiere of the Batman movie *The Dark Knight Rises* became a horrific intersection of media and real-life violence. Laurie's brother was a Denver SWAT team member who responded to the carnage. He said that survivors were milling around outside aimlessly, in shock, many stained in blood. On that dreadful night, the place where many young people saw violent media became the same place for deranged student James Holmes to produce real-life terror, slaughtering twelve people and wounding seventy others. When we asked Laurie's brother if he had to go inside the theater, he said he wasn't needed there and thus chose not to. We were relieved that he wasn't required to endure seeing the ghastly scene, yet so many others had no choice.

The Internet

The web is an important source of educational information for youth. But because Internet content is unregulated, virtually anything can be seen. Most teens report that parents don't know which websites they've visited. Kids can illegally download movies and music, buy substances and weapons, view real-life homicides (such as beheadings of hostages), and join hate or terrorist groups. They don't need to search for harmful content to be exposed: search engine home pages can show disturbing news photos and pop-up ads can show pornographic or other sexualized images. The Internet also provides a way to connect with other people, good or bad.

Social Media

Using social media (texts, instant messages, Instagram, Twitter, Snapchat, and Facebook) has benefits for youth. It can help kids find friends and support systems, practice social skills, foster independence, communicate about school activities and social justice concerns, and explore identity. Teens who electronically communicate with only *real* friends report less depression and fewer social problems.

However, social media also has risks. It can feed drama, reduce family connection, take time away from more productive activities, expose kids to inappropriate or harmful content, and facilitate bullying. Research shows that higher levels of electronic communication compared to face-to-face interactions are linked to reduced empathy and sense of well-being. Multitasking with social media or TV during homework harms learning and productivity, and academic difficulty is a risk factor for being affected by aggression. Sharing personal information electronically is harder for youth to resist and to understand the dangers of, and identity theft can occur. It allows nearly unlimited access to peers, increasing their influence, as well as dangerous adults posing as children. Also, since kids are immature decision makers, many have suffered consequences of making or forwarding inappropriate statements and pictures.

Sexting (sending and receiving of cell phone text or photo messages of a sexual nature) has negative legal, social, emotional, and behavioral consequences for youth. Estimates vary greatly according to how sexting is defined in surveys and how students understand terms like "sexually explicit." In one recent study, more than half of youth reported sexting as minors when sexts were defined as containing wording or photographs that were "sexual in nature." Estimates appear much lower (1% to 7%) when youth are specifically asked about messages containing nude or nearly nude material, as in a recent study.

Why do kids sext? Common reasons are as part of romantic relationships (including as a way to control a partner in dating violence), trying to start a relationship, impulsive thrill seeking that is common in adolescence, and as a joke. More than 20% of youth who appear in or create sexual images, or receive such images, report feeling upset, embarrassed, or afraid as a result. Although most images aren't forwarded to other people, about 10% apparently are, sometimes with disastrous consequences.

Your kids need to know that possessing or sending sexually explicit images of themselves or other minors is a crime, and they need to delete and never retransmit them—many youth have been charged with child pornography and registered as sex offenders. It also may be a crime to make obscene comments, requests, suggestions, or proposals, or to describe sexual acts electronically even when portrayed in a cartoonish nature. If your child is sharing explicit material, it's a warning sign to intervene and assess for other risk-taking behavior.

Modern Music

Like other popular media, rock, heavy metal, rap, and emerging genres often portray violence, sexualized female portrayals, and drug and alcohol use. Experts are concerned that listening to lyrics or watching music videos with depressing, sexualized, violent, or substance use content creates or increases young people's dangerous behaviors and thoughts, including aggressive and violent ones against self or others. But it's also possible that kids with problems prefer certain types of music.

Here is a sampling of research findings. Kids who prefer heavy metal music more likely have conduct problems, depression, and delinquency. Listening to heavy metal and some rock music has been linked to risk of suicide. Adolescents exposed to music videos in all genres appear more likely to use alcohol. Rap music has been found to contain the highest levels of violence, hate lyrics (misogynistic, racist, homophobic), and graphic rape lyrics. Exposure to rap videos has been shown to increase drug and alcohol use in young listeners. Young males exposed to violent rap and sexist videos were more likely to accept and report likelihood of perpetrating violence, including against women.

Tragic Real-Life Events in the News

Knowledge of world issues makes our kids very anxious. Most broadcast news programs are full of graphically depicted violent crime stories. Following 9/11, studies showed that levels of anxiety and fear in children and adults were directly proportional to the amount of time spent watching news coverage of the event. Prolonged fear is linked to many problems, such as substance use, anxiety, depression, and PTSD. The more they see and hear about disasters, crime, and terrorism, the more anxious kids get.

Electronic Game Playing

Computer, phone, and console gaming have become a big part of life for many youth (and adults). Playing nonviolent games in limited amounts can safely help develop hand-eye coordination and concentration and can be something friends and family do together. But very frequent video game play of all types is linked to depression, anxiety, and addiction.

There's evidence that there are critical developmental time periods when it's far easier for children to learn things like language, social interactions, and impulse control. In his book *Why Do They Act That Way?*, David Walsh discusses practical implications of brain development for parents, including that when experiences are narrowed due to excessive time spent gaming, youth can miss the window of opportunity to learn skills that help people form healthy relationships. Furthermore, a recent global meta-analysis by top researchers reported indisputable evidence that playing violent video games is a causal risk factor for reduced empathy and prosocial behaviors like helping, and increased long-term aggressive thoughts and behaviors. Here is the bottom line: the more teens play violent games, the more they make violent decisions, including when provoked.

Not convinced of the dangerous effects of playing violent games? Well, consider that playing these games gives children good feelings of pleasure and success when they cause harm to others, at a time when their brains are making permanent decision making and emotional connections. This is particularly true when the game permits the player to be a shooter (that is, to see things as the shooter sees them).

No, not all players of violent video games become school or workplace assassins, but many school shooters spent large amounts of time playing violent games and were fascinated by guns. In the book *Stop Teaching Our Kids to Kill*, Lt. Col. Dave Grossman describes the case of Michael Carneal. Michael was only fourteen years old when he opened fire on a high school prayer group. He had never fired a real gun before, yet he had greater deadly accuracy than the average law enforcement officer, delivering five head shots and three upper torso shots. He learned how to shoot to kill as many people as possible from a video game similar to those used for training purposes in the military.

Violent game play has even stronger effects on a child's personality when images and messages are frequently repeated, harming and killing other characters is rewarded, and when gaming is combined with social isolation and sleep deprivation. Experts believe that media exposure may have a cumulative effect with other risk factors, such as underlying aggressive or antisocial traits, to produce the worst outcomes. In other words, just because all violent game players don't become mass murderers doesn't mean that young people with other risk factors won't be more influenced by games to act violently.

So, while we hear game players and entertainment industry officials claim that violent media doesn't *cause* violent behavior, it's very clear from thirty years of research that this exposure is a significant risk factor for aggression.

Warning Signs of Media Harm

These warning signs pertain to behaviors in preschool and school-age children and indicate that electronic media are most likely harming your child or contributing to a serious problem:

- Identifying with violent, villainous characters or media figures by speaking like them and reenacting violent scenes.

- Hurting (or threatening to hurt) animals.
- Threatening to or physically harming people.

These three warning signs are the most critical warning signs that you need to take away all violent media *now* and get help. Here are other worrisome signs that you need to reduce or stop your child's media use and get your child help:

- Signs of dependence or addiction. These include angry reactions when you try to reduce or stop use, often *wanting* but also *needing* to use in order to avoid uncomfortable withdrawal symptoms (being anxious, irritable, or shaky), lying about amount of use, not wanting to do much else, and losing friends or jobs because of media use. Research is finding chemical brain changes from screen exposure that are linked with behavioral changes, including addiction and sleep problems.
- Dropping grades.
- Social isolation or difficulty relating to people.
- Depression and anxiety problems.
- Sharing images, texts, or posts that are sexually explicit or involve self-harm.

Even if your kids seem to be OK right now, you can help prevent problems promoted by media exposure and greatly improve communication and relationships with your kids by using the advice in this chapter.

Managing Media to Minimize Risk

Professional groups caring for families strongly recommend that parents regulate children's media use because studies show better behavior and emotional health with lower exposure. You can reap the following benefits from your efforts: better grades; less arguing; less aggression, including bullying; lower chance of drug and alcohol use; less anxiety, fear, and depression; less profanity and vulgar behavior; and better sleep, which means better mood, which is good for everyone!

Because risky content is so embedded in media, experts have long recommended restricting screen time for children. But because of continued increases in media use by youth, the American Academy of Pediatrics (AAP) is in the process of updating its recommendations, emphasizing things like content management, co-engagement, and modeling more than time limits. Formal, updated guidelines were not available at the time of this writing, so the following recommendations are based on research, proposed AAP guideline changes from an October 2015 AAP News article, and information from other national organizations.

Early Childhood and Digital Media

More than 30% of children first play with mobile devices when still in diapers. According to the AAP, for children under age three, face-to-face, two-way communication and live presentation of information is essential and far superior to digital media for learning and socialization, which are protective against victimization and perpetration of aggression. That said, starting at age one, it appears that limited exposure to age-specific language-teaching *interactive* videos (such as video chat, or coviewing with kids and asking questions or commenting about content) can benefit learning. But at this age children need to interact with the presentation to learn (they can't learn by just watching), and face-to-face verbal interactions and hearing people speak live still work better and are critical for language development. Starting at age two, developmentally appropriate educational media in small amounts can help kids learn language and problem solving, but must not be overused to the detriment of live social, nurturing, and physical play and having books read to them.

Coviewing all media with infants and toddlers is essential to ensure that content is appropriate, prosocial, and nondisturbing, and to encourage interaction with educational content. Be aware that research shows that the amount of screen time during early childhood correlates with attention difficulties (which may also be true for older youth), a risk factor for aggression. But don't feel guilty if you need to park little ones in front of a prescreened video for a few minutes so you can get something done—just keep it to a minimum.

How to Limit Harmful Content and Screen Time for Kids

Although content may be more important to monitor and manage, kids still need limits on time spent with media, to promote life balance. It may be helpful to know that many kids use screen media (as well as music) as a way to relieve stress, boredom, and loneliness. So helping kids with these issues may reduce their need to use media—and this support is important anyway. Also, studies show that the more TV and movies parents watch, the more kids watch with and without parents, so it helps to limit your own use, keeping in mind that what might be OK for *you* to see may be very harmful to your kids.

Talk about how media content affects how people in your family feel and act (for example, ask your kids how seeing people harmed or frightening scenes affects how they feel compared to seeing people helping others or experiencing good things). Talk about how media takes time away from other stuff kids could be doing, like homework, chores, reading, sleeping, talking to people, and family and school activities. We have tried to keep in mind that the time we spend with screen media is time taken away from face-to-face interactions and other activities with our kids, other relationships, and taking care of ourselves and households. The AAP News article states, "Attentive parenting requires face time away from screens."

Studies show that discussing the risks of high screen time and harmful content can help kids decide to reduce exposure because they realize the benefits. (Wow—that's cool.) Even first graders can learn that TV teaches people many things, good and bad: how to act, look, spend money, express emotion, and solve problems. Notice when kids make good media choices and praise it. Encourage small children to talk to the TV when they see someone make a bad choice and to choose real-life heroes instead of screen characters. Ask older kids how media make them feel and help them reach their goals.

To help you stay connected with your kids, designate "unplugged" times (such as during meals and at bedtimes) and zones (such as the kitchen, car, or yard) in which no one is allowed to use media, including cell phones. Turn off the TV when no one is actively watching and mute commercials using the remote. These are straightforward, easy things to do to decrease screen time that kids usually respond pretty well to, especially when you don't eat during their favorite show.

Watch TV and movies with your kids when possible. Doing this helps you know what they're being exposed to and allows for discussions about healthy and unhealthy content. Prescreen or research TV shows, movies, apps, and games that your children may be exposed to when you're not around (see our resource section). Look beyond star ratings posted when possible. For example, Common Sense Media and the Parents Television Council give content information such as positive messages and responsible themes as well as violence, sex, language, and substance use. When evaluating media, look for prosocial content such as friendly, cooperative, and sympathetic characters helping others and solving problems nonaggressively, and positive stories about the world and its cultures. Parental TV controls aren't very effective: we've found that blocking R-rated movies also blocks fun unrated content, such as old television series. See our tips on media industry ratings later in the chapter.

Lastly, at the time of this writing, the American Academy of Pediatrics still recommends not allowing children to have TVs, electronic games, or Internet access in their bedrooms as an effective way to reduce harmful content and screen time. But alas, your kids will probably see removing devices already in their bedrooms as unfair punishment and greatly resist it. What that means (no, it doesn't mean that you can't do it) is that you'll want to explain that you're doing it out of concern for them and not as a punishment. It will also help to replace this privilege with others. If you can't get yourself to remove bedroom media screens, at least minimize the harmful content (such as only allowing approved DVDs and nonviolent games) and ensure no use after bedtime. It appears best to have your kids park their phones, laptops, and tablets overnight in your room.

Internet and Smartphone Safety

Experts have recommended that Internet access only be allowed in a central place, to make monitoring easier. But the explosion in mobile laptop, tablet, and smartphone use in youth has made monitoring much more difficult. A 2015 Pew Research Center study reported that 73% of teenagers have smartphones and 24% admit to almost constant use.

Nevertheless, it's a parent's right and responsibility to monitor online activity (websites used and time spent) but it's important that kids know it will be done. There are monitoring apps and programs available but kids can figure out how to get around them, so don't let these give you a false sense of security. Parents still need to spot-check what kids are looking at, and ask about topics being searched and if they've seen anything disturbing. Make it clear that you won't ban all Internet activity if they share concerning content with you—that's a common reason that kids don't tell adults about problems. Kids younger than eight should only be on websites with very strong safety features.

Chat rooms are dangerous because influential strangers, including sexual predators and hate group members, can connect with your children. Teens with conflicts at home more often become victims. If a chat room is being used, set high privacy settings and make it one that allows you to specify who they can chat with.

Look through browsing history for violent or hate websites. According to research, youth who reported that many, most, or all of the websites they visited showed real people fighting, shooting, or killing were five times more likely to report engaging in seriously violent behavior compared to those reporting that none of the websites they visited showed these scenarios.

Tell kids that you don't approve of illegally downloading music, movies, programs, or the like, because that is stealing. Some kids view getting around regulations and laws online as a game, and some grow up to be perpetrators of scamming and hacking.

Be aware that apps can be very misleading, such as appearing to be a calculator but actually containing harmful content and allowing secret communications. Thus, it seems advisable to only allow apps to be downloaded on devices with your password after you've investigated them.

Social Media Safety

Middle school friends Amanda, Chloe, and Karina were spending the night at Amanda's house. They were on Chloe's Facebook page chatting with friends, giggling about cute boys, and generally having innocent fun. Suddenly, an official-looking message appeared saying that they had violated Facebook policies and the police would be notified unless the girls clicked an external link. The girls were scared and didn't know what to do. Amanda went to her parents and told them what happened. Recognizing the message was potentially dangerous, her father helped to block Chloe's account so only people she invited could contact her. The girls did the right thing. They stopped their activity, told an adult, and blocked future inappropriate contacts.

Parents can play a pivotal role in making social media on computers and smartphones beneficial but not dangerous. Kids are tech-savvy and can delete things and find ways around software and apps that parents use to monitor or block content. Therefore, although it's recommended that you use parental media management technology, your best defense is educating your kids about appropriate communication and the dangers of receiving and sharing harmful content.

First, model and discuss online etiquette: treat digital interactions like face-to-face interactions and discuss appropriate content and showing empathy. Second, discuss inappropriate content, such as profane, sexual, unkind, or untrue texts, tweets, posts, comments, and pictures, which are common in tween and teen social networking. Give your kids safety advice. They need to avoid making, responding, or forwarding such content, because it's permanent, can be passed on to anyone without their knowledge, can get them into a lot of trouble, and can hurt people. If they're sending, receiving, or looking at anything they wouldn't want you to see, it's a warning sign that the content is inappropriate and could harm them. Again, clearly state that you won't take away access when they share content that concerns them and that you'd like them to share anything that makes them feel uncomfortable, worried, or threatened, and that they shouldn't respond to it. Most websites allow reporting inappropriate content.

If your family comes across content indicating that someone is planning an assault, suicide, or homicide, call either 911 or your local law enforcement agency's nonemergency phone number, depending on how urgent you think the threat is. Police should also be notified if your child has been threatened with serious bodily harm. Read about cyberbullying in the next chapter.

Set up social networking apps, profiles, and pages with your kids to check the content they're thinking about posting and learn about privacy settings. On Facebook, for instance, "friending" each other gives you something to chat about but it may be possible for users to block certain friends (you) from seeing all posts. On websites and apps, have your own account that allows you to see your children's content and review their friend or contact lists. Ask about people you don't know. Discuss how strangers can still see pages, so kids need to be very careful about what's on them. Ask what relatives or employers would think about their posts. Posts, pictures, and videos can be passed around and come back to haunt users, even after deletion. Also, content can be altered and forwarded without a user's knowledge.

Write down a list of information that must not be put online. Dangerous choices include making a selection to post one's location, or typing in an address, city, full name, Social Security number, school, phone number, bank account or credit card numbers, or full names of friends and family or where they work. Pictures should not contain clues as to where children live or go to school. Share your concern about sending pictures of themselves, and before they're in high school, you might want to require your permission to do so.

Young users' friend or contact lists should only include people they actually know, not friends of friends (who are then strangers). Firmly forbid meeting anyone in person who they've only talked to online or by phone or text unless it's in a public place with a trusted adult present. Studies suggest that most youth share their passwords with friends, so it's good to say why they shouldn't: friends may use your child's account for harmful purposes.

Many parents wonder at what age they should allow their kids to text. If you want our advice, wait as long as humanly possible! The drama, loss of face-to-face interactions, distraction from more productive activities, costs, and risks of bullying are substantial. On the other hand, texting, like other social media, has the benefits we reviewed. Rules for texting such as appropriate times and amounts can help (you can keep tabs online with your carrier). Many kids text in the middle of the night, so again, you may want phones turned in to you at bedtime.

We believe, and many experts agree, that it's a parent's responsibility to randomly survey children's texts, Facebook, instant messages, pictures, and other electronic communications. But tell your children you'll do it first and get their passwords. Checking is especially important when your child's behavior is concerning or changes detrimentally, or you suspect risky behavior or danger. Tell your kids you trust *them*, but not other people. We recommend regular surveillance beginning at onset of use, gradually decreasing to spot-checking as they demonstrate safe use of social media and there are no signs of trouble. This can teach kids how showing responsibility increases your trust.

What if they won't give you their passwords? Tell them that because you're a good parent, responsible and concerned for their safety, you won't be able to let them use their phones and the Internet unless they do. Wise parents don't allow their children to be alone with people they don't know much about. Well, cell phones, the Internet, and social media websites are common ways that kids communicate with friends *and* people they don't know well. There's software to monitor children's Internet and social media activity that notifies you only of negative activity (see our resources).

Managing Aggressive and Violent Content Specifically

Because exposure to violent or frightening media content can psychologically damage kids, and because kids tend to imitate and approve of what they see (including acts that are risk factors for being affected by aggression and violence), we make the following recommendations depending upon a child's age.

Children Under Age Eight

Children under age eight can't tell fantasy from reality very well, so it's really important to minimize how much they see or hear about violent or scary things. (By the way, this age group appears most vulnerable to learning bad behaviors seen in media.) Well-meaning parents may believe that watching scary shows with their young kids and saying certain things like "That's not real" can alleviate fear. However, before age eight, doing this doesn't help and when parents discuss frightening content (even to reassure children), it can actually *increase* fear up to fourfold. That's because young kids can't process information from parents logically, so these comments might increase their attention to violent and scary things. Or, if parents frequently watch violent shows, watching TV together may increase their exposure, which increases their fear. Covering their eyes and ears doesn't work either—children tend to imagine what happens.

So, simply turn off inappropriate content, saying, "This isn't good for us." Pay attention to their fright reactions—just because *you* don't find something scary doesn't mean *they* don't. But do make positive comments about helpful and kind behaviors in scenes. If your kids end up exposed to violent images or characters acting inappropriately, make disapproving comments rather than asking what they think. Children this young can't process questions while viewing very well.

Keep in mind that even educational shows can contain graphic, disturbing violent images and scenes, particularly shows about historical events, so it's a good idea to check these out before or while the child views it. Watch unfamiliar screen content with small and elementary school–age children.

Ages Eight and Up

For youth aged eight to about fourteen, you can just turn off harmful content and explain why, or you can keep watching or listening as a way to start a learning discussion, provided that you think the content is appropriate enough. To teach disapproval and reduce imitation, make comments or ask questions about scenarios. If you don't speak up, your kids will interpret this as your approval of what they're seeing.

Commenting that you don't like how people are behaving works much better than saying that a scenario isn't real. So for example, when watching a criminal threatening people with violence, it's better to say, "Nobody likes people who act like him," or "That's not cool," than to say, "Real people don't do that—she's pretending," or "That's fake." But for fictitious, scary content, telling kids age eight and older that a scene or event isn't real *does* help reduce their fear, and that's a good thing.

On the flip side, you'll want to avoid making positive comments about violent content. For example, while watching an explosion, don't say, "That was awesome!" (even if you do think it was pretty cool). Or if a good guy shoots some bad guys, hold back on saying, "He showed them," since that gives the impression that violence is justified to solve problems.

It helps to give children credit for realizing that people are responsible for what happens after they make a bad choice (behaviors have consequences), even in little ways kids come up with. For example, if you say that a guy was dumb for slugging someone to show how he felt, and your kids say yeah, say, "I'm proud of you for knowing that imitating violent guys would be bad." Don't correct their negative comments about aggressive characters unless they are very inaccurate.

For older adolescents, watch and listen to things together when possible. As opposed to younger kids, asking teens questions about content works better than your comments. That's because older teens view parents' disapproving comments about scenes as condescending (and, you know, parents really don't know much). So if you're concerned about content, ask questions before, during, or after a show, even if you didn't see the show together. Ask what they think about it. For instance, if a man pulls out a gun because someone is stealing his car but ends up getting shot by the thief, you could ask, "What would you do if your car was getting stolen?" Listen and then tell them what you think (you might say, "Too bad that guy used a gun to try to save his car. He could have let the thief go, reported it, and lived").

Research has shown that the more realistically and graphically violence is shown, the more likely it is tolerated, learned, and psychologically effective. There are other aspects of violent content that make it more likely for kids to approve of and imitate it: perpetrators are attractive, are looked up to, or enjoy hurting others; lack of accurate pain and suffering for victims; and infusing humor or sexual material. Sexual content and humor are particularly dangerous when they associate positive feelings with hurting other people. We think you'll agree that all these scenarios are quite common today, even in shows made for children. We need to find a way to persuade the entertainment industry to reduce these most harmful aspects of violent material.

You'll want to comment on these elements with kids aged eight and older, using questions for teens. For instance, when a violent character is portrayed as attractive or powerful, you could remark that the perpetrator looks weak like a coward because he doesn't know how to talk it out but has to rely on fighting, or that real criminals don't usually look that good and are outcasts of society (or ask teens what they think about the character). When seeing a criminal go unpunished, you could state that (or ask if) the perpetrator should have been or normally would have been jailed. When a character intentionally wounds innocent people, you could say that this is never (or ask if this is ever) an OK way to solve a problem. If violent scenes do not portray accurate levels of pain, distress, and harm, you could point out that (or ask if) a real victim in that situation would likely die or end up in a wheelchair, or be in more pain or unable to talk. You could address humor infused into violent scenes by saying that it isn't funny when people get hurt, and they wouldn't find it funny if it happened to them.

About Media Ratings

More violent and other harmful content has gradually filtered into movies, TV, and games rated for younger people. Even G-rated movies contain fantasy characters and violence that small children find very frightening and influential. And ratings only limit what is actually shown, not what's hinted at (you see a knife, but the scene fades out before it's used). Yet kids imagine actions easily, which can be just as damaging as seeing the actions happen. Therefore, most parents don't trust ratings, with good reason.

When movies are rated PG-13, surveys show that most parents don't think they're appropriate for their teenagers. The other interesting thing about ratings is that kids are often enticed to see a show just because it's rated for older people. Teens are anxious to join the adult world, and look to media as a friend and adviser on how to act in it—but media are now dangerous role models doling out harmful advice.

But because using ratings is better than nothing, pay attention to them without solely relying on them to make your decisions. Really think twice (or thrice) about letting your kids, including teens, see R-rated movies because they contain high amounts of profanity and vulgarity, substance use, sexualized characters, and disturbing, realistic violence. Studies show that seeing R-rated movies increases alcohol use in kids, and increases the risk of using marijuana sixfold. Poorer grades in school and more behavior problems are also associated with increased viewing of R-rated and PG-13 movies.

The good news is that these problems are reduced when parents prohibit these movies, especially in preteens. If your child argues that he or she is old enough, or that friends have seen an R-rated movie, explain your reasons for forbidding it: say, "I know it seems unfair, but what you see can hurt you. Other parents may not realize this. I could preview it and make sure it seems OK before you see it or we can find another movie." An NC-17 rating indicates that only adults should see it due to excessive levels of explicit sex, language, or violence—we find this a concerning rating since seventeen-year-olds are still kids, not adults.

For popular music, heed parental-advisory warnings—they really do indicate large doses of harmful content, such as violence, drug use, criminal activity, and sexual assault. Check out your kids' music every once in a while (even if it hurts). You can remove and offer to replace content that you find dangerous.

Watching the News and Talking About News Events

You can help your kids deal with life in these scary times and ease their fears by managing media coverage of tragic events and by letting them watch you handle your emotions in healthy ways. Again, watching violent and scary things with children younger than eight and saying things to try to reduce their fear doesn't work. So experts advise against allowing kids younger than eight to see any scary or violent news content. But even eight- to twelve-year-olds can have long-term worries from seeing violence, especially when content is presented as news rather than fiction. So we agree with researchers who say that most TV news isn't appropriate for children younger than age eleven. This probably also applies to violent historical events in educational shows.

With kids age eleven and up, it appears best to limit their news exposure and watch it with them. Crime, natural disaster, school shootings, and terrorism stories are the most harmful, because they're so unpredictable. But there are ways you can help your kids be less affected and fearful after hearing about tragedies.

Finding the Words

· ·

How you react and talk about tragedies helps kids cope. By the way, not talking about it makes it worse. First, ask, *What do you know about what happened?* Empathize with their feelings (*Yes, it is sad, isn't it. And I can see why it's scary to you*) and clear up any misconceptions that made the event seem worse. If they ask if you're afraid too, it's best to say, *No, not really, because I know we'll (or you'll) be OK.* It's important not to express much fear because it increases children's fear. Instead, note positive aspects (*There are so many people helping the victims*), and say, *Nothing like this has happened where we live*, if that's true, which works better than saying that there's very *little chance* of it happening here. Or if a similar event *has* happened nearby, say, *But there are steps being taken to make sure that it won't happen again.* For small children, say, *I won't let anything bad happen to you and will keep you safe.* For older kids, discuss safety measures, and what officials are doing to help.

Limit time spent talking about bad world events unless children want to keep talking, and limit watching news coverage of events. (Many adults feel better by spending less time watching and talking about depressing events too.) Praise children when they say something that helps them cope ("I'm proud of you for talking about it," and "I like what you said about that") and challenge dysfunctional views. Help them find ways they could help victims and keep routines going. If your child continues to express fear, anger, or sadness a month after an event, and it's interfering with ability to function, it's a warning sign that you need professional advice. Children who are part of violent events need professional help right away to adequately cope.

Video Game Management

Parental monitoring of game playing is generally low, with almost half of young teens reporting that parents never limit playing time or check ratings. In light of the strong evidence of harm, experts recommend that youth not play games in which players are awarded for killing or intentionally harming human or other living targets (even cartoonish ones). Regarding ratings, even E-rated (E for everyone) games may reward players for hurting a character and almost all T (teen) games reward players for inflicting wounds. M-rated (M for mature) games are not recommended before adulthood because they contain the highest doses of the most explicit violent and sexualized content. Consider replacing harmful games with less violent ones, or even better, games that are nonviolent and prosocial. Here are other tips:

- To enable monitoring, allow game play only at a central place in your home.
- Set a time limit on play so your kids have more time to interact with people.
- If you allow violent game play, play these games together so you're aware of content and time spent, and talk about it (for example, when characters are hurt, ask or state how real people such as your child would be affected). If your kids say they know already (or don't agree), it helps for them to hear it from you anyway.
- Seek out nonviolent games and play them together as a way to have fun and stay connected.
- Youth can become addicted to games, so watch for the warning signs of addiction that we mentioned earlier in the chapter.

Making a Family Media Plan

Even though it's impossible to know everything about kids' media lives, wise parents make management plans with their kids. Here are things to remember as you do: (1) approach it as a time-management and life-balancing plan made out of concern for your kids' well-being and happiness; (2) give your school-age kids input from the beginning; (3) plan gradual changes over time instead of all at once; (4) include *your* non-work-related screen time (sorry, but this will help your kids buy into the plan); and (5) while older kids will say that media aren't influential, they're counting on you to do what's best for them.

A great way to prepare for a family media meeting is to have everyone in the household write down the following for one week: what they watched, played, communicated, and listened to, and for how long and using which device (or record this information yourself for young children). This will help everyone evaluate how time is spent and which entertainment is most important. For TV, identifying your favorite shows that you don't want kids seeing can help you plan for alternative child activities during that time or to record shows for private viewing later. Planning encourages worthwhile viewing (instead of automatic viewing) and gives you more free time.

Review everyone's electronic media diaries and set rules that everyone interprets the same way, specifying limits on time spent on which device or media, when it can be spent (such as no noneducational media before homework is done or on a certain weekday, no social media while doing homework, no screens, including cell phones, during meals, mute commercials, TV can only be on when someone is actively watching a show). Also, specify types of shows, music, websites, and games that are or aren't allowed, and if a child's choice is not approved, replace it with something less harmful that he or she would probably like. Compromise when you safely can. Once you decide on rules, write them down and put them in plain view.

The good news is that children can learn from prosocial content (helping others, cooperating for a good cause, showing empathy, and seeing other people's perspectives) and benefit from uplifting content (overcoming adversity and experiencing good things). This content has been shown to improve children's moods, sleep, and helpful behaviors, so include it in your media plan using your children's input.

Studies show that children respond fairly well to many media changes, such as not watching TV during meals, removing background TV (the TV is on when no one is actively watching), setting time limits, and eliminating programs that kids view as pointless, but avoid making your rules too restrictive (such as allowing hardly any violent or sexual content for adolescents). That'll probably backfire as resentment and make kids want to see objectionable content even more, which they'll probably do elsewhere. Also, we think that even when your teens spend their own money, you have the right to approve their purchases, because you have the job of protecting them.

Write down specifically what will happen when someone follows the rules (rewards, extra or continued privileges) as well as what will happen if not (loss of privileges with that device, loss of allowance, getting an extra chore). Not allowing screen media in bedrooms makes it much easier to make sure the rules are followed. When you can't monitor or regulate exposure and you're concerned about previous noncompliance or trouble related to media, reset devices to work with your password or take away or hide power cords, including smartphone chargers.

Once you think your adolescents have established healthy viewing, cell phone use, and other media habits, and you've seen them make reasonable choices over time, let them decide on media. Studies show this works as long as you still spot-check and discuss or restrict content or time spent when you think it's best.

How to Approach Other Parents About Their Children's Media Use

When very concerned about media use by children of relatives or close friends, have several short conversations with the children's parents. You could simply bring up the new information on media that you've been reading and how you're making changes with your own kids. Be very careful not to criticize but just act concerned about their children. You may meet resistance, but it's worth a try. Suggestions for approaching parents about your child's media use in their home are on page 17.

Childhood is now filled with large doses of harmful media content that can potentially be more influential than parents. Congratulate yourself on efforts to block electronic media from detrimentally molding your children's emotional health and behavior while reducing their risk of being affected by violence and aggression. If needed, help motivate making media changes by asking how media fulfill your family's desires and goals and what you all might be missing out on by using it so much.

We hold a collective power that could sway the entertainment industry to provide safer products: if we don't use or allow our kids to be exposed to music, games, television shows, and movies with harmful content, and don't support their advertisers, their production and sale could be greatly curtailed. On the other hand, research supports that prosocial media can teach valuable altruistic lessons—let's demand increased production of media that families can feel good about sharing.

5

Bullying and Putting a Stop to It

One's dignity may be assaulted, vandalized and cruelly mocked,
but it can never be taken away unless it is surrendered.

—Actor and author Michael J. Fox

Emmet Fralick was a friendly, popular fourteen-year-old boy. Leaving a note that said he was being tormented and could no longer take the bullying, he shot and killed himself in his bedroom. Emmet would be beaten up unless he repeatedly paid a gang of teenage bullies. A sixteen-year-old girl was sentenced for extortion and assault in connection with his death.

A child tormented by bullying can violently strike out, even by suicide, homicide, or both. While most victims don't, and some may think of bullying as "just part of growing up," bullying is now recognized as a cause of serious, multifaceted harm. Bullies may become aggressive and violent adult perpetrators and their victims often suffer long-term consequences to mental health that raise the risk of aggression and further victimization.

In this chapter, we'll describe different types of bullying and ways to prevent them. You'll learn how to recognize and handle when children you care about are being bullied as well as what to do if your child or one you care about is a bully. First, we want to make sure we are all speaking the same language about this significant, complex problem.

What Bullying Is

Bullying is comprised of the following elements: (1) unwanted aggression that is intended to create distress, fear, intimidation, humiliation, or other harm in a targeted victim; (2) perceived power imbalance—bullies are perceived as being physically or socially stronger; and (3) often repeated over time.

Bullying can cause physical, psychological, social (reputation and relationship), and educational harm, and destruction of a target's property. Bullies don't need to confront their victims in person but can use peers or technology like text messages or social media; this is called *electronic aggression* or cyberbullying. But over 80% of all bullying occurs in front of others, and bystander actions can be very influential in promoting or discouraging bullying. Shockingly, most middle school bullies are rewarded by peers with increased social status.

A child can be both a bully and a victim of bullying. These "bully-victims" appear to have even greater negative outcomes than kids who are only bullies or only victims.

Let's look at parts of the definition to help you decide if behaviors you see constitute bullying. Many bullies claim that victims don't care about their actions, but the "unwanted" part of the definition means victims want it to stop. So, when two kids are playfully taunting each other and both are enjoying it, this doesn't constitute bullying. "Aggression" means the intentional use of threatening or harmful behaviors regardless of whether or not the intent is to injure. Swinging a bat at someone (which is threatening) or actually hitting him with it can both constitute bullying. "Power imbalance" means bullies use personal or situational characteristics to their advantage: physical size or strength, academic standing, popularity, money, and accomplices. Bullies often target kids with disabilities or different sexual orientations—anyone they perceive as being different or weak.

Victims may not recognize, describe, or express what they have experienced as bullying, but that is where informed parents can help. Regarding being "repeated over time," one episode of severe unwanted aggression intended to harm still counts as bullying, but bullying generally recurs.

Which Behaviors Are *Not* Bullying

Roughhousing between two willing participants is not bullying. Although no one enjoys it, it's also not bullying for one- to four-year-olds to act out when they're uncomfortable, angry, or don't get what they want by yelling, hitting, or other aggression. Toddlers and preschoolers aren't developmentally capable of controlling these behaviors but need to learn how to as they grow older.

Fights between kids without a power imbalance and when no one appears frightened or threatened isn't bullying. Aggression meeting the criteria for bullying committed by persons eighteen and older is often classified as criminal assault.

Types of Bullying

Bullying can be *direct*: physically or verbally confronting victims directly, often in front of others. It also can be *indirect:* hurting victims without direct confrontation but through peers, which frequently involves relational aggression. *Relational (or social) bullying* harms a victim's reputation, acceptance, and friendships. It includes purposefully leaving someone out of an activity with the intent to cause distress; spreading lies, gossip, rumors, or embarrassing stories or pictures; and forcing other kids to be mean. *Physical bullying* includes pushing, hitting, kicking, throwing objects, spitting, tripping, destroying property, and making unwelcome gestures. *Verbal bullying* includes insults, name-calling, threatening with words, taunting, excessive teasing, and making sexual or embarrassing statements. Bullies commonly threaten others to get something from them (like money, possessions, or homework). All but direct physical bullying can occur through electronic media, or cyberbullying.

Cyberbullying

Cyberbullying is the newest form of bullying and a growing problem. The website www.stopbullying.gov defines it as bullying that takes place using electronic technology (sending texts, voice messages, and images) and social media (like Snapchat, Instagram, Facebook, YouTube, and Twitter). It's done either by sending content directly to a victim or indirectly (sending content to peers) that threatens, excludes, embarrasses, humiliates, or spreads rumors. Cyberbullies can also be strangers who pose as someone else, but most victims personally know their bullies.

The effects of cyberbullying can be more devastating than face-to-face, direct attacks. Harmful messages can spread quickly to large numbers of people. Victims are often unaware when it's happening. Since cyberbullies are less likely to make their threats during school hours, kids are often home and alone when bullied—so it feels like an invasion of their safe place. Cyberbullies have more time and are more willing to say bad things online than during face-to-face attacks. Social media can also be used to recruit other bullies. By creating phony accounts, cyberbullying can be done anonymously, leading to further anxiety about who is responsible.

Hazing

Rather than excluding someone, hazing is an organized form of bullying that requires dangerous or humiliating behaviors from someone who wants to join a group. The nature of the activities required for group membership is often unknown to the target before the activities occur and they are usually limited in time and severity. However, many cases involve physical and sexual assault, substance abuse, and even death.

A sports team appeared to be a good place for Jacob to make friends and keep busy. When he told his parents about repetitive taunting he endured on and off the court—like the time teammates purposefully made no seat available on the bus and then all screamed at him to sit down so the bus could leave—his parents discussed ways to cope so that Jacob was able to tolerate it even though the coaches knew what was happening and did not intervene.

One day, he told his parents he wanted to quit playing and also wanted to transfer schools. Jacob was reluctant to reveal what happened. But a strong relationship, parental concern, and patience helped him open up. Although he hadn't personally experienced the team's longtime hazing ritual, his best friend had. Jacob had witnessed other boys endure it too. He knew it was just a matter of time before they got to him. It turned out that older boys on the team would corner younger players and assault them with digital anal penetration.

The severity of hazing activities condoned by coaches speaks to their quality of character. Hazing must be reported by parents and the athletic director should also be involved and held responsible. If it constitutes assault or other illegal activity, like it did with Jacob's team, it should be reported to law enforcement.

How Often Bullying Happens

For many reasons, getting reliable numbers is difficult. Victims are reluctant to report and if they do, it often remains a "private matter" within a family, school, or organization. Schools can be reluctant to report bullying because they don't want to advertise their problem. They may lose good students and jeopardize their standing in the community. Furthermore, schools risk having to face angry parents or the publicity of an investigation while their teachers and staff are already overwhelmed by the pressures of being educators.

General estimates of bullying in the United States range from 10% to 33% of school-age children being victims and 5% to 13% being bullies. Research consistently shows peaks in bullying behaviors during times of change when children are establishing a social hierarchy, such as the transition between elementary and middle school, and between middle and high school. Bullying and victimization also increase when individual children transition from one school to another, which is one reason that moving bullies or victims to different schools may not work. In a recent US Department of Education study, bullying declined from 37% to 22% as children progressed from sixth to twelfth grade.

Most children "age out" of physical bullying by middle school, but relational and verbal bullying increase with age until early high school. With the ubiquity of communication technology, cyberbullying is a method that bullies have increasingly used to harm kids. In a large, multiyear review, the Cyberbullying Research Center reported in 2015 that, on average, 26% of kids acknowledged being a victim and 16% admitted to engaging in it.

Differences Between Boys and Girls

Boys and girls are equally likely to become victims of bullying, but boys are more likely to be bullies as well as bully-victims. While boys use more direct, physical aggression than girls, both use indirect bullying, relational bullying and cyberbullying equally. Emerging research on sibling bullying suggests boys and girls are equally likely to offend.

Kids who bully others may be hard to recognize—they're often good, well-respected, popular students. In her book *Odd Girl Out*, Rachel Simmons aptly describes covert aggression performed under a "good girl" guise, even bullying close friends to achieve power. Girls commonly bully by humiliation, gossip, rumors, lies, exclusion, sharing secrets, and creating drama, and they use technology more often than physical means. Female bullies often repetitively tease their victims about weight, appearance, relationships, and intellectual ability. Most do their bullying in groups, victimizing and pressuring members to also engage—and most are afraid to speak up or stop it.

Where Bullying Happens

Bullying happens everywhere—in homes, schools, school buses, public transportation, and on the streets. Face-to-face bullying is more likely to happen when kids are without adequate adult supervision, including when adults are around but are uninvolved, unaware, or condone the behaviors. Schools have more bullying when supervision is lacking and rules on bullying are poorly defined and inconsistently enforced. Bullying is more likely to occur when the majority of students belong to a specific, identifiable demographic group. All things being equal, bullying appears to be less common in schools with fairly evenly distributed diversity than in schools where one ethnic group has a clear majority.

Home Bullying by Siblings

Although this chapter deals mostly with bullying by peers outside the home, research suggests that kids are far more likely to bully a sibling than a peer. Being bullied at home by siblings and other family members is very damaging to a child—home is a place where children are supposed to feel safe and cared for. The detrimental effects of being bullied by a sibling may be even greater than being bullied at school because there's a misperception that fighting between siblings is normal, benign, and even useful. Consequently, sibling bullying is more likely to continue and escalate before it's considered by parents to be a legitimate problem. Kids who are bullied both at home and school fare the worst. Also, it's common for children bullied at home to become bullies at school. Therefore, parents should not dismiss sibling aggression as "kids will be kids."

Next, we'll discuss the negative impacts of bullying, whether it's by a peer at school or a sibling at home.

How Children Are Affected by Being Bullied

Immense physical, psychological, social, and academic harm can result from repeatedly being bullied by peers or siblings. Kids and parents may not recognize how harmful these events are until later. Victims often avoid school and develop aches and pains (real and imagined) to avoid facing bullies, resulting in grade erosion. Disordered eating, substance use, and sleep problems are common aftereffects of being bullied. Recent research has even found that the brain activity of victims is different from nonbullied peers. Victims may become anxious, depressed, or both, withdrawing from others and feeling badly about themselves or acting out aggressively due to anger. Sadly, these same characteristics make kids more likely to be bullied.

Effects of being bullied don't end in childhood. Victims suffer more physical and mental health problems as adults, including loneliness, agoraphobia (fear of open places), depression, and anxiety. They're also more prone to suicide attempts. Victims are not only more likely to develop delinquent behaviors as teens but also more likely to become violent later in life.

Bullying and Suicide

Does being bullied cause kids to commit suicide? The short answer is no; not directly, anyway. There are many other factors that more directly predict suicide. But being bullied can result in emotional and mental health problems that lead a person to consider suicide. In other words, being bullied increases risk, but psychological and other support from home, friends, and school can prevent children from resorting to suicide. Bullied children receiving emotional support from at least one other person are much better off than those who don't. Suicide risk is significantly higher, however, when children are bullied for being lesbian, gay, bisexual, or transgender (LGBT).

So we don't want parents or children to think that suicide is a normal or natural reaction to being bullied. Suicide risk may increase *if* there is no intervention. Following widespread coverage of a bullied victim's suicide, there can be an increase in suicide attempts from a phenomenon called *contagion*, as we discussed in chapter 3. Experts are recommending that the term "bully-cide" not be used because it is misleading and can imply that bullying causes suicide.

How Bullying Affects All of Us

Does being bullied result in retaliatory attacks? Though many school shooters appeared to have been bullied, very few bullied children retaliate with deadly violence. What does affect society is victims' higher rates of depression, anxiety, and truancy. There's evidence that bystanders who repeatedly witness bullying are also more likely to develop these symptoms.

Victims and bullies use higher levels of public assistance, costing taxpayers. Both groups also have higher risk for suicide, relationship conflicts, and substance abuse. Bullies have more trouble keeping jobs and are twice as likely to behave violently, four times more likely to have multiple criminal convictions, and four times more likely to be diagnosed with ASPD than nonbullies. Despite these grim statistics, it's important to note that most bullies do not become criminals and with proper support and intervention, we can significantly reduce the problem! Let's begin by discussing how to know if your child is being bullied.

Warning Signs Your Child May Be Getting Bullied

If any of the following are happening with your children, you should be concerned that they are being bullied:

- Increased moodiness, secretiveness, or withdrawal.
- Increased agitation or emotional outbursts.
- Increased worrying or anxiety.
- Becoming agitated or afraid when seeing classmates in public settings.
- Beginning to bully siblings or others.
- Avoidance of going to school or school activities (frequently sick or truant).
- Vague physical complaints like stomachaches or headaches.
- Avoidance of less structured school settings (recess, lunch room, school bus, after-school organizations, or sports).
- Sudden changes in friendships or exclusion by current friends.
- Unexplained decline in grades.
- Sleep difficulties.
- Noticeable changes in mood after talking on the phone or looking at media devices.
- Loss of money or possessions, or possessions get broken or destroyed.
- Bruises or soiled or torn clothing.
- Reluctance to show arms or legs to you (such as covering arms with long sleeves when it's warm outside) or unexplained scratches or cuts on skin.

- Making negative statements about themselves or their schools, friends, lives, or futures.

Readers may note that many of these warning signs can be related to other problems, such as depression and substance abuse. Be concerned and seek help regardless of the cause of these signs of distress.

Which Children Are More Likely to Be Bullied?

Victims generally don't do anything to provoke bullying. They're often picked on because they're perceived as being different. Kids who have developmental disabilities or mental disorders such as ADHD, autism spectrum disorder, learning disabilities, or speech problems are often targeted. Those who appear physically or socially weak are also at risk, as are those quick to anger or tears. Children who have depression, anxiety, and lower self-esteem may appear more vulnerable to bullies and thus become targets.

Kids may also be bullied because they're shy or socially isolated, or become targets due to religious affiliation, race, socioeconomic status, or sexual orientation. Recent research shows that 80% of LGBT youth report being harassed due to their sexual orientation, 40% receive physical threats, and 18% report being physically assaulted.

Why Don't Bullied Children Tell Parents or Other Adults?

In her book *The Bully, the Bullied, and the Bystander*, Barbara Coloroso describes reasons that bullied children may suffer in silence, such as fear of retaliation, feeling ashamed of not being able to handle it, and not thinking that anyone can or will help. They also may fear rejection or ridicule from parents, friends, or other adults like coaches and teachers or may be embarrassed by what the bully is saying and don't want others to know. But victims are more likely to confide in an adult if a peer bystander tells an adult first, or when they believe that adults will actively respond.

How to Bully-Proof Your Child

Family life qualities that protect against the effects of bullying include supportive and affectionate relationships, open communication, and parental involvement. Research shows that parental involvement in the classroom decreases bullying in elementary school, but overprotective, hovering parents can actually increase bullying regardless of age. According to a 2013 study, kids who were most resistant to becoming depressed after being bullied were socially connected boys with high self-esteem and low levels of family conflict.

How to Talk About Bullying with Children

It's important for adults to empower children with knowledge and the ability to ask for help. We recommend asking all children, "Do you know what bullying is?" Praise them for their knowledge and add any further information they should know. Then ask, "Do you know anyone who is being bullied?" That opens up the conversation even if children don't want to talk about their own situation. If they say that "a friend" is being bullied, you can talk about it in terms of their friend. Also ask kids what their friends are like, what they do together, and how they treat others. Talk about what it means to be a good friend and ask whether they think the kids they hang out with are good friends. If you're concerned that your child is being bullied, talk about it.

Finding the Words

If you're concerned your child is being bullied, say, *Sometimes kids are afraid to tell their parents when they're being bullied, but because I love you, I need to know. Have you ever been bullied?* Help normalize your child's experience by saying, *This happens to a lot of kids.*

If your child seems reluctant to talk or indicates fear that telling you will make it worse, say, *It helps to tell because bullies often pick on kids they don't think will tell. It's not telling that makes it worse.* If your child is being bullied, say, *It isn't your fault and you don't deserve it. This happens to other kids too. It isn't about you—it's about (the bully).* Then ask, *Do you feel you can defend yourself and deal with this?* Whether the answer is yes or no, say something like, *I will help you until it is better. I don't expect you to handle this all by yourself—you're a kid and shouldn't have to.* It's crucial that you believe and do not make fun of your child's concerns.

Some researchers suggest kids are more likely to disclose bullying if they think that their school won't suspend the bully (because the victim won't fear the retaliation that often occurs once a bully returns to school). Schools that put bullies on behavioral plans before suspending them may have higher rates of victim disclosure.

Ways to Make It Better and Help Children Cope

How adults act when bullying is disclosed can have a huge impact on children's adjustment. First, listen without judgment, believe them, and help them understand that it's not their fault. Make sure children feel accepted and supported by other family members and encourage family discussions about bullying experiences. It should be out in the open. Have kids make a plan with you on how to deal with a bully, whether it is a sibling or an outside peer. When you address bullying head-on, you communicate that you believe and care about them and that they have nothing to feel ashamed about.

Help kids see that the reasons for being bullied reside with the bully, not them. Research shows more negative outcomes when victims attribute the cause of bullying to something about themselves (such as being annoying and unlikeable) rather than characteristics of the bully (so insecure that he or she needs to be mean to others). Some bullying treatment programs have victims write about what they experience and discuss why they think it happens. Whenever they blame themselves (thinking they were bullied because no one likes them), therapists help victims consider other more healthy explanations (such as getting bullied because of not making eye contact and appearing vulnerable). Parents can do this too!

For many reasons, it's important to support children's academic achievements and extracurricular activities—show up for them. You'll be more aware of what's happening to your kids and they'll feel more willing to disclose to you. Ensure that your kids are in situations where there's sufficient adult supervision, and if they ever talk about feeling helpless or wanting to hurt themselves, don't leave them alone, and follow our suggestions from chapter 3.

Things Parents and Other Adults Do That Make Bullying Worse

When adults see bullying, they need to stop it right away by moving victims to safety and then report it to the appropriate parties (parents, school staff, or police when it constitutes a crime). But there are things adults can do and say that can actually make the situation worse for victims:

- Telling kids to ignore it. This minimizes the problem and tells victims that bullying will stop if they pretend it's not happening, even though the bullying will usually increase before it decreases. But ignoring or walking away from the bully in the moment *can* be an effective temporary strategy to prevent it from escalating.
- Saying things like, "Suck it up!" or "Don't be such a wimp." These kinds of statements blame the victims instead of the bullies. In contrast, it helps to say, "I will help you fix this. For right now, try to let it roll off your back." Bullying should not be treated as an expected rite of passage into adulthood, because it isn't.

- Encouraging victims to fight back. This escalates the problem and may lead victims to get suspended from school or be physically harmed. Remember, with bullying there is usually a power differential. That said, when faced with serious bodily harm, physical self-defense that permits escape is warranted.
- Confronting bullies with threats and criticism (or confronting parents of bullies) usually escalates the bullying. Read more about talking with parents later in this chapter.

What Children Can Do When Facing a Bully

Ask victims what would help them feel more safe and in control. Minimize changes they need to make in their daily routines or it may feel like punishment. There are things children can try when directly confronted by a bully: (1) calmly and politely tell the bully to "please stop" or "please let me go" while looking into his or her eyes; (2) say something totally unrelated ("Yeah, I hate taking tests, too"); (3) give them a compliment (like how cool their shirt is); (4) agree with them ("Yeah, I'm short, but I'm working on that"); or (5) laugh and say, "That's a good one." This should be followed by calmly walking away. It's important to not show emotion (anger, fear, or tears), because emotional reactions reinforce the bully's behavior.

Because bullies are more prone to pick on kids perceived as being vulnerable, have children practice walking straight and tall with their chins held high. If children can't say anything to a bully, or feel it wouldn't be safe, have them stand by you, another adult, or another group of kids. Encourage them to avoid areas where bullying is known to happen.

What Children Can Do When They See Other Kids Being Bullied

Victims aren't the only ones hurt by bullying. Children who witness bullying (bystanders) are also harmed. They may become angry, fearful, or guilty—all negative impacts on how they feel about school and learning. Discuss what kids can do when they witness bullying. Bystanders can help reduce bullying in the following ways:

1. Don't laugh at, smile, agree with, or give attention to the bully.
2. If you know the bully, or feel it's safe, say, "Let's stop—that's not cool (or funny)."
3. Go tell or get a trusted adult, like a teacher.
4. Create a distraction, such as saying to the victim, "Hey, I heard your name called over the intercom to go the office," "Come and help me with (something)," "Hey, let's walk to your next class together," or "Your teacher called for you."
5. Show sympathy for the victim. Ask him or her, "Are you OK?" Later on, call or text the victim and say something like, "I felt bad for you today. You didn't deserve that. Can you talk to your parents about this?"
6. Say hi, talk to, or even befriend victims. Research shows that having just one supportive friend can significantly reduce the negative effects of being bullied.

Cyberbullying Defense

Kids need our help to safeguard their activities on cell phones and online. They have limited ability to make good decisions on the content they disclose about themselves and others, how it might be used, and how to defend themselves against cyberbullying.

It's important to have regular cyber-safety talks, as described in chapter 4. Here are things to tell kids about cyberbullying:

1. Definition: using technology like cell phones and the Internet to be mean.
2. Don't post, write, say, or send anything unkind, critical, or embarrassing about someone. Don't say anything electronically that you wouldn't say to a person's face.
3. Consider any post, text, picture, voicemail, and e-mail to be permanent and possibly passed on to others. A friend may not stay a friend and may not keep secrets.
4. Don't give out passwords (except to you) because it's hard to know who can be trusted long-term.

5. Tell a parent or another adult about anything seen or heard that is sad or disturbing about another person or your child, or may be bullying. Tell kids not to delete, forward, or respond to concerning messages without talking to you first.

6. Cyberbullying involving students should be reported to the school, so show the evidence before deleting it. Once reported, delete future related messages without reading them.

7. You won't take away their tech devices for telling you about concerns—this is a common reason cyberbullied kids give for not telling their parents.

8. States have laws on cyberbullying. You can find your state's laws on the web, at www.stopbullying.gov/laws.

9. Report cyberbullying to law enforcement if it threatens violence, contains child pornography or sexually explicit messages or photos, contains photos or videos of people in places they would expect privacy, or constitutes stalking or a hate crime.

There is a small but increasing trend of cyberbullying in elementary kids. For this and other reasons, we recommend waiting as long as possible to give young children texting and online social media privileges, to delay headaches and risks. Also, teach kids how to block perpetrators and report cyberbullying to social media websites and Internet service providers involved.

Speaking with a Bully's Parents

In general, meetings between parents of victims and bullies should be with school officials. Your child probably is not the only one being bullied. Chances are good that the bully is experiencing other difficulties at school, so his or her parents may be defensive when approached. Independently approaching parents and asking them to stop their child from bullying yours can make matters worse. Parents of elementary school children tend to be more responsive, perhaps because they have more influence over their children. Schools tend to prefer letting teachers or principals handle school bullying first, before parents get involved.

If you know the bully's parents and feel the need to say something, you could say, "Boy, it seems like our kids don't get along right now. I wish they could." This is an opening for a discussion that won't make them as defensive as compared to asking them to make their kid leave yours alone. If you don't know them, but see them often at school or other events, try introducing yourself as your child's parent and ask how their child is doing. Depending on their response, you may be able to introduce your concerns. If the parent seems preoccupied or defensive, you may need to wait until later. It sometimes works better to form an acquaintance relationship first.

Asking Teachers to Intervene

Besides giving kids the skills to deal with bullying that we've discussed, ask teachers who are most likely to witness it to intervene. If that doesn't resolve the issue, then request a meeting with the principal (more on this on pages 132–133) and the bully's parents. In the meeting, don't accuse but act concerned and say you'd like the behaviors to stop. It gets more complicated when the bully has dropped out or changed schools but still has access to your child. In situations like that, the police may need to be involved and can be helpful.

Why don't teachers always intervene, regardless of being asked? Reasons could include not noticing, being overwhelmed with all the other pressures of teaching, or fearing that the school won't appropriately deal with it. Perhaps it's because they haven't had adequate training to deal with bullying or they too have been traumatized by students' (or parents') threats and other aggressive behaviors. Teachers and other school personnel are increasingly facing threats of violence or actually being assaulted in or around schools.

School Responses to Bullying

Research suggests best practices for dealing with bullying on a school-wide basis as well as with individual bullies. Ask your school administrator if an antibullying program is in place. Successful school bullying prevention program elements will be addressed at the end of the chapter, where they will be combined with an advisory list of preventive parenting actions.

Management of a Bully by School Personnel

We suggest that school personnel approach bullies from a place of concern for what is happening to them, rather than being punitive. This may lower their defenses and make them more receptive to intervention. Asking a bully, "What is wrong with you?" may exacerbate behavior, but asking, "What has happened to you (or how are things going for you)?" or gently asking, "What were you thinking about when you (bullied someone)?" can start a productive conversation. Bullies have often been traumatized at home, making them more emotionally reactive, so they may not be able to respond in a controlled, logical manner. Telling parents, "We'd like to help you help your child stay in school, stay out of trouble, and have a better school experience" works better than saying, "Your kid has a problem and you need to fix it."

Research indicates that zero-tolerance plans where all bullies are suspended or expelled regardless of the circumstance have been shown to create more problems than they solve. When bullies return, they often retaliate against victims. It's better to get bullies engaged in prosocial behaviors in school than get them kicked out. Schools and parents can develop individualized discipline and support plans that have bullies make restitution to their victims. It's important for the plans to also address some of the underlying issues related to bullying (such as seeing actions of others as hostile, abnormally elevated or low levels of self-esteem, poor social skills, and academic problems). Connecting bullies and their families to needed support services like counseling can also help.

Engaging bullies in changing the school's social climate is useful. Asking for their ideas to combat bullying and create a culture of kindness will help increase bullies' ownership of possible solutions. They need praise when showing others respect or for being a "good friend." All kids are more willing to listen to adults if they feel respected and liked by them. Teachers may assign bullies to do reports or classroom presentations on aspects of bullying and possible solutions.

Several actions have been shown to worsen bullying. These include when school personnel and other adults see bullying and don't intervene, and placing bullies in groups to work on their behavior. Also, having children meet with bullies to resolve the conflict can further traumatize victims, especially if the bullying occurred recently; bullying is not a conflict resolution situation—it is a victimization situation. Meetings between bullies and victims should only occur under very controlled circumstances and when both want the meeting.

State Laws on School Bullying Intervention

Despite the challenges of directly dealing with bullying, schools have been held legally liable for knowing about bullying and not intervening. While forty-nine of fifty states have antibullying laws (what's going on, Montana?), the laws are remarkably fragmented and inconsistent. Some laws only apply to public schools, allowing private schools to be exempt. Others make it difficult to prosecute unless the bully targets someone due to a protected status (race, religion, disability, gender). What happens when a child who is being bullied does not fall into a protected group? Most state laws require or encourage schools to discipline bullies, but there is much variability as to how.

Talking to School Officials When Your Child Is Bullied to Get a Response

School staff may help get bullying situations satisfactorily resolved. Set up meetings with supervising adults (teachers, principals, counselors, coaches) and discuss your concerns. Don't criticize or threaten, as this may make them defensive and harm your cause. You want to keep lines of communication open. Ask them to work with you to set up a plan for action and then discuss the plan with your child. School officials won't be able to disclose discipline or services given to other children, even bullies. Continue meeting with them until the issue is resolved.

If you're having trouble getting a satisfactory plan in place, or believe bullying is being ignored, you can try saying this to school officials: "I feel like we're not getting anywhere. Who can I write to at the district administration level to start a paper trail on this situation?" If unsatisfied with the plan or progress, you can meet with your school superintendent or even correspond with your state's Department of Education officials. Parents can ask the state to investigate their concerns.

When School Officials Meet with You Because Your Child Is Bullying Others

Parents of bullies often don't recognize how their actions contribute to their child's bullying behaviors. When meeting with school officials, hopefully you'll be approached from the perspective of offering support, not criticism. If you feel criticized, it's really important not to let this cause your natural defenses to erupt because this can keep you from seeing the situation for what it really is and helping your child. Some parents don't act due to their own aggressive tendencies or their desire to protect their children's (or families') reputations. They may not understand the harm inflicted by bullying or the danger to their child. Don't let this happen to you or your child; rather, take strides to improve your life and your child's life by following the strategies in the last section of this chapter.

Warning Signs That Kids May Be Bullies and How Parents Can Help

Kids who bully have learned to use aggression to get what they want, have power over their peers, elevate their social status, or make others miserable—and they often seem to enjoy doing so. Although mean actions may be impulsive, they're usually planned and intentional. Repetitive aggression against children, including siblings, is the most important warning sign that a child is a bully. Here are other risk factors for becoming a bully:

- Often quick to anger.
- A need to win.
- Unrealistically positive views of themselves—research suggests many bullies rate themselves as being more popular than they actually are.
- Not feeling connected to their school, family, or community. This lack of connection can result from feeling disrespected and mistreated.
- Poor academic progress.
- Poor social skills (while some bullies have poor social skills, others can be quite charming).
- Friends who either condone aggression or are bullies themselves.
- Lack of empathy.

Research has shown a dangerous progression in boys. It starts with sibling aggression at home, leads to bullying at school, delinquency, and deviant peer affiliations by middle school, and then sexual harassment and dating violence in high school. Thus, it *is* important for parents to manage sibling conflict at home instead of expecting kids to "work it out."

Family Characteristics Linked to Bullying Behaviors

Certain parent and family characteristics are also linked to childhood bullying: use of harsh discipline, lack of parental warmth, prejudice, excessive teasing, domestic violence, condoning violence, and substance abuse. These are common features of a bully's home life. When parents bully their children, or interact with hostility, coldness, accusations, or disinterest, they teach their children to treat others badly. Child abuse and neglect are also linked to bullying behaviors.

Parents can teach kids to be bullies by saying that people who are strong and tough get what they want and everyone else is weak. A patient once told Laurie she was concerned about what happened to her four-year-old son. He was playing with his five-year-old cousin and when the cousin became angry at having a toy taken from him, he hit her son in the mouth and knocked out his front teeth. When the woman discussed the event with her brother (the cousin's father), he replied, "Well, I don't want my son to be a wimp." This father's response reflects a direct, powerful lesson to his son that violence is an acceptable way to solve conflicts. He may not realize he not only condones bullying but also increases his son's chance of becoming an adult perpetrator of violent crime. We suspect this father engages in violence at home.

But we mustn't be fooled into thinking that all bullies come from high-conflict homes. Children from "good" homes can become entitled, selfish, or bored and become bullies, especially when they're not taught empathy and prosocial values. All homes, including privileged ones, can have disturbed family relationships that promote bullying. The most effective bullies (who hurt others the most) often go unrecognized. They are polite to adults, get good grades, and are involved in school or community activities while tormenting others. They have good emotional recognition and social skills and use them to manipulate others. This just means that the old adage "You can't judge a book by its cover" also applies to bullies.

How Parents Can Help Their Child Who Bullies Others

If a child you care about is bullying others (including siblings), you can greatly reduce these behaviors. Similar to the approach we suggested with school personnel, saying, "What is wrong with you?" doesn't help, but asking, "What has happened to you (or how are things going for you)?" or "What were you thinking about when you (bullied someone)?" can start a good conversation. Discuss your child's specific bullying behaviors and ask what he or she gets out of harming others. Keep in mind that bullies frequently lie and play the victim to manipulate parents into inaction, so check the facts. Figure out ways to help with underlying problems, such as self-aggrandized views, low self-esteem, anger, prior trauma, or academic troubles. Tell your child, "Bullying is not OK. I won't let you grow up not being able to get along with people because this will make you unhappy and get you into a lot of trouble. I'll help you fix this." For a child who is bullying siblings, also address underlying issues such as jealousy or greed, and tell the child how important it is to have a close relationship with his or her siblings.

Focus on teaching conflict resolution skills (see page 8) and empathy (ask kids how their victims felt, or how they would feel if it happened to them). Use consistent, nonharsh discipline methods for aggression and bullying. Because parental conflict and disrespectful treatment of family members is linked to bullying, also work to decrease these experiences for your kids. When kids see parents working to change their behaviors, they'll be more willing to work to change their own.

All sibling conflicts don't meet the definition of bullying that we discussed earlier. But if they do, or you wouldn't let a neighbor treat your child the way a sibling is treating your child, it suggests bullying behavior and that you need to intervene. First, it's important for parents to label this behavior for what it is, therefore signifying that sibling bullying is not normal. Say, "You are acting like a bully, and you will not treat your sister that way." Establish a house rule of "no hurting" where everyone knows there will be a consequence if the rule is broken (such as replacing intentionally broken possessions, or doing chores or something special for a bullied sibling). If sibling bullying continues or escalates in severity, it's time to get professional help. Bullying may indicate other problems in the family, so family therapy may be recommended.

Antibullying Program Components for Parents

Various antibullying programs have been developed to help address the problem in schools. While it's beyond the scope of this discussion to review all the research on these programs, it appears the programs with highest success rates include parents in the process. The interested reader can get much useful information on such programs by going to www.stopbullying.gov.

The good news is that there are elements of antibullying programs that you can implement at home, some of which we just mentioned. Here are others:

1. Create a home climate that is supportive, respectful, and accepting of individual differences, and a place where aggression is not acceptable.

2. Set clear expectations for respectful behavior, focusing more on encouraging good behavior than discouraging bad. It's especially important to praise bullies for positive behaviors. Consistency is crucial, not only in expectations from morning to night but also from person to person. Get all adults involved in your child's life to be on the same page with regard to bullying.

3. Help children learn what's expected by labeling their behaviors: "When you say someone is stupid, that's being disrespectful and we're not disrespectful in our family," or "Not making fun of your little sister's school project was very nice and I love it when you're nice."

4. Increase supervision whenever and wherever aggression has happened in the past. You don't necessarily need to be physically present. Research shows that kids are less likely to engage in aggressive or delinquent behaviors when parents do phone check-ins after school.

5. Recognize times when your children are particularly vulnerable to bullying (such as entering middle school and high school). During these times, increase your levels of supervision and support.

6. Intervene when you see bullying to support and make sure the victim is safe. Children are reluctant to intervene when they witness bullying if they notice that adults don't intervene.

7. Lastly, relationship building and conflict resolution are important skills for all children to learn, especially in regard to preventing or treating sibling bullying. Helping bullies understand nonverbal communication (facial expressions or changes in tone of voice), and to control their impulses by talking out loud about what they're doing and why in order to monitor and modify their own behaviors is beneficial. Teaching these skills to aggressive children while young and reviewing them regularly will provide greater opportunities for success.

Bullying is a significant cause of suffering in places where children should feel safe: in their homes, schools, and neighborhoods. Its damage extends into adulthood and permeates society, strongly contributing to physical, emotional, and behavioral problems, including aggression and violence in our nation. Yet there are ways that parents and schools can combat it successfully. Please see our resource section for more assistance. We can and must join together to stop the harm—now.

6

School Violence and How to Support School Safety

Violence in our schools can never be tolerated. When children pass through the schoolhouse door, they should find safety, not violence.

—Elizabeth Dole, former US Senator
and head of the Red Cross

As of the end of February 2016, there have been at least 170 school shootings since the heartbreaking tragedy at Sandy Hook Elementary School. The vast majority of these resulted in intentional and unintentional injuries, suicides, and homicides not related to self-defense.

Any given school can expect a school student homicide every six thousand years, and these are more frequently the result of gang violence and personal disputes than random mass homicides. Less than 1% of youth homicides happen at school and that hasn't changed over the last decade. Although we are shocked and frightened by mass school shootings, they are relatively rare. This chapter will discuss school shootings as well as more common types of school violence, their risk factors and warning signs, and how they can be prevented.

School-Related Violence

The good news is that research shows progressive reductions in school violence overall and that schools are relatively safe places to be in terms of risk of death. However, aggression and violence remain unacceptably common—children deserve safe places to learn, and teachers and staff deserve safe places to work.

School violence is defined by the CDC as youth violence happening on school grounds, on the way to and from school or school-sponsored events, and during school functions. Studies indicate that the following are common causes or risk factors for school violence:

- Negative school environments (including bullying, disconnection, and academic failure).
- Cultural socialization of males as aggressive.
- Poverty.
- Violent communities.
- Gang involvement.
- Abuse or violence in families.
- Beliefs in violence or prejudice.
- Ineffective parenting.
- Impulsivity.
- Substance use.
- Media violence.
- Social isolation or peer rejection.
- Availability of firearms.

Surveys show that parents generally agree with these underlying causes, which also raise the risk of youth violence outside of school. Throughout this book, we provide advice for recognizing and mitigating these risk factors.

What Types of Violence Happen in School?

School-related aggression and violence include acts like bullying, electronic aggression, shoving, fighting, assault, theft, destruction of property, sexual harassment, sexual assault, rape, and attempted rape. In a 2013 national survey, high schoolers reported the following occurred on school property one or more times: 8% were in a physical fight and 7% were threatened or injured with a weapon during the prior twelve months; within the last thirty days, 7% didn't go to school because they felt unsafe and 5% carried a weapon. In 2012, there were almost 750,000 victims of school violence.

Aggressive and violent acts affect not only students but also staff, teachers, and administrators, by making them feel unsafe and interfering with their jobs. About 9% of teachers report being threatened with injury and 5% report being physically attacked by a student. Experiencing and witnessing school violence can lead to alcohol and drug use, depression, anxiety, prolonged fear, and suicide.

A 2001 CDC study investigated school-associated violent deaths, including suicide and homicide accomplished by any method, from 1994 to 1999. In more than half of the incidents, a potential warning sign in the form of writings, notes, threats, or other actions preceded the event. Homicide perpetrators were seven times more likely than their victims to have shown evidence of suicidal thoughts, plans, or previous attempts, and twice as likely as victims to have been bullied.

During the CDC study time period, incidents involving single homicide victims decreased while incidents involving multiple victims increased. The most common homicide motives involved interpersonal disputes (over 45%) and about one-fourth were gang related. Perpetrators (nonstudents included) were significantly more likely to have the following histories compared to their victims: criminal offenses, gang membership, delinquent friends or being considered a loner, or using drugs or alcohol on a weekly basis. Students who perpetrated homicidal acts were more likely to have seen the principal for fighting or noncompliance, and less likely to have been involved in school activities compared to victims. The most common times for deaths to occur were around the time that school starts, the lunch hour, and after school hours.

How Are Mass School Shootings Different?

Compared to more common violent events, mass school shootings are relatively rare but very disturbing. Characteristics of perpetrators who kill multiple victims at random appear to differ from what was found in the 2001 CDC study discussed above, and we'll review these after we answer common questions.

First, do school shooters just snap? Do they act impulsively, making a quick decision to act? As we discussed in chapter 3 for Adam Lanza, evidence strongly shows that these events are almost always planned well in advance.

Second, are there warning signs before attacks? After the shooting at Columbine High, the Secret Service, in collaboration with the US Department of Education, conducted the Safe School Initiative (SSI) study on school shootings and attacks from 1974 through May of 2000. The study report published in 2002 concluded that warning signs were almost always present prior to attacks.

Prior to 80% of events, peers (friends, classmates, or siblings) actually knew that attacks were being considered or planned yet rarely told an adult. Peers may have known details or heard that someone was thinking about bringing a weapon to school, or just that something big or bad was going to happen. Many attackers were actually assisted (with obtaining weapons or ammunition, or tactical planning) or encouraged by other students to carry out their plans.

Prior to 90% of events, at least one adult, such as a school staff member, parent, or police officer, had been concerned about the perpetrator's behavior. In three-quarters of cases, at least three people (kids or adults) were concerned. Shooters often intended to harm specific targets, but very few threatened them directly beforehand and these targets often didn't end up being harmed. This supports the need to investigate students who pose a general threat rather than waiting for a threat to made against a specific person.

Third, why do school shooters do it? Most perpetrators had a grievance against someone or an entity. The most common motives for attacks were revenge, trying to solve a problem, and to get recognition or fame. Many attackers described being bullied to a level qualifying as criminal harassment or assault. Compared to victims, perpetrators of school-related homicide were seven times more likely to have talked or written about committing suicide or to have already attempted it.

Fourth, where do shooters get their weapons? Firearms were predominantly obtained from home, friends, or relatives of the perpetrator. Most perpetrators had used weapons before.

Can We Predict Which Students Will Be Violent at School?

The risk factors for all types of school violence were listed at the beginning of this section. But presence of one or more risk factors in a student's situation in no way predicts that he or she will be violent at school—most students with risk factors won't be violent. Although school shooters may have some of these risk factors for youth violence, there is variation.

All studies to date have been unable to determine a composite of characteristics—a profile or type of person—that would reliably predict who will perpetrate school shootings. Both the SSI report and an FBI study of school shooters published in 2000 could not identify a profile of school shooters and advised against using their findings as a profile or checklist of warning signs. Other than most school shooters being white males, no accurate profile could be determined based on things like personality, family structure, and academic status. Other research supports the notion that it isn't possible at this point to make a simple list of warning signs that a student will be violent or that violence will occur at school. Doing this can be dangerous because it may result in violent students being overlooked or innocent students being erroneously labeled.

Despite not being able to develop a profile, once a threat or concerning behavior has been identified, there are proposed ways to use characteristics of a student and his situation as part of a threat assessment procedure to prevent school shootings. In this way, characteristics and behaviors may serve as risk factors for school shootings when examined together.

What are these characteristics and concerning behaviors found to be associated with school shooting cases? Let's look at findings from the SSI study first. In this study, 70% of the attackers felt persecuted, bullied, threatened, attacked, or injured by others prior to the incident. About 80% had histories of suicidal thoughts or attempts, and 60% had documented histories of feeling severely depressed or desperate. One thing that almost all mass killers have in common is that by committing their acts, they purposefully end life as they know it, as discussed in chapter 3.

Most had no history of prior violence or criminal behavior but were known to have had difficulty coping with what they viewed as a significant loss or failure. What this means is that while it's hard to identify someone who will be a mass murderer, it's easier to identify someone who is in distress and perhaps at risk of hurting himself or others.

Certain other personal and situational characteristics of students may be associated with mass violence. According to the FBI and other studies of school shooters, there seem to be recurrent elements in these events that can help assess the level of danger. Therefore, these characteristics constitute other risk factors for committing mass violence at school:

- Evidence of preoccupation with death, violence, hatred, or end-of-the-world themes, either in writings or preferred media use.
- Fixation on injustices he thinks he has experienced.
- Depression or uncontrollable outbursts of anger.
- Narcissism or exaggerated sense of entitlement or superiority, which actually may mask low self-esteem.
- Alienation, isolation, or a small sect of friends who are into violence or extremism.
- Lack of empathy.
- Consistent blame of others for disappointments or failures.
- Distrust of other people or paranoia.
- Inappropriate heroes like Satan, Hitler, and other school shooters.

Regardless of association with possible school shooters, these characteristics reflect a troubled child and are warning signs that the child needs professional help.

Family factors commonly found in studies of school shooters include turbulent relationships and weapons kept in the home and accessible to the student. Parenting factors include not recognizing or addressing what others would find disturbing behavior or responding defensively to inquiries, not limiting or monitoring media use, not setting appropriate limits on behavior, allowing excessive privacy, and knowing little about activities and relationships of the student.

School dynamics that were often found included tolerance for disrespectful or bullying behavior of students, school officials and students promoting a "pecking order" where some students were more valued, and a "code of silence" under which students felt they shouldn't report other students' concerning behaviors to authorities. We examined underlying perilous thoughts in chapter 2 and exacerbating factors in mental illness, likely involved in some mass shootings, in chapter 3.

How Can Schools Assess and Manage Threats to Keep Kids Safe?

In order to prevent violence, students, parents, and staff must be educated about and encouraged to report concerns for violence. And information obtained needs to be assessed quickly, because attacks often happen soon after students become aware of the potential.

According to the SSI report, threat assessments should be triggered not only by a direct threat of violence but also when a student's behavior or communications are concerning for violence. The student characteristics in the last section may be used to aid threat assessment. In the aftermath of widely covered school shootings, most schools and universities have developed threat assessment teams that often involve faculty, staff, students, psychologists, counselors, and community professionals.

Both the FBI and SSI reports make recommendations for how to assess direct threats, defined by expression of intent to harm people or act violently against someone or something. Direct or specific threats must be investigated, including those not related to possible shootings (for example, members of one gang have indicated they would attack any member of another gang who shows up at a dance, which could result in danger to others present).

While *threat assessment* is used to assess possibility of school attacks, a different process called *risk assessment* is used to evaluate general aggression and violence in youth. Risk assessment also involves determining whether a situation could pose a problem if the conditions were right (if we had a school dance and members of competing gangs attended, what is the likelihood there would be conflict?). But generally, risk assessment deals with more abstract "What if?" type problems and threat assessment deals with more tangible "How seriously do we need to take this?" situations.

A direct threat to a student, group of students, or school can be reported by anyone (a student, teacher, bystander, or parent) and so can concerning behaviors and communications. Most people who make specific threats ("You're gonna die," "I'm going to kill everyone in the lunchroom") have no intention of actually doing what they say. But teams must evaluate the credibility of every threat they become aware of by interviewing the person making the threat as well as people who are close to him or her and examining evidence.

The FBI study describes a categorization of threats from low to high risk based on how direct, specific, and plausible they are. They recommend using a threat-assessment method that combines determining this threat level with an investigation of personality and behaviors, and family, school, and social factors, such as those described in the last section. The FBI and SSI reports agree that the more direct and detailed the plan, the greater the concern.

But less than 20% of school shooters communicated a direct or conditional threat ("I'll blow up the school unless I get what I want") to a target before an attack. Therefore, it's crucial to assess whether a student *poses* a threat of violence in school even when a threat hasn't been made.

What types of behaviors and communications pose a threat and should raise concern about a student's potential for violence and be reported? Most obvious are verbal, electronic, or written statements containing school attack ideas, plans, and preparations. But more generally, any type of communications indicating interest in any of the following: harming people; poisons or bombs; inappropriate violent heroes, such as other school shooters; and homicidal or other types of revenge, even when nonspecific about method or targets. Concerning behaviors also include seeking weapons, practicing using weapons, suicidal communications or behaviors, and talk of bringing a weapon to school.

It's recommended that there be a single point of contact for reporting threats and concerns to a school, which should be widely publicized, frequently monitored, and anonymous, given the code of silence in students. When assessing threats or concerns, information is gathered by team members to try to determine the level of risk. The following things about a student may be investigated, according to the SSI study and other research:

- Motivations and goals behind the concerning behavior.
- Communications about attack ideas and intentions.
- Inappropriate interest or fascination with school attacks, weapons, or mass murderers.
- Planning, rehearsing, or recent weapon procurement.
- Mental state, such as hopelessness, desperation, despair, rage, signs of being out of touch with reality, or suicidal behaviors.
- Means to carry out an attack, including weapons and cognitive ability.
- Recent losses in relationships or status.
- Consistency between communications and actions.
- History of being bullied.
- Presence or absence of a trusting relationship with one adult.
- Receptiveness to using violence to solve problems.
- Other factors that may increase or decrease the likelihood of an attack.

Threat assessment teams make recommendations for how to respond to a threat depending on its severity. The team may call on school violence detectives or other law enforcement departments who may coordinate investigations, including whether the student has access to weapons. When finding that a student has ideas of an attack, inquiry should include his investigation of and attention to weapon access and use and communications about weapons. If the person has the means to carry out the plan (has access to weapons) or is in the process of acquiring the means (is purchasing weapons or building bombs), the greater the concern.

Throughout the process the team also keeps potential victims informed and offers support as needed. We don't often hear about the hard work and success of threat assessment teams because if they're doing their jobs well, there are no major incidents.

State laws differ in their mandatory reporting of threats. Some states don't require automatic charges to be filed, which may allow police, school officials, and parents to work together to remedy less serious offenses committed by students who don't have a history of delinquency so they aren't subjected to the harmful effects of court involvement. Studies show that criminal court involvement increases subsequent arrests and school dropout rates. Therefore, experts recommend that low-level offenses be diverted away from police action and court intervention. All persons involved in threat assessment should be educated in normal child and adolescent development, how histories of trauma or disabilities affect behavior, diffusion of volatile situations and people, and recognition of signs of abuse.

What About Gang-Related Violence in Schools?

On average, 20% of students aged twelve to eighteen say their schools have gang members, with higher numbers in urban schools and lower numbers in rural and private schools. Female membership is increasing, as are juvenile crimes committed by females.

Gang members may engage in drug dealing at school and violence against rival gangs. According to the National Gang Center, gang-related bullying, assaults, thefts, and harassment, and other incidents involving gang members can easily erupt into more serious situations unless there is an appropriate response by school personnel. Therefore, personnel should be trained to recognize threatening situations and formulate a response plan. Gang membership prevention and handling of gang-related incidents, including bullying, are best handled by schools, in partnership with a task force that is formed specifically for these purposes and that includes members of law enforcement.

School Violence Prevention

The good news is that schools can prevent violence by reducing bullying, implementing antiviolence programs, and improving things like classroom behavior management, student supervision, and school social culture. Luckily, prevention of violence does not require prediction. Just like preventing car accidents that we can't predict, we can prevent bad outcomes from school violence by identifying and addressing risk and protective factors.

A 2006 survey indicated that parents agree with components of prevention and intervention programs shown to be effective by research. The most productive programs promote student trust and communication, problem and conflict management skills, positive peer relations, and interpersonal skills. This is as opposed to enacting harsher punishments and using security measures like metal detectors and placing armed guards in schools. Parents also generally agree that character education, including anger management, empathy, and perspective taking, should be incorporated in school curriculums, and they believe that arming teachers would be harmful.

Safety Measures in Schools

Although it isn't possible to prevent all school violence, there are measures, in addition to risk and threat assessments, that can reduce it. Regarding the physical structure of buildings and grounds, crisis communication, staffing, and procedures, there's a guide to best practices for school safety recommended by school principal groups. It's available online and can be found in our resource section. Involving teen students in the process of establishing and enforcing safety policies helps, because adults are often unaware of how kids will respond or whether something may not work because kids don't have the same perspective.

Schools throughout the nation have implemented security measures in response to violent events. Because there's a perception that schools are unsafe, many schools today are equipped with security devices similar to those at banks, airports, and courthouses. Children walk through metal detectors and have bags searched while cameras record activity. Most doors may now be locked to outsiders.

While lock-down drills have become widespread, some students have been subjected to gruesome drills complete with armed SWAT team members running through the school and students posing as bloody gunshot victims. We think that by attempting to portray a realistic massacre, students who witness this may be as or more traumatized compared to escaping a real event, when most wouldn't have seen the bloody aftermath. We also believe this is ill-advised because it can make children believe it *will* happen at their school, since they have "seen" it happen.

Multiple national organizations, including school psychologists, school counselors, and principal groups, recommend against metal detectors, security cameras, and armed guards at schools, and arming teachers or anyone but school resource officers. The reasoning is that these things undermine learning without evidence of improved safety, and they may increase fear and feelings of being unsafe at school. These organizations also collectively emphasize the need for positive, consistent discipline strategies for students as well as positive climates.

School Policies That Promote Safety

Enforcing certain policies for students can promote safety. These may include forbidding gang colors, certain clothing, whistles, gestures, and symbols; requiring all coats to be kept in lockers during school hours and shirts to be tucked in so weapons can't be hidden; enforcing drug- and weapon-free school grounds; and enacting effective antibul-lying policies. You might ask how parents are involved in or could be helpful in your school's security.

Although acting to prevent violent crises is much better for every-one, we need school crisis intervention plans. It's good to check that emergency measures are in place not only for disasters like fire, floods, and tornadoes but also for weapon attacks, large scale fights, gang violence, student abductions, and suicides. All schools should have crisis policies for each of these events devised by broad committees of professionals. You can ask to see these policies or have them described to you.

Basic components of crisis policies include protocols on what, when, and how things are done and by whom, such as the follow-ing: mobilizing students to safe places; interschool communications; mobilizing police and medical assistance; reporting incidences to law enforcement, students, parents, and community; and training of all involved parties.

Changing School Culture

A CDC report on effectiveness of programs states that schools with less violence and misbehavior and more respect for teachers use firm discipline that is fair, and have teachers and administrators who act in a supportive manner with students. A healthy, supportive, inclu-sive school culture can prevent violence, not only in school but also in society once students enter it as adults. To become supportive, inclusive places where students can find help for problems, schools need to have trauma-sensitive training, and enough counselors, school psychologists, and before- and after-school programs. Yet, funding for these essential supports for students and schools has been reduced. The potential savings from strengthening them are enormous in terms of reducing societal violence and mental health costs.

A school culture that prevents aggression and violence promotes respect, clearly doesn't tolerate bullying, and reflects the belief that violence doesn't solve problems but makes them worse. Safe school cultures are ones where youth encourage each other to tell when a student is in distress and can rely on adults to respond appropriately. All students should feel that there's at least one adult at school with whom they can safely talk about their concerns and from whom they can seek support and advice.

Why Suspensions and Zero-Tolerance School Policies Are Bad Ideas

Zero-tolerance policies focus on automatic punishment via suspension or expulsion for breaking rules at school, whether intentionally or unintentionally, no matter the reason or situation. These policies have resulted in huge numbers of suspensions. During the 2011–2012 school year, more than eight thousand preschoolers were suspended in the United States, often because they behaved, well, like preschoolers!

Students have been suspended for tardiness, disrespectful behavior, bringing medications to school, and bringing items that were misconstrued as weapons. These policies often transcend common sense and cause harm, which is why multiple national school organizations recommend against their use.

We knew of a homeless eight-year-old boy who lived with his mother in a car and accidentally grabbed a backpack with kitchen utensils from the car instead of the identical-appearing school backpack. When he got to his classroom and opened up the bag of utensils, which contained a knife, the school's zero-tolerance policy called for automatic expulsion, adding to this boy's trauma.

The Federal Gun-Free Schools Act, enacted October 20, 1994, requires that schools expel any student who brings a gun to school (often without an investigation) and to report all violations to local law enforcement officials. School chief executive officers are, however, given the power to modify the expulsion requirement on a case-by-case basis. While it would be appropriate to suspend a student for bringing a gun to school, this law began the zero-tolerance movement, which has been extended to many other behaviors.

Zero-tolerance policies focus on using punishment to change behavior—but punishment doesn't work for troubled, aggressive children and traumatized ones like the eight-year-old homeless boy. Experts on school violence say we need to move from punishment models to prevention, taking into account a student's history and situation. With zero tolerance, discipline means suspension from learning, and from positive connections with other people.

Why is suspension a bad idea? Don't intentionally misbehaving kids deserve to get kicked out for a while? Yes, misbehavior calls for a consequence, but not having to go to school and getting to just hang out at home is not likely to be punishing. It feeds a cycle of academic and behavioral failure, risk factors for becoming victims or perpetrators. When students return further behind on schoolwork, they may act out because they feel like they can't or don't have needed resources to catch up, and get suspended again. Suspension also further socially isolates and disengages misbehaving kids from involvement and sense of belonging to the school, and often leaves them unsupervised, other risk factors for violence.

A better approach for all concerned is to focus on reversing the behavior rather than worsening it through suspension. Giving misbehaving kids a behavioral remediation plan along with appropriate individual counseling, support, and chances for supervised prosocial involvement with other kids can turn them around. However, when you put a bunch of misbehaving kids in group therapy, they can feed off each other, resulting in worse behavior.

The US Department of Education recommends that suspension and expulsion be reserved for serious infractions and as a last resort, while equipping staff with alternatives, including effective discipline strategies. The American Psychological Association Zero Tolerance Task Force encourages schools to use threat assessment as an alternative to zero-tolerance policies. Unlike zero tolerance, threat assessment promotes resolution of the problems that led to threatening behaviors in the first place. Threat assessment can lead to appropriate and proportionate discipline and support.

Through threat assessment, unnecessary harmful expulsions and suspensions can be avoided. For the eight-year-old boy just described, following a threat-assessment protocol instead of zero tolerance would have prevented his unnecessary and harmful expulsion from school. Using threat assessment rather than zero tolerance also increases children's willingness to ask for help and report concerns, and reduces bullying while improving the school's climate.

Role of School Police and Resource Officers

People working at or attending schools or school functions feel safer when security or law enforcement officers are present. School resource officers are assets who promote safety, address drug and weapon possession and other crimes, are part of threat assessment teams, and reduce the chance of unwitnessed crimes. However, their most important contribution may be in forming positive relationships with high-risk students to feel the pulse of potential trouble and deter violent actions. It's important for officers to be friendly to all students, and to appear approachable and caring about the students and school.

In light of incidents of possible mishandling of students by resource officers, officers should be focused on protecting students from physical harm and crimes against them, according to the US Departments of Justice and Education. That means that school discipline issues that do not involve any student safety risk or serious crime should be handled by educators, not by officers.

Preventing School Violence Also Prevents Societal Violence

According to the National Crime Prevention Council, we can all help prevent youth violence at schools by placing violence prevention programs in every community, teaching youth how to manage anger and handle conflicts peaceably, and keeping guns out of the hands of unsupervised kids.

Violence Prevention Programs Benefit Everyone

Training during the many formative years spent in school represents a huge opportunity to reduce societal aggression and violence. Large research studies show strong, far-reaching benefits of school-based violence prevention programs at all grade levels. When all children (not just those considered high-risk) receive this education, it reduces not only violent and aggressive behavior but also depression and anxiety. The potential broader benefits beyond the school environment, such as reduced crime and antisocial behavior, can't be ignored.

Community Support of Schools Can Reduce Youth Violence

Members of the community can create or support after-school programs, including recreational and sport activities. They can enable services such as job training, child care, family support, and mental health care in response to student need. Initiatives to decrease youth access to weapons, drugs, and alcohol and to provide student employment opportunities give at-risk youth a different and better future. Community entities can and are carrying out violence prevention programs. See our resource section.

Parents' Roles

Please see the recommendations for helping children cope with hearing news of tragedies, including school shootings, on page 109. Warning signs that your child is not coping with aggression or violence at school well enough and needs professional help come from the American Psychological Association. These include change in the child's school performance or relationships, panic or excessive worry, refusing to go to school, sleeplessness or nightmares, headaches or stomachaches, and loss of interest in previously enjoyed activities. There may be a delay in these signs, so keep watching for them.

Surveys show that parents believe that they (and other parents) are most directly responsible for preventing violence, including school shootings, and that they're the best solution to the problem. Research suggests they're correct. We can support efforts to curtail gang membership in our communities and bullying in our schools. We can maintain close connections and involvement in our children's lives so they'll share what's going on. Then we can help them cope with stresses, losses, and failures, and become aware of student behaviors concerning for violence. We can actively manage our children's behavior at school, and work with teachers and administrators if they express concern. This helps teachers focus on teaching rather than classroom behavior management and gives children a better learning environment. We can support academic achievement and extracurricular activities. Individual actions and partnerships between students, parents, school personnel, and communities can significantly reduce school violence, to benefit our kids and society.

7

Hazardous Friendships and What to Do About Them

There's something about childhood friends that you just can't replace.

—Lisa Whelchel, *The Facts of Life* TV series actress, singer, songwriter, author

Latisha's parents worried about her. Although she did OK in middle school, she was struggling in her first year of high school and had trouble making friends. They breathed a sigh of relief when she found a friend named Shauna to hang out with. A few weeks later, Latisha was acting like a stranger—she was starting to swear and wear revealing clothing. Latisha's parents had been noticing that Shauna behaved this way and were discussing what to do when they got a call from the police department asking them to come and pick up their daughter. She'd been caught shoplifting. Latisha reported that Shauna and her friends had done this before and that it was "no big deal."

Children need friendships with other kids to feel good about themselves and to create a sense of belonging in the world. Early in childhood, time spent with kids around the same age surpasses the amount of time spent with parents, and as childhood progresses, having friends is a large contributory factor to happiness. Fortunately, decades of research has clearly shown that peers can influence each other in good ways to promote prosocial behavior.

But unfortunately, kids can also influence each other detrimentally, promoting aggression, antisocial behavior, crime, substance use, depression, and weapon use. Thus, being around aggressive or delinquent peers increases a child's risk of being a perpetrator or victim of aggression or violence, especially in adolescence.

This chapter reviews the impact of peers on children's behavior and character as well as protective factors against negative peer influence. We offer suggestions for getting kids socially connected to good peers, monitoring friendships to determine if they're healthy enough, warning signs of dangerous friendships, and how to intervene while protecting children's development of autonomy.

The Strength of Peer Influence

When sixteen-year-old Evan Ramsey told his friends that he wanted to kill himself, they encouraged him to take out a few other people too. One friend showed him how to load and shoot a brother's shotgun the day before the carnage, and a second friend offered to take photos, but in his excitement forgot to use the camera he brought to a balcony until the shooting was almost over. Many other kids knew about the planned attack and assembled to watch it. Ramsey claimed that he really only wanted to scare a few kids who had been bullying him, but his friends encouraged him to expand the hit list to fourteen people. He shot and killed a principal and a student, and wounded two others at Bethel Regional High School in Bethel, Alaska, in 1997.

Eric Harris and Dylan Klebold met in middle school and their friendship blossomed while at Columbine High. They appeared to have similar interests: computers, violent video games, petty theft, vandalism, drinking alcohol, and writing about dark, violent topics. Some experts believe that Dylan would have been unlikely to plan and carry out a massacre alone. He was very depressed, angry, and grandiose, and may have viewed Eric as a strong compass to look to for direction. Eric was seething with rage and may have portrayed a mass homicide as a solution to Dylan's problems while viewing him as a gullible accomplice for his violent plans.

Some psychopaths and mass murderers are indeed "loners" with few or no friends, whose social disconnection feeds dysfunctional thinking, leading to antisocial actions. But having friends can be falsely reassuring, leading parents to believe that their children aren't capable of violence. The stories just mentioned illustrate the strong influence of children's peers. Kids who hang out with aggressive, antisocial, manipulative, disrespectful friends can be swayed to act similarly. For kids like Evan and Dylan, friendships and peer affiliations may have fostered the transition of depressed suicidal thoughts into homicidal actions.

Although extreme, these are useful examples of peer influence. We'll discuss the more common, insidious ways that friendships can harm our kids, as well as how friendships can help them.

Two Types of Peer Pressure and How They Work

As a normal start to separating from parents, adolescents need peers' approval. By peer, we mean anyone about the same age, friend or not. Peer pressure is how kids affect what peers believe, feel, and do. Coercion is an uncommon kind of peer pressure that does what its name implies: pressures by force, daring, or threats to get kids to do bad things.

The term peer pressure is a misnomer because, most commonly, kids want to do what others are doing in order to fit in and impress peers. So they aren't pressured by anyone but themselves. This is the strongest way that peers affect each other and why most antisocial behavior by teenagers occurs in groups. Latisha may have pressured herself to do what Shauna wanted in order to stay friends or fit in with that group.

Peer pressure can make kids who don't tend to harm others volunteer to humiliate or bully new members of a group through initiation activities called hazing (see page 117). Conversely, peer pressure can change the behavior and beliefs of troubled kids in good ways if members of the group are prosocial.

How do kids negatively influence each other's behaviors? They may encourage each other by laughing when others engage in or talk about deviant adventures (such as getting drunk or vandalism) or by suggesting deviant behaviors. Threats of exclusion or use of praise further motivate kids into action. They may do these things to satisfy needs for attention, social status, or friendship, and may not be aware that they are negatively influencing each other. But the same influential process can happen to promote positive experiences.

Does hanging out with aggressive kids increase the chance that a nonaggressive child will become aggressive (in other words, can kids be socialized to be antisocial)? Or do aggressive kids just choose to hang out with similar kids (select them as friends)? It appears that age affects the answers to these questions. From about ages twelve to fifteen, when kids are still sorting themselves into friend groups, it appears that both things happen. But when kids are around sixteen, they've usually chosen who they hang out with, making those peers more influential. So from ages sixteen to about twenty, it looks like socialization (influencing kids to be more like their group of friends) is a more important factor in determining how kids turn out (antisocial or prosocial). After age twenty, peer influence starts to dissipate because emerging adults are more resistant to these pressures.

This socialization process can act in a mutual manner, like a feedback loop, with long-lasting effects into adulthood. So, Latisha may have had tendencies to behave the way Shauna did, and their mutual influence on each other may have resulted in escalating, troubling behaviors.

Research clearly shows that kids have an increased rate of drug and alcohol use when their friends use these substances. There is strong evidence that hanging out with juvenile delinquents increases the risk of aggressive and violent behaviors, from rule breaking, theft, and bullying to violent crimes. In fact, one study showed the impact of peer behavior to be stronger than some indicators of parent-child relationships and parents' antisocial traits. In contrast, being part of a peer group that disapproves of antisocial behavior directly protects kids from involvement in delinquency and violence.

Types of Influential Peer Groups

Common ways that kids consider themselves connected with others include being in the same grade at school or part of an activity group, such as a club or team. But what we'll talk about here are different close connections between kids in groups.

Cliques

Cliques are technically groups of three to ten friends who frequently associate with each other, and aren't always based on reputation (such as jocks or nerds). By late childhood and early adolescence, nearly all youths report being members of cliques. When comprised of prosocial individuals, cliques can be good for kids. They can provide group support and a sense of belonging. But being excluded from friendship by a group can really hurt. Being excluded from a clique often leads to depression and loneliness.

More problems arise when cliques have aggressive behaviors, which kids may understand better when referred to as "mean" cliques. That's what many kids, parents, and researchers refer to when using the term clique, and that's what we'll focus on here. Warning signs of an aggressive clique include when members pressure each other to include only certain types of kids, associate only with other members, participate only in specified extracurricular activities, dress a certain way, and participate in mean or bullying behaviors. The aggressive exclusion perpetrated by these cliques differs from the common, incidental type that happens to everyone: aggressive exclusion is a type of bullying done with a pattern of intent to harm by shunning or hurting feelings and often involves planning and noticeably whispering about or laughing at an excluded child.

Aggressive cliques are dangerous peer groups. First, research shows that *relational aggression* (rumors, lies, and exclusion) and direct physical and verbal aggression within group members is high when cliques are considered by peers to be on the extremes of popularity (either very popular or unpopular). Thus, aggressive clique members harm each other, often to elevate their social status over other members, and kids who hang out with relationally aggressive kids become more relationally aggressive themselves. Second, aggressive cliques can also exert high levels of aggression against kids outside the clique. Research shows that aggressive kids tend to cluster in groups (cliques) known for bullying. These groups are often not united by real friendships but by coercion and need for popularity. Members can be cast out for unknown reasons, for not conforming, or by preference of the clique leader.

We recommend that parents explain what mean (or you can call them unhealthy) cliques are, and that almost every school and large student activity group has them. Tell children you expect them not to be a part of these types of cliques, just like you won't allow them to be bullies. If not accompanied by meanness or bullying, being excluded from cliques is part of growing up and rejection is part of life. However, bullying is *not* an acceptable part of growing up, regardless of whether it occurs in or outside of a clique.

At the end of this chapter, you'll read about supporting kids when they've been rejected by friends. If your children get rejected from an aggressive clique, they also need your support. Tell them about unhealthy cliques you remember from when you were growing up. If you had wished to be a part of one, you might say something like, "I was so jealous of those girls because they were close and popular and it hurt my feelings to be excluded. But later I realized that those girls weren't that cool, and I would have had to make sure I did everything the way they wanted to stay in, including acting stuck up, excluding other friends, and being treated meanly (so being in the most popular group would have harmed you). It would have kept me from making nicer friends and doing other stuff I wanted to do. It's hard to believe it now, but it won't matter at all when you grow up."

Build healthy levels of self-esteem and empathy to protect kids who have been excluded by an aggressive clique and to prevent them from becoming involved in one. If kids feel insecure, explain that being a member of such a clique can give them a false sense of confidence and belonging, which won't help them gain real respect or long-term friendships. In the realm of friendship, help your child find one or more kind, supportive friends who will treat him or her well (because your child deserves this) and to move on to new friends when needed.

Gangs

Gangs are groups of dangerous, violent young people, generally aged eight to twenty-two, who claim ownership of a part of town they call their turf, where they perpetrate aggressive acts and often make money illegally. They sell drugs, steal, deface property, use threats (extortion) to get money or property, fight other gang members, and commit homicides. It's like an organized crime club for young people. Kids, including large numbers of girls, most commonly join when they're thirteen to fifteen years old (but may join as young as nine), and are most heavily recruited in public schools. Gangs recruit and exploit younger kids for riskier jobs because they know the judicial system will be more lenient on them.

Gangs are active throughout the United States. In 2012, the National Gang Center reported approximately 850,000 gang members who belonged to more than thirty thousand gangs. It's very difficult to estimate the proportion of violent crimes that gangs commit, but one estimate is that 13% of annual homicides are gang related. However, in some highly populated city communities, gangs may be involved in more than half of all homicides. Gang membership is also significantly linked to committing many other crimes.

In the 1970s, Laurie's family had a close friend, Carl. Their families would often get together for meals and church activities. Carl was a kind, hardworking father who along with his wife was raising five children, including an adopted daughter. Late one night, after hearing repeated car honks in front of his house, Carl rose from bed and went outside to see if someone needed help. He died of multiple gunshot wounds on his front lawn. Police presumed his murder was part of a gang initiation ritual. The shooter was never identified.

Kids join gangs for many reasons: peer pressure from friends, excitement (they're bored), money (they're failing or feel rejected in school or jobs), sense of belonging, fear and need of protection, family members are in the gang, and the need to feel respected (they have low self-esteem). Some kids join because they don't have a home to go to that provides food, safety, and support.

Here's a real-life story we heard at a joint conference by the American Psychological Association and American Bar Association on community violence. Marvin, a twelve-year-old boy, got suspended from school after a friend encouraged him to steal another child's money to buy food. He didn't have enough to eat in the apartment where he lived with his mom. If he'd gotten any attention there, it was from his mom's boyfriend's fists. His mom cared more about getting high than about her son and didn't want to upset her boyfriend, so she would often push Marvin out of the house. Marvin felt in danger on the streets and had met a guy who said Marvin could come over if he needed help. So in desperation, he went. He got food, a clean place to sleep, and positive attention from the man, who turned out to be a gang member. Wouldn't many of us have done the same in this situation? Marvin's story illustrates child neglect and abuse as risk factors for gang membership.

Perpetration of crime is a well-known part of gang life, but what is less well-known is the link to victimization. While kids often join for protection (and joining does reduce their risk of simple assault), youth in gangs are actually at increased risk of being victimized by robbery and serious violent crimes like aggravated assault (assault with intent or actual serious bodily injury, often with a weapon), including by one's own gang as part of initiation rites.

How to Counteract Dangerous Peer Influences

The good news is that there are many things parents can do to help kids resist negative peer pressure.

Have Warm Family Relationships and Use Positive Parenting Practices

Research shows that positive, nurturing parent-child relationships, and nonharsh discipline, monitoring, and supervision are protective factors against negative peer influence. These also reduce the chance your children will *want* to associate with friends who have behavior problems.

Strong family relationships make kids less likely to want to disappoint you and do risky things just to fit into a group (the most common type of peer pressure). Also, having a strong relationship will make children more likely to tell you when they're feeling pressured to do things they don't want to do (the other type of peer pressure). Combat this pressure by practicing ways to say no firmly but politely. If your son is asked to steal something, he could say, "Nah, not really into that," or "My parents always find out what I do for some reason, so I have to be careful," or whatever seems comfortable. Talk honestly about how harmful behaviors can mess up kids' lives (like what a criminal record means for someone's future). If pertinent, use personal mistakes as lessons, saying that you want a better life for them. A close relationship will also make it more likely that children will follow the limits on character and behavior that you set.

Find Your Child a Mentor

If the parenting measures described aren't happening consistently, another positive adult, or mentor, can make a remarkable difference for a child. A mentor is a trusted adult friend who guides and supports youth via a long-term, consistent relationship. A mentor can be a teacher, relative, family friend, or a member of a mentoring organization. He or she can be a strong source of support for children's behavioral development, especially when parents have limited time or there are family or community troubles.

Research shows that when children have just one adult who supports them, it can help promote protective self-esteem and prevent psychological and behavioral problems, including aggression and violence. Most research on mentoring of adolescents shows significant reductions in delinquent behaviors, physical fights, and substance use. Kids report that mentors help them feel supported and deal with problems and anger. But as you can guess, when kids are "mentored" by adults who engage in problem behaviors, it can worsen youth's behavior. Check out the community section of our resources to find your child a mentor or to support mentoring organizations that make positive impacts on children and communities.

Promote School Achievement and Supervised Group Activities

Kids who do better in school are also better able to resist peer pressure to commit crimes and behave violently. So get your kids the academic help they need to make adequate progress.

Get your kids involved in one or two activities with other youth. Participation in a supervised activity, such as sports, school music groups, community organizations, clubs, and religious youth groups, has been shown to be protective against aggression and violence, partly by helping kids connect with nondelinquent, prosocial friends. Activities give your children a greater selection of friends and can be a source of protective self-esteem and opportunities to learn to work with others.

Latisha's parents insisted that she look into all the student groups at her school to see which ones might match what she was interested in. She liked messing around with pictures using Photoshop. They had to reward her to do so, but she showed up for a meeting of the yearbook committee and made a friend there. This friend was kind and fun and not into disrespect or breaking the law. Latisha started down a better road. One club made a huge impact.

Work to Help All Your Children Get Along

Siblings are peers too, and can act as friends. Those who have problems with aggression and antisocial behaviors or substance use can influence other kids in the family to behave the same way. Conversely, strong relationships with good siblings make positive impacts on a child's behavior and can be a beneficial source of support and companionship. That's another reason to work on sibling relations and not allow your kids to be mean to or bully each other.

Monitor Friendships and Act When Needed

Children need prosocial friends to support their mental health and self-esteem, practice social interactions, and reduce chances for victimization and perpetration. Friendships help kids develop interpersonal skills like sensitivity to others, and help them manage life's transitions. Having supportive friends appears especially important for children whose family relationships are less positive. Even if your relationship is good, friends can become more important and a bigger influence than parents. Therefore, the kind of friends a child has is very important.

Let's talk about how to help your child find a supportive friend and how to monitor and manage aggressive or dangerous friendships. Abusive romantic relationships will be covered in chapter 8.

Helping Your Child Find at Least One Friend

Being friendless or rejected by peers increases risks of mental health issues like depression as well as victimization and antisocial behavior. Although having friends is important, the number of friends isn't. Being likeable and accepted by classmates who aren't considered friends can be a better indicator of ability to get along with people than how many friends a child has. Likewise, being aggressive can be a strong predictor of not being able to get along with others despite having many friends.

A child doesn't need a whole bunch of friends because research supports the value of having just one good friend who is prosocial (positive, helpful, and gets along with people) and not involved in delinquent activities for good emotional and behavioral outcomes. This is not to say that kids need a "best friend" to do well (in fact, at least one-third of elementary school kids report having no best friend), but it appears that only one good friend is needed to help children learn to interact in socially acceptable ways. However, having more than one friend appears to be even better, especially given frequent changes in friendships that occur in childhood. Help your children find good-enough kids to hang out with and support their ability to be together.

Tips for Getting Kids Socially Connected

There are things you can do when your child isn't finding a good friend. Research shows that kids who can self-regulate their behaviors and emotions get along better and are able to form high-quality, caring, positive peer relationships. So if your children have emotional or behavioral issues, helping regulate these is crucial. Making and keeping friends also requires social skills, such as perspective taking, recognizing how someone is feeling, understanding intentions and desires in others, social problem solving (see page 56), and face-to-face conflict resolution (see page 8).

Frequent moves to new towns or neighborhoods can make it very difficult to form meaningful friendships. When this happens, kids will need help connecting with others and keeping in touch with old friends. In any event, here are things to try when your children need a friend or you're concerned about them being too isolated:

- Teach social skills if you've noticed deficits. Make gentle comments that may help your child connect with others: "I noticed you didn't say anything when you saw your teammate. He may think you don't like him. Next time you could say hi, and maybe ask him if he's looking forward to your team's practice." Point out when your child seems rude, bossy, gets upset at others, whines, is very negative, or blames other people for troubles.
- If your child is shy, practice meeting other kids and making small talk: "Start by simply saying hi (best while making eye contact). Give a compliment ('Cool haircut' or 'I like your shoes') or comment on something you have in common ('I hope this teacher won't give much homework,' or 'I wonder if the bus will be on time'). Saying hi and talking to kids makes them feel good and helps you and them make friends." Let them know it's OK if kids don't say anything back, because they may be shy too, and to try again later.
- Reduce socially isolating activities like electronic games and Internet use.
- Get your child involved. Being involved in adult-supervised activities in and outside of school reduces violence and delin-

quency while promoting social skills. But keep in mind that some activities may connect kids with antisocial peers (as demonstrated by stories of assault and rape involving members of high school and college sports teams and fraternities).

- Suggest that your child ask someone from a class or club over to your place or out to dinner and offer to drive, feed, and pay. Call a parent from your work, place of worship, or neighborhood, and invite his or her child for games, movies, or dessert.

What can you do when kids resist involvement? You can make getting to do something else contingent on involvement: "You'll check out the club or you won't use the Internet," or "If you join the team you can have (something the child wants)." Help identify activities that your child has interest in or aptitude for to increase the chance he or she will get and stay involved.

Monitoring Friendships While Avoiding Intrusion

Monitoring has been shown to reduce a child's association with delinquent peers and to buffer a negative peer's effect on adolescent behavior. Monitoring friendships can mean asking questions of your children, their friends, and their friends' parents, as well as supervising activities. Monitoring makes your kids less likely to participate in delinquent group activities.

We covered intrusive monitoring in chapter 1. For friendships, this would be intruding or intervening when there's no sign of trouble with your children or their friends. This could mean doing the following when there's no indication of danger: listening to conversations, regularly reading e-mails and texts instead of recommended spot checking, joining kids when they're hanging out with friends when you haven't been invited, or asking for every little detail about events with friends.

Today's unlimited contact between older kids using electronic devices can potentially increase a friends' influence and feed drama that wastes energy and time. Computer and text message contact can also hurt friends, since kids find it easier to "say" things in e-mails, texts, and Facebook that they regret and would not have said face-to-face. Be ready with advice if electronic communication seems, well, unseemly (see chapter 4).

Healthy Friendships

It's normal for older kids to act as if time with friends is more important than time with you. (We just have to get over it.) Get to know your teens' friends early and well enough to assess their possible impact on your child—whether they're basically good or could be dangerous. As long as you think friends are generally good kids (to us, this would be those who aren't doing illegal things, being disruptive at school, using illegal substances, being disrespectful, mean, or deceitful), help them get together and include them in your family activities.

Beneficial friendships are ones that provide fun and support to children and are free of excessive drama (worries about who said what to whom and who is friends with whom, repetitive hurt feelings or lies, or relationships that are great one day and bad the next). A sign of being in a healthy relationship is wanting to be together and enjoying it—but not feeling pressured or a need to be together. In a healthy friendship, kids feel accepted for who they are.

Warning Signs of Dangerous Friendships

While beneficial friends can promote protective self-esteem and happiness, bad friends with dangerous beliefs and behaviors can encourage the same in your kids. If your teens say "everyone is doing" something you don't agree with (like painting graffiti, stealing, cheating, drinking, or doing drugs), it often means that everyone they hang out with is doing it. If friends are doing risky things, your child is likely doing the same.

The following behaviors in a friend are warning signs that he or she is a bad influence:

- Cruelty to people or animals.
- Encourages lying to parents or sneaking away to do things you wouldn't approve of.

- Bad-mouths or disrespects parents (calls you or his or her own parents disrespectful names like idiot, cusses about parents, claims refusal to do what parents ask or that your child doesn't need to listen to or obey you).
- Gets in frequent trouble at school or is dropping out.
- Has unsafe behavior or beliefs (is aggressive or violent, uses drugs, is involved with a gang, gets drunk, talks about hating life or people, or manipulates others).

Your child may give you clues of a dangerous friendship too: being secretive, being repetitively upset, disrespecting you after being with a friend, negative changes in behavior or outlook on life, and drop in grades or completion of assignments soon after becoming friends.

Another way that kids can be harmed by friends is via a type of aggression called manipulation. Warning signs of being manipulated are when attention and approval seem contingent on giving things to a friend or doing what he or she wants. As opposed to manipulation, peer pressure is more direct (saying, "You're a chicken and you can't join if you don't . . . ").

Manipulators play emotional mind games in which they act like victims to compel others to give in to what they want. They don't have true friendships but rather use people for their own gain. Inducing guilt is a common strategy: manipulating youth try to make a child feel guilty, and in order to reduce this uncomfortable state, the child will do what the manipulator wants. For example, a manipulator may say, "I can't believe you'd choose staying home to see your visiting grandparents when you said we'd hang out over here (or do homework together). I'd never do something like that to you and I thought our friendship meant more to you." Manipulators often use threats or induce fear ("Since you don't really care about me, let's just plan on not seeing each other for a while") and lies ("Ann and Tracy agree you aren't a friend we can count on") to get their way. Kids may also manipulate by blaming others to avoid any responsibility for relationship problems and twist their own actions into being another child's fault.

When confronting such manipulation, your child could say, "Give me a break. My grandparents only visit twice a year and I didn't know they were coming. You're being unreasonable (or selfish)." Manipulators will act hurt that someone would say such things about them, or may claim that their lies or other bad behaviors are just misunderstandings. One thing is clear—manipulators seldom admit when they're wrong. In his book *Character Disturbance*, George Simon describes many warning signs of being manipulated. If you're concerned that someone is manipulating your child, it's time to explain how manipulation differs from healthy friendships and to steer your child away from that person.

How to Intervene in a Dangerous Friendship

First decide whether you should suddenly take away access to a friend, or instead slowly withdraw opportunities for interaction. Reasons that might prompt you to suddenly forbid your child from being with someone are threats to safety (a friend is violent, in a gang, deals drugs) or other serious behavioral concerns, such as the warning signs listed on page 171.

If you decide to take away access to a friend right away, tell your child he or she can't see this friend for now because you're concerned for his or her well-being. Say, "I'm worried about you and won't let other kids harm you and your chances for a good life." Talk about what to say to the friend: "I'm too busy to hang out the next couple weeks," or "My parents told me we can't hang out for a little while. Sorry." Get your child busy with other peers, home and family activities, and homework, and spend extra time together. If your child is extremely upset because he or she can't see a friend who's using drugs, it's a warning sign of possible drug addiction.

As opposed to suddenly taking away access to a dangerous friend, other friends may be worrisome to you because their influence seems to be changing your child in harmful ways. The sidebar below discusses how to talk about your concerns.

Finding the Words

If you want to separate your child from a friend who is a bad influence, do it gradually. First, express your concern: *How's it going with you?* Listen to the response and then say, *I'm worried about you because you're changing in ways that might put you in danger.* If you're asked what you mean, specify what you see: *You're disrespecting the family and your grades are getting worse (you're angry and aggressive, using drugs, stealing, withdrawing). Why do you think that's happening to you?* Listen, and then say, *Your friend seems to act that way too. Do you think she has anything to do with it?* Make it your goal to help your child see why a particular friend or group of friends is bad for her and why she'd be better off having different friends. In other words, it's best if children think they've figured this out themselves. Do this by commenting on how a friend behaves or seems to think: *I noticed how Maria was mean to her sister. I wonder why she does that and what it says about her. I wouldn't want a friend that treats people that way*, or *I wonder why your friend needs to get her way, and if she can't, she gets mad and hurts people*, or *I wonder why she thinks it's OK to cheat and lie*, and *I'm worried that she might change you.*

Focus on reducing the time your child and the friend have together. Get your child busy with other things during the times they would usually hang out or play. So if you don't want them to hang out after school, say something like, "I need you to come home alone after school this week and do your chores and homework. If I call the house and you're not there, or I find out your friend is there, you won't be able to hang out this weekend." You'll need to make sure this happens (at least at first) by dropping by the house to get something or having a trusted friend or relative do so. If needed, set a rule that they're only allowed to be together when you're around and enforce it with consequences.

Escaping Gang Life

Sadly, gang life is often a familial cycle. Children need to know what gangs are, what they do, why kids join, and what happens to members. They need to understand the greatly increased risk of personal violence and incarceration. Gang members have trouble getting good jobs and may be forbidden from leaving the gang.

Experts recommend starting to talk about gangs when children are around age eight. Prevention also includes enabling school success by getting them help with homework and learning difficulties. Keep them busy and away from gang members. Help them find friends through supervised school and community groups. Affectionate family connections, high monitoring, and consistent, nonharsh discipline protect kids from joining gangs. Community early childhood programming and social and family support programs also prevent gang membership. There is help for members who want to leave. See our resource section.

Supporting Kids When Rejected by Friends

When your child feels bad because of a friend's or clique's rejection, your support is very important. Being rejected is a risk factor for depression and acting aggressively. Rejection also makes some youth more vulnerable to negative peer influences. You don't have to solve anything, but just listening and giving some basic information can really help. Tell her or him, "We all get rejected by people we want to be friends with. But we find other friends. And anyway, who we're friends with changes for most of us while we're growing up. Friends come and go." There may be reasons for rejection that have nothing to do with your child and are out of his or her control.

Rejection can, however, result from unresolved friendship conflicts. Repeat rejection could indicate that your child has trouble with this. Youth generally need to think they can figure out how to fix friendship conflicts by themselves—so don't jump in with advice on every conflict. But it helps to give them an adult's perspective when repetitive problems arise or you're asked for advice. When your child shares an uncomfortable situation, listen without judgment. Ask what he or she would like to do about it. If the plan sounds reasonable, praise your child for talking it out and say that you'd like to know how it goes. If not, make suggestions. Be there for him or her if things don't work out.

If your child is unable to make friends or is frequently rejected, it's a warning sign of needing professional help, either with social skills or management of emotions or aggression. Friendships are critical components of your children's ability to form a positive self-image and to gain social maturity by learning to get along with people. Friends with good character traits such as kindness, empathy, and the ability to have fun can be powerful, positive influences. We hope this helps you know when and how to guide children in the realm of friendship while otherwise allowing kids to figure things out themselves. Experiencing success in friendships as children will give them the confidence to forge healthy relationships throughout adulthood.

8

Sexual Aggression and Violence and How to Reduce Your Child's Risk

It's not a matter of Dad sitting down with his preadolescent son and incorporating "Don't be a criminal!" into the "birds and the bees" talk. . . . It's about teaching our boys to actively *oppose sexual violence.*

—Kate Harding, author of *Asking for It*

On the night of August 11, 2012, in Steubenville, Ohio, a sixteen-year-old girl incapacitated by alcohol was repeatedly raped by the local high school's football players. Their friends watched and then spread related photographs and videos on social media. Evidence from more than a dozen cell phones revealed that the girl was sexually violated over the course of several hours in at least two party locations, and showed her being carried by two boys between locations with no one appearing to intervene on her behalf. The jocular attitude of the assailants and witnesses was particularly disturbing—a judge in the case described the evidence as profane and ugly. One student offered money for someone to pee on the girl as she lay vomiting in the street. Tweets of student witnesses included, "If they're getting 'raped' and don't resist then to me it's not rape," "Some people deserve to be peed on," and "Whores are hilarious." There was a video of a young man chuckling in front of several other students, saying, "You don't need any foreplay with a dead girl. . . . She's deader than Caylee Anthony. They raped her harder than that cop raped Marsellus Wallace in *Pulp Fiction*. She is so raped right now." The group laughed for twelve minutes.

How is it possible that seemingly normal kids would find sexual acts with an incapacitated peer funny or cool, and acceptable to film or photograph and share as if it were entertainment and worthy of bragging about? Similar incidents from the news have ended in suicide of victims.

Sexual violence and abusive romantic relationships (dating violence) devastate many of our youth. After describing them, we'll review risk factors, warning signs, and how you can protect your kids from being victims or perpetrators while promoting healthy dating and sexual activity choices. We'll also discuss major stimuli for these problems—sexualization of girls and promotion of sexual aggression in boys—and provide ways to minimize them.

Sexual Violence

To protect children from sexual violence, first we need to understand its definitions and scope. It's common to think of sexual assault and rape when hearing the term sexual violence, but it's now more broadly defined by the CDC: a sexual act that is committed or attempted by another person without freely given consent of the victim, or against someone who is unable to consent or refuse. Thus, it includes all unwanted sexually aggressive actions, and when these actions happen in school or a youth's workplace, it's often called sexual harassment.

Types of Sexual Violence

There are many types of unwanted sexual acts encountered or perpetrated by youth today. The variety of terms used can be confusing and overwhelming, so we've tried to simplify them. Keep in mind that some of these terms overlap in scope. Although it can be uncomfortable to think about these things affecting your children, knowledge is a first step toward protective power:

- Unwanted noncontact sexual experiences. This type of sexual aggression includes unwanted sexual comments, exposure to nude images or watching others in sexual acts, and indecent exposure. Perpetrators increasingly use technology via filming or photographing of victims.
- Unwanted intentional sexual contact, directly or through clothing, of a victim's genitalia, anus, groin, breast, inner thigh, or buttocks, or forcing a victim to touch the perpetrator.
- Nonphysically forced penetration of a victim. This may be accomplished by coercion: verbally pressuring (asking repeatedly for sex or saying the victim doesn't love the perpetrator enough), intimidating through fear, threatening (to leave, spread rumors, or treat the victim badly if noncooperative), or by using authority.
- Completed or attempted alcohol- or drug-facilitated penetration. This means that the victim was unable to consent due to intoxication, incapacitation, or lack of awareness or consciousness because he or she voluntarily or involuntarily used drugs or alcohol. Drug-facilitated sexual assault or rape is when victims are given drugs without their knowledge in order to facilitate those crimes.
- Sexual assault. Although this term is sometimes used to include rape, legally it constitutes the wide range of offenses distinct from rape. It is defined as attempted or completed sexual contact of a person who doesn't want it or is unable to consent to it, and that may or may not involve force, including verbal threats.
- Rape. According to the FBI, rape is defined as "the penetration, no matter how slight, of the vagina or anus with any body part or object, or oral penetration by a sex organ of another person, without the consent of the victim." This is regardless of gender or physical force and may be committed via coercion or alcohol or drug facilitation. Attempted rape is attempting to do this. These crimes are believed to be greatly underreported, especially by males, because of shame and fear.

- Being forced to penetrate someone else, including the perpetrator. This is an act of sexual violence even if not completed.

As a parent, you also need to know what legally defines consent for sex so that you can share this knowledge with your older kids. Consent is freely given words or easy-to-see actions indicating agreement to have sex by someone who is legally and functionally able to do so. Reasons for not being able to give consent include intoxication from drugs or alcohol (not functioning normally or not being conscious or aware), otherwise being unconscious or asleep, young age or illness, mental or physical disabilities, or inability to refuse because of physical force, threats, coercion, or misuse of authority. Child sexual abuse is a form of sexual violence, as are forced prostitution and sex trafficking. It's important to know that even when consent is initially given, if it is ever withdrawn during the act, continuing sexual activity then becomes sexual assault or rape. Physical resistance by the victim is not required to demonstrate lack of consent.

Teens also need to know the age of consent for sexual intercourse in their state. What has been referred to as statutory rape is now addressed through sexual assault or sexual abuse laws. All states specify the age that a minor (under age eighteen) is considered able to consent to intercourse, making it illegal for anyone to engage in it with someone below that age, other than a spouse. Some states specify how many years older a sexual partner has to be in order to be guilty of sexual assault or rape, or if a crime occurred because the older person was in a position of trust or authority.

Sexual Assault and Rape

Sexual assault and rape are tragically common acts against youth. In a 2013 survey of high school students, almost 11% of girls and more than 4% of boys reported that they were forced to have sexual intercourse at some time in their lives. Of the nearly one in five women in the United States who report being raped, 37% report first being raped between ages eighteen and twenty-four, 30% between the ages of eleven and seventeen, and 12% when they were ten years old or younger. In a survey study, almost 20% of female college students reported being victims of completed sexual assault (defined as including rape) by their senior year.

Although girls are thought to be seven times more likely to be raped than boys, it is believed boys are less likely to report being victimized. There is also evidence that sexual violence by females against males is underreported. According to a 2012 study of college males, more than 50% reported at least one experience of sexual victimization since age sixteen, with 21% reporting unwanted sexual contact, 12% reporting coerced oral, vaginal, or anal sex, and 17% reporting completed rape. Other studies indicate that 27% of male rape victims say they were first raped at age ten or younger. Almost 5% of men in a national survey reported that they were made to penetrate someone else at some time in their lives.

Although child abductions are horrific events that make the news, strangers are least likely to rape children and teenagers, and the great majority of sexual violence happens at the home of the victim or the offender. Child and adolescent victims reportedly know their attacker more than 90% of the time. Nearly 60% are acquaintances and 35% of child sexual attackers are actually family members. Thousands of juveniles are arrested for rape each year.

The devastating impact of sexual assault and rape attempts and completions is clear. Victims suffer long-term physical and emotional harm, including fear, depression, anger, anxiety, PTSD, and suicidal thoughts and actions, especially when rape is completed or results in other physical injuries. Victims are thirteen times more likely to abuse alcohol and twenty-six times more likely to use drugs. They are much more vulnerable to being victimized again in the future.

Risk Factors for Sexual Violence Victimization

What things make it more likely for a child to be victimized by sexual violence here in the United States? Although sexual violence can't be predicted and happens to many kids without any risk factors, there are some things that make it more likely. For example, young age: between one-third and two-thirds of all victims are fifteen years old or younger. Knowing other risk factors may help you persuade your kids to change what is alterable to promote safety. These include alcohol and drug use (making youth less likely to see or act on warning signs and placing them in settings of increased risk), hooking up (sexual activity of any kind with acquaintances or strangers), having higher numbers of sexual partners (which may result from being victimized before), and cohabiting with a romantic partner at a young age.

Other risk factors include being sexually abused as a child, being raped before, and living in poverty, although sexual violence happens across socioeconomic levels. Having friends who drink alcohol or use drugs and having sex as young teenagers increase the risk of sexual victimization. Deplorably, gay, lesbian, bisexual, and transgender youth appear to have significantly higher rates of being sexually assaulted compared to heterosexual youth. Youth who have an accepting attitude toward violence, are bullied, or have a conduct disorder are also more likely to be victims. Family cultures that blame victims without punishing perpetrators, concentrating instead on restoring what they misperceive as lost family honor, increase victimization of female members.

Warning Signs for Becoming a Perpetrator and Protective Factors

So how can you tell if a child you know has a higher than average risk of perpetrating sexual violence? Research shows that certain conditions raise the risk, and here is a summary of the long list of these warning signs. Of course, perpetrators may not appear to have all or even most of them, but the more that are present, the more concern you should have.

Warning signs of perpetration include general aggressiveness and acceptance of violence, low empathy, alcohol and drug use, juvenile delinquency, conduct disorder, bullying, impulsiveness, early sexual initiation, multiple sexual partners, use of sexually explicit and violent media, preference for impersonal sex, belief in traditional gender roles, and prior physical, sexual, or emotional abuse. Poor parent-child relationships (especially with fathers), growing up in emotionally unsupportive or physically violent families, and having sexually aggressive or delinquent peers raise the risk. Men who commit sexually violent crimes often believe in male entitlement to sex and the normalcy of sexually predatory behaviors, therefore justifying violence against women. In his book *Guyland*, author Michael Kimmel discusses possible underlying reasons why nearly two in five college males report that they would commit sexual assault if they could be assured they'd get away with it. One is pressure to "keep up with the Joneses," or sexual pressure.

As you've probably guessed, protective factors are often the opposite, such as empathy, emotional health and connectedness, and parents who use reason to resolve family conflict.

How to Help Your Kids Prevent Being Victimized or Perpetrating Sexual Violence

The prevalence of sexually violent incidents, such as the one described at the beginning of this chapter, illustrates an appalling lack of respect for human dignity. We parents are in the best position to make meaningful changes and to arm our children with protective measures. This discussion relates to youth in middle school and older. For protection of small children, please see chapter 11.

To reduce your child's risk, first examine the alterable risk factors and warning signs for becoming victims or perpetrators and work on those that may be occurring with your child or are being modeled by you or another parent. A strong parent-child or mentor-child relationship and addressing changes out of concern for the child's welfare will increase their acceptance and effectiveness.

You can help reduce boys' risk of becoming perpetrators of sexual violence by doing several things:

- Use gender-balanced parenting roles (i.e., parents share in child rearing and home responsibilities).
- Nurture kids and encourage empathy.

- Use nonviolent conflict resolution.
- Talk about the damaging nature of stereotypical sex roles and your disapproval of sexual violence.
- Talk about rape myths (such as women who dress provocatively or drink too much deserve to be raped).
- Set rules on sexual activity.

Girls are much more likely to be victims of sexual violence than boys, reflecting a lack of respect for the gender. So it seems logical that we can significantly attack the problem by teaching boys to respect people who happen to be female. Learning respect (or disrespect) for females begins in the home, when kids watch how Dad and other men treat Mom and other women. Boys who learn to be respectful are reprimanded when they speak disrespectfully to females at home, and are told that it's unacceptable to speak to them that way. Have him apologize and state a more appropriate way he could have interacted. Limit media that treat women as sexual objects, show women being assaulted, and glorify power over women (or when you see these common media depictions, say that you think they are dangerous and wrong).

Here are other measures that can help prevent victimization and perpetration:

- Tell your kids it's never OK for someone to frighten, pressure, or force them into having sex and that you want to know if it happens. If they report this kind of event, it's very important that you don't blame them, but believe and protect them. Abusers may say they love their victims or just can't help themselves. They may threaten kids to keep them silent.
- Make it very clear to your kids that when someone says no, it means no. For boys, no means no even when a girl dresses provocatively, flirts, seemed attracted and receptive to them, or has been a long-term girlfriend. No means no even when consent was given initially and then she says "stop" during a sexual act, or when she has consented at a prior time.

- Kids need to know that rape and accusations of rape happen more often when the perpetrator or victim is under the influence of drugs or alcohol.
- Monitor your child's activities and limit unsupervised time with other teens and adults. Know your teen's friends and their parents.

Suggestions for Teen Party Safety

You can help your kids prevent assault, or being accused of committing it, by discussing party safety—even if you don't believe they go to parties, or that there's any danger. Also, be aware that when kids ask for time alone with other kids, there's a higher chance of sex and illegal activities such as drug and alcohol use. It's best to permit only supervised parties where children are in your home or the homes of other parents who you trust will intermittently check and work to prevent dangerous activities. Don't be afraid to call the parents or stop over if you have any concerns. We contend that unsupervised coed high school parties with underage drinking are no longer acceptable due to their high-risk nature.

Even if you trust your children not to go to parties without permission, they need to know safety basics in case they end up at one, or still choose to go to one (it could happen). Make sure that your boys know that drinking alcohol puts them at risk of being accused of sexual assault, especially when girls making accusations were also drinking. Tell your girls that drinking or drug use increases their risk of being sexually assaulted. Because sexual assault most often happens to girls at the hands of boys, we'll discuss safety from that perspective.

Encourage girls to arrive at and leave parties with the same group of friends. (In the sexual assault case described at the beginning of this chapter, the intoxicated girl reportedly left a party at the protest of her friends.) They should move about the premises in groups, not alone. Tell kids not to leave drinks unattended to prevent someone from putting drugs in, and never to accept drinks from boys unless in a new container that is opened personally.

Talk about being responsible like adults (assigning sober designated drivers or arranging cab rides) and tell them never to leave an intoxicated friend alone. Friends can help friends prevent assault—someone who is sober needs to watch activity vigilantly and stop a friend from leaving with someone else. Give your teens an "out": if they ever feel uncomfortable with what's going on and want you to pick them up, they should call you. You can even come up with a code (like "I've got the flu"). Make this offer unconditional with no questions asked (until possibly later).

Talk about ways they can stop assaults as a bystander. For instance, if a guy appears to be doing something sexual to an incapacitated or otherwise nonconsenting girl, bystanders could pull a fire alarm, turn on the lights, turn off the music, call the police and then say "Dude, somebody called the cops," spill a drink on him, warn him that she's been drinking or is high so he'll get in trouble, or physically pull him or her away. They can call or text an adult. Have an agreement with your children and their friends: if they're ever concerned about their safety, you want them to call you at any time.

Self-Defense for Attempted Rape

Youth need to know what to do when faced with rape—not to scare them, but to protect them. Contrary to past beliefs, there is now some research indicating that it can be beneficial for victims to verbally or physically resist attackers. Resistance reduces the chance that a rape attempt will be completed without significantly increasing risk of other serious physical injury, and it aids recovery.

All of the following are effective:

- Screaming to scare the offender or to attract attention.
- Verbally threatening the attacker with harm.
- Physically attacking by hitting, kicking, or biting.
- Struggling, running away, hiding, or calling 911.

These protective actions appear to reduce rape completion by more than 80%. In contrast, other actions like cooperating, stalling, arguing, reasoning, and pleading may actually increase rates of completed rape. Also, although screaming to attract attention or get help appears protective, screaming from pain or fear may increase rape completions, possibly because it feeds the offender's desire for control over the victim. Despite these results, victims should use their own judgment as to whether violent resistance may be more dangerous in a particular situation. Also, never blame a victim who did not resist—studies show that even black belts in martial arts can freeze in rape situations. In her book *Rape is Rape*, Jody Raphael also describes the very common response of mental disassociation during rape, in which the mind "has to go somewhere else to be able to survive."

What to Do If Your Child Is Sexually Assaulted or Raped

It's very important not to make the victim feel responsible or guilty, no matter what, because he or she could not have done anything to provoke or deserve the assault. We can never be fully prepared for these events.

Report sexual assault, rape, or attempted rape to local law enforcement immediately. Rape victims shouldn't shower, change clothes, or wash up in any way, and should go to an emergency room (not urgent care or doctor's office) to have a medical evaluation as soon as possible. It is best to collect evidence within twenty-four hours, but some states allow it to be done up to seven days from the time of assault. Internal exams are necessary to collect samples and evidence. Victims may choose to initially get this medical evaluation without reporting it to police. Victims greatly need their parents' and friends' continued support over time. They also need follow-up medical and psychological care.

Dating and Dating Violence

Dating in adolescence can be fun, helping to shape interpersonal skills and feeding self-esteem and adolescent adjustment. But dating can also be a source of angst (over how the relationship is going and how partners treat each other). It also commonly turns violent, even in early adolescence, and that is what we'll focus on here. First, let's look at what healthy dating relationships are like.

Healthy Dating Relationships

Teaching youth about healthy dating relationships helps them recognize signs of danger from dating violence. In addition to observing good adult relationships at home, children can learn what healthy relationships look like through discussion. Healthy romantic relationships are marked by open communication and decision making between two equal individuals, as well as mutual trust and respect. Partners are not dependent on each other for everything. Conflicts are resolved by talking instead of manipulation or violence. Physical involvement is at a comfortable level for both people. We recommend telling your kids that regardless of looks, talents, and abilities, everyone deserves mutually caring, respectful relationships when dating.

Dating Violence

As opposed to healthy dating relationships, dating violence is a pattern of behavior with intent to harm, or using abuse to control, frighten, or maintain power over a dating partner, regardless of gender. This is linked to many negative long-term effects; victims of dating violence are more likely to binge drink, attempt suicide, have physical fights, and be in other violent relationships in the future.

How common is dating violence? Overall, about half of teens in romantic relationships experience physical or psychological abuse as part of dating violence. It happens just as often in middle school as in high school. Overall, boys and girls appear to be equally victimized. Some young people are both victims and perpetrators of multiple types of dating violence, and some couples engage in mutual violence. Just as with bullying and abuse, there are multiple methods that teen perpetrators use to harm or control dating partners.

Depending on the study, 10% to 35% of students who date in middle or high school report being punched, slammed into something, pinched, kicked, slapped, pushed meanly, or injured with an object or weapon on purpose by a dating partner one or more times during the prior year. This is physical dating violence, and girls, not boys, are more common perpetrators.

Emotional or psychological dating abuse attempts to harm a partner's self-worth. It includes name calling, humiliating, controlling who partners can see and isolating them from friends or family, frequent texting asking what partners are doing, and jealousy. Up to 50% of dating teens report being victims. Dating violence can also take the form of stalking to harass or induce fear.

Cyber dating violence (electronic aggression) includes frequent texting to monitor a partner's activities as mentioned previously (a quarter of dating teens say their partners text them hourly from midnight to 5:00 AM) and sending intimate photos as is described later. About 25% of dating teens report being victimized in this way.

Sexual dating violence includes taking intimate photos or sharing them without consent. It also includes unwanted sexual acts: about 13% of dating teens report being kissed, touched in sexual areas, or coerced or physically forced to have intercourse against their will. More girls than boys experience this.

Sexual Coercion by Dating Partners

As we discussed earlier, sexual coercion is basically nonphysically forced sex. Discuss with your kids starting in early middle school that being coerced into having sex with anyone indicates a dangerous relationship and is not OK. What are the warning signs of being coerced? Your child may feel pressured, obligated, or shamed into having sex or afraid of not going along with it. Some of the common ways girls may be coerced include when boys intentionally exaggerate feelings for girls, point out how money spent entitles them to sex, or say that sex is how girls prove their love. Boys may claim that sex is a normal male need or react emotionally or threaten to break up if girls don't agree to it.

What is meant by date rape? Many experts recommend that this term not be used, for many reasons. First of all, rape happens to victims who aren't dating their perpetrators but just met them or have in actuality *never* met them. Second, date rape has been used to refer to rape facilitated by alcohol or drug impairment of the victim (using drugs commonly called date rape drugs), which again can happen to victims who are not dating the perpetrator. Therefore, *substance-facilitated sexual assault* and *substance-facilitated rape* appear to be more accurate terms to describe these crimes. The drugs used by perpetrators are also known as "club drugs" because they tend to be used at dance clubs, concerts, and "raves." These drugs are used to facilitate other crimes against youth, such as robbery and physical assault.

Risk Factors for Being Victims of Dating Violence and How to Protect Your Kids

First, you need to know that certain teenagers are more likely to be victimized by all types of dating violence. Those who are sexually active, have had multiple sexual partners, are involved in delinquent activities, use drugs or alcohol, have been exposed to domestic violence, and whose parents have used low monitoring levels are at increased risk. For forced sex specifically, studies show that teens in dating relationships are more likely to be victims when they've started sexual activity earlier in adolescence, had multiple sexual partners, or used alcohol and drugs including marijuana.

Why does early sexual activity increase risk? It places vulnerable teens in private settings at an age when they haven't developed the skills of evaluating risk and assertiveness needed to resist pressure or stop unwanted activity. By the way, sexual activity early in adolescence can be a consequence of childhood sexual abuse.

There are things you can do to protect teens against victimization by dating violence. First, work on minimizing the risk factors. Also, help them form supportive, quality friendships, have close relationships with them yourself, and share dating violence knowledge and warning signs along with tools that we'll suggest for getting out of abusive relationships.

Risk and Protective Factors for Perpetrating Dating Violence

Many characteristics of a child point to elevated risk of harming a dating partner. This long list includes depression or anxiety; aggressiveness; belief that violence in dating is acceptable; alcohol or drug use; being sexually active in middle school and having several partners; having aggressive friends; use of violent media; parental conflict or domestic violence; and parental lack of warmth and involvement, psychological control, low monitoring, harsh punishment, and physical child abuse.

Nearly one in ten adolescents reported in a recent study that they had perpetrated some type of sexual violence, and 4% of all youths surveyed said they committed attempted or completed rape. In three out of four instances, the violence was committed against a dating partner. Coercive tactics like pressure and making the victim feel guilty were used more often than physical force, and in cases of rape, vaginal sex predominated, except at younger ages, when oral sex did. Alcohol was reported to be a factor in the minority of assaults. The mean age of first perpetration was sixteen, and girls claimed to have perpetrated these crimes also. Blaming victims and seeing them in negative terms were common and perpetrators hardly ever received consequences. There were clear links to consumption of sexually explicit and violent media.

To protect your kids, examine the list of risk factors and work on ones that might be changeable. Protective factors for youth include believing that dating violence is wrong, empathy, better grades, and positive relationships with parents.

Warning Signs That Your Child Is in an Abusive Romantic Relationship

All of the following indicate that your child may be a victim of dating violence:

- Doesn't want you or friends to spend time with a boyfriend or girlfriend.
- A dating partner puts down your child in front of others and your child makes excuses for it.

- A boyfriend or girlfriend frequently demands to know what your child has been doing and with whom, and acts jealous.
- Seems to do things so a partner won't get angry.
- Being secretive about whom he or she is dating or what happens during dates.
- You're seeing negative mood changes when a dating partner is around.
- Unexplained bruises or other injuries.
- Evidence of depression after beginning to date someone.
- Dating someone three or more years older—there is a significant risk that your child is being sexually coerced.

If any of these warning signs are apparent, find out what is happening.

Why do young people stay in abusive dating relationships? Victims may not believe they deserve good treatment (due to low self-esteem), may feel they need to put up with abuse to gain the attention or status they seek through the partner, or may think that having a partner is more important than being treated well. They may not understand what abuse looks like in dating relationships, and how it differs from healthy relationships. They may mistake control for love or caring, or even excuse physical abuse when accompanied by caring words.

It's also common for victims to think treatment will improve with time, although it often gets worse; people treat their dates best early in relationships when they're trying to impress. Your child may have been threatened not to break up or may think a partner's behavior can be changed. Victims may also be pressured by peers to stay in relationships.

Warning Signs That Your Child Could Be Committing Dating Violence

Your child might be perpetrating dating violence if you notice things like these: shows uncontrolled or frequent anger toward a partner, insults him or her, tries to control how a partner dresses or acts, is constantly texting to monitor the partner's activities, or damages a partner's property. Also, if you hear that your child insists on walking a partner to classes or threatens to harm a partner (or himself or herself) in the event of a breakup, these are warning signs of perpetrating dating violence.

How to Help a Child Leave an Abusive Dating Partner

If you see warning signs, your child needs your help. Kids may not tell parents what is happening out of embarrassment, denial, or fear, so you'll need to actively seek information.

Finding the Words

Pick casual times, such as when you're driving or eating, to bring up the subject of dating violence. Don't start by putting your child on the defensive by saying, "We need to talk." Simply say, *I'd love to hear about any worries you have about dating. I won't judge what you say and it's my job to help you deal with problems.* Perhaps ask, *So what do you like about him (or her)?* It will likely take several conversations to figure out what is happening, so keep following up. When you notice elements of abuse, you could say, *I just worry that he doesn't respect you (is trying to control you, you seem almost afraid of him). What do you think?* and *No one deserves to be treated that way, including you.*

During conversations, gently bring up the differences between abusive and healthy relationships without criticizing your child's choices or opinions. Don't criticize the abusive partner—just express concern that your child deserves to be treated better and you worry about his or her safety. Point out elements of abuse over time and that a much better relationship could be enjoyed by choosing someone healthier and safer. Try to let your child conclude that a partner is bad for him or her and isn't worth it, and praise your child when that happens. Victims need reassurance that they don't deserve it and it isn't their fault.

Be prepared for your child to resist your concern and make excuses for the abusive dating partner's behavior: "He just acts that way because our relationship is so intense (or his feelings are so strong)"; "She was just joking when she said that"; "He was drunk (or high)"; and "Well, I shouldn't have made her mad (provoked her)." Discuss what your child can say to a partner to end the relationship. For example, "My parents say that we need to take a break," "My parents are worried about us," "It worries me that . . . " and "You deserve to be happy in a relationship and it looks like being with me is stressful, so I need to let you go."

There are laws against dating violence that are state specific, and some may allow a minor to get a protective order against someone. The National Dating Abuse Helpline can give you support at (1-866) 331-9474. Continue to be there to help your child dissolve the relationship. Tolerating dating abuse greatly raises the risk that children will have abusive partners throughout their lives.

Helping Your Kids Make Safe Dating Decisions

The prevalence of dating violence indicates that, just as with other risky activities, kids need parents' help in making good dating decisions. But dating doesn't mean the same thing today compared to when many of us were growing up. The stages are so complex that, well OK, we had to ask our daughter what they are—again. It might simply mean communicating by cell phone or Facebook ("we're talking") followed later by group dating before eventually going places alone together ("dating"). Being in "a thing" means hanging out but not being exclusive, and they don't want to put a label on it. Being "in a relationship" implies exclusivity, kind of like the old "going steady" term, when they might say they have a boyfriend or girlfriend. There you have it in a nutshell, and it may be different in your neck of the woods, and will likely change in the future. In any event, when discussing dating with your child, first see if you're talking about the same animal.

The choice to date for adolescents is often influenced by peer pressure, as is the decision to become sexually active and to have sex with multiple partners. Kids today need our help dealing with sexual pressure. Children as young as nine are being asked if they have a girlfriend or boyfriend. Your son may feel pressured to have sex with a girl to "be a man." The average age of first sexual intercourse is 17.4 for girls and 16.9 for boys. Kids benefit from hearing what parents think. Explain how being a man means being responsible, strong, and caring. It isn't manly to use girls for sex or to let other kids pressure him to do it. It's interesting that boys who are pressured to have sex often abstain afterward because the pressure is off, as if to say, "There—I did it."

Some research reveals that sexual activity is occurring among progressively younger adolescents. Early sexual activity increases the number of sexual partners, and both are risk factors for sexual victimization. Six percent of females reported initiation of intercourse prior to age fourteen, and experts generally consider sexual activity as developmentally inappropriate when it occurs before and up to age fifteen.

Here are risk factors for early sexual activity, a precursor to being a victim of dating violence: lower grades, alcohol and other substance use, depression, low self-esteem, and having friends who are sexually active. Depressed girls may seek sexual encounters in order to obtain intimacy, although it's widely believed that early sexual activity may predate depression. Feeling the need to have a partner or intimacy can also be predictive of dating and sexual activity in young teenagers. Girls who've been neglected by parents and who have poor self-esteem often seek boys' affection and approval by having sex early, mistakenly thinking it will improve their self-worth. When parents indicate that sex at younger ages is appropriate or that it's what they did, it's no surprise that it's significantly linked to kids initiating sex at younger ages. Insufficient parental warmth and support along with intrusive control and infrequent or restrictive discussions about sex also increase early sexual activity.

Early dating is a clear indicator of early sexual activity, and early sexual activity likely exposes young people to unwanted sex because of underdeveloped assertiveness. Early attention to romantic relationships can interfere with a carefree, full childhood by being a source of drama and worry. We've found that when parents give their kids an excuse for not being able to date ("My parents won't let me date until I'm older"), kids are actually relieved—the pressure is off.

Because adolescent dating often involves violence, and because it can divert attention away from other peer relationships and activities that are protective against violence (like academic achievement and extracurricular activities), consider setting an age at which you will permit your child to date—many experts recommend age sixteen. Then set up ground rules concerning curfew, date activities, effect on school grades, supervision, and respecting your wishes. Using concern and compromises by allowing for some choices to be made by your teenagers will most likely result in compliance with dating limits. Get to know their dates and reach out to their parents. Encourage and facilitate group dating.

Better parent-child relationships with warm and open communication are linked to postponing intercourse as well as less frequent intercourse and fewer sexual partners. Sharing values of delaying intercourse and restricting sexualized media content help delay sexual activity. In contrast, perceiving that friends or most kids are having sex (which is most likely untrue) and frequently being home alone predict sexual activity.

Romantic Relationships Versus Hookups and Friends with Benefits

You might have questions or concerns about casual sex outside of romantic relationships, which many youth engage in today. Young adults are increasingly having sex outside of romantically involved partnerships: research estimates that 50% to 80% of late adolescents to young adults have engaged in some type of casual sexual activity, from kissing all the way to intercourse, outside of a romantic relationship. Hookups generally mean brief sexual encounters with someone not well-known (not romantic or dating partners). Kissing is the most common hookup activity and intercourse is the least common (perhaps occurring in one-third of hookup encounters). Booty calls generally mean a previous arrangement for nonpaid sex without any commitment.

Trying to study these casual sex situations is difficult because there's considerable overlap in descriptions. For example, it's unclear if it's even necessary to be a friend first in a "friends-with-benefits" arrangement, and only one-half of folks having sex with people who are considered friends report it to be a friends-with-benefits situation.

During his freshman year at college, our son had two eighteen-year-old friends, Sam and Rick, who were roommates in another dorm. One afternoon, Sam called our son in tears, distraught that Rick had just been charged with rape of a female student whom he invited to his dorm room after a party. Sam had just finished being interrogated because he was in the room at the time of the alleged assault, trying to fall asleep in the other bunk. All three students had been drinking. Sam was terrified that police didn't believe his assessment that there was mutual consent and questioned his interpretive ability because he was inebriated at the time of the event. Our son tried to reach Rick, but the next news of him was from Sam the next day. Rick was found dead from a self-inflicted gunshot wound in a field near campus.

What really happened that night will likely remain unknown, but the story exemplifies the fact that having sex outside of romantic relationships heightens the risk of becoming a victim of aggression and violence. Up to one-third of casual sexual experiences involve aggression, emotional and sexual more often than physical. Higher frequency of sexual activity outside of romantic relationships is associated with more substance use, including drinking before and during, and having sex with someone who's using drugs. The frequent use of alcohol and other problems affecting consent during hookups increase the risk of sexual violence.

Males and females apparently don't differ in motivations for hooking up: physical, sexual, or emotional gratification, because others are doing it, peer pressure, or to initiate a romantic relationship. But, men tend to look more favorably on sex outside of romantic relationships and women are significantly more likely to want a romantic relationship to emerge. Regret after encounters is common (up to 70%), especially in women. A quarter of young men and one-half of young women feel negatively after hooking up, and females who hook up are more depressed than those who don't. Having sex with nonromantic partners is associated with lower self-esteem in both genders.

Ask your kids what they think of these types of sexual relationships. Listen and tell them what you think and worry about. If it's occurring under the age of eighteen, we contend that parental intervention is needed, given the risks to and immaturity of child participants. If you find out that your emerging adult children (eighteen and above) are engaged in these types of activities, you may want to express your concern for their well-being as a springboard to discussion. As stated in an article in the American Psychological Association's *Monitor*, "Sexual hookups provide the allure of sex without strings attached. . . . However, developing research suggests that sexual hookups may leave more strings attached than many participants might first assume."

Sexualization of Youth

As opposed to healthy sexual development, sexualization imposes dangerous beliefs and sexual behaviors on youth. Although sexualization happens to both boys and girls, the process appears particularly prevalent and harmful for girls given its negative effects on boys' beliefs and behaviors—abundant evidence shows that it promotes aggression and violence against girls and women.

The American Psychological Association's Task Force on the Sexualization of Girls explains that any one of the following indicates sexualization: (1) her value is only based on her sexual appeal or behavior; (2) her sexiness equates with a narrowly defined, unrealistic standard of physical attractiveness; (3) she is not a person but an object (a thing) to be evaluated and used by others for sexual purposes, thus being objectified; or (4) sexuality is imposed on her (forcing her to be sexual, including by using authority). Although less common, these components of sexualization also apply to boys.

How Sexualization Happens

So what causes girls to think that their value is based on sexiness and narrowly defined physical attractiveness and that they are objects to be used by someone else for sex? Research points to the following culprits: media, society, peers, parents, and girls themselves.

Research clearly shows that all media forms, such as music, television, and movies, much more often *objectify* females than males, and this has increased over time. Objectifying female characters means to speak about and show them as objects or tools used for sex and emphasizing body parts rather than whole people with thoughts, interests, and feelings. Entertainment media are much more likely to present women in revealing clothing than men, emphasizing bottoms and breasts as well as sexual readiness over personal attributes, even when they are portraying professional characters.

Typical kids now grow up with high daily doses of media full of sexualized females included as decorative objects. Because youth tend to believe that media reflect real life and approve of what they see, this likely increases boys' and girls' acceptance of the belief that being attractive and sexual equates to a female's value. Research shows that heavy exposure to sexualized images causes depression and low self-esteem in girls, both risk factors for victimization.

Many merchandising examples of sexualization of girls can be found (scanty, sexy clothing even for young girls, sexually dressed Bratz dolls). Parents can promote sexualization by buying these kinds of products, or doing things like supporting and paying for plastic surgery of their minors or entering them into little girl beauty pageants dressed like adult sexual figures. Parents can also promote sexualization by modeling it with their attitudes, behaviors, and styles.

Both girl and boy peers can inflict media's unrealistic and narrow beauty standard on other girls, escalating the impact. Girls can pressure each other into dressing sexually and promote this as the pathway to power with boys, although it is quite the opposite because sexualization makes girls more vulnerable and can limit their opportunities and achievements.

Girls can sexualize themselves by trying to emulate sexy celebrities or friends with their clothing, styles, and behaviors. Girls may perceive that sexualized images are rewarded with attention and popularity while fearing social rejection if they don't attain a sexualized image, causing them to place great emphasis on looking sexy, even at young ages. They also may constantly assess their bodies to try to conform to narrow standards of attractiveness. When girls objectify themselves, research shows they're more likely to endorse sexual stereotypes of women (being sex objects and submissive), and to equate their personal value with other people's appraisal of their sexiness or physical attractiveness.

Essentially, sexualization may function to keep girls "in their place" as objects of sexual attraction and beauty, while at the same time promoting aggression and violence against them, as you'll see in the next section.

How Sexualization Is Linked to Sexual Aggression and Violence

Many studies show links between female sexualization and both victimization and perpetration of sexual aggression and violence. For girls, objectification is associated with lower self-esteem, depression, and early initiation of sexual activity, all risk factors for victimization. When objectified girls fear negative evaluations of their bodies, they may focus more on their partners' judgments rather than their own safety and assertion of their own desires.

For both boys and girls, objectification of women has been associated with having stereotypical beliefs on femininity and masculinity, and acceptance of rape myths, sexual harassment, coercion, and interpersonal violence, including dating violence. When boys and young men have stereotypical beliefs about women's roles, they're more likely to be aggressive with women. Stereotypical masculine gender roles, such as being dominant and aggressive, are linked to sexual aggression and rape. Studies show that when victims are objectified, observers don't have much empathy for them. When women are thought of as objects, it's also associated with men's likelihood to commit rape or other sexual violence.

Pornography, which often objectifies women, is very commonly viewed by tweens and teens. More than 40% of twelve- to seventeen-year-olds and 70% of fifteen- to seventeen-year-olds report exposure. This is unfortunate, because when boys view pornography, especially of a violent nature, it increases their risk of committing sexual offenses. Interestingly, girls who view pornography are significantly more likely to be victims of sexual harassment or assault.

Research results point to the sexualization of our entire culture, which promotes gender inequality by designating women as sexual objects and men as sexual predators, while justifying sexual violence.

Sexual Exploitation: Child Sexual Abuse, Sex Trafficking, and Child Pornography

These deplorable acts are all extreme examples of sexualization in which sexuality is imposed on children who are treated like objects and used for sexual acts by cruel adults. They often involve physical, sexual, and psychological abuse and violence.

Experts believe that viewing sexualized and objectifying portrayals of girls or adult women made to look like girls—both more common in media now—may lead to acceptance of child sexual abuse, pornography, prostitution, and sexual trafficking of children. By definition, prostitutes are sexualized because they're objectified and treated as sexual products. Under the age of eighteen, prostitution is legally considered sexual abuse and described as commercial sexual exploitation or child prostitution.

In 2014 there were more than fifteen hundred reported cases of sex trafficking of minors under the age of eighteen. Just as with other cases of sexual abuse and violence, most cases likely go unreported.

Estimates are that up to 325,000 American young children and adolescents are at risk of being exploited commercially for sex every year. Under federal law, anyone under the age of eighteen who is induced into commercial sex is a victim of sex trafficking, regardless of the circumstance. Coercion and physical and sexual violence are common ways that traffickers control or groom minors to become sex workers while essentially enslaving them. Perpetrators often target youth who are poor, vulnerable, and living in unsafe situations, such as homeless or runaway kids with histories of abuse and neglect.

Warning Signs That Sexualization Is Affecting Your Children

It's normal for adolescents to be insecure about their looks and spend quite a bit of time enhancing their physical appearance, but when it appears to be the most important thing to the exclusion of other activities and priorities, it's a warning sign of sexualization. When kids frequently express concern about not fitting into narrow ideals (six-pack abs for boys, large breasts and tiny waists for girls), it's another warning sign. Here are others: pornography use, speaking about women or men as body parts or in derogatory or stereotypical terms, acceptance or preference for media highlighting assaulted or objectified women, being pressured by peers to dress or act sexually, and for girls, expressing concern about looking sexy or wanting to buy sexualized toys, products, and clothing.

How to Minimize Sexualization of Your Kids and Fight Sexual Exploitation of All

Encourage your kids to insist on having full childhood experiences by avoiding sexualization as you describe what it means. Ask kids why they think some girls try to dress or act sexy, as a way to start a discussion and introduce information. Also do the following:

- Share media experiences. Watch TV and movies and read magazines together. Ask kids what they think about sexualized images and situations ("What do you think about how she is dressed (is acting around that guy, or her posture)?" "What do you think about how he's treating her?" "Who is sending that message and why?"). Say what you think about content. Because kids are more anxious about their appearance after viewing typical body ideals, simply suggest that they not pay attention to bodies in media. But don't analyze specific body characteristics (like criticizing breasts for being surgically enhanced) because this may increase attention to those characteristics. This also applies to muscles and ab-madness in males.

- Help girls understand how sexualization harms them. Contrary to media messages, how "hot" or sexy girls are doesn't matter compared to things that can give them real happiness and power, such as confidence, self-respect, educational and other achievements, supportive relationships, and having fun.

- Help infuse self-respect into girls. Tell them to expect respect and to be valued for characteristics other than appearance, just like boys do. Challenge pressure to make appearance and attracting men a woman's most important quality while men are exalted more for character traits like work ethic, financial success, sensitivity, and success in sports or career. Ask your kids what they admire other than appearance in people and what qualities they like in themselves.

- Build self-esteem in girls. Comment on your daughter's skills, personality, physical characteristics other than beauty, work ethic, academic progress, and character attributes. Tell her that these things matter so much more than her appearance—to you and to worthy future partners. Help her focus on body competence (what she can do with her body other than sexually) instead of appearance. Help her build nurturing connections with peers.

- Help boys understand sexualization and how idealized physical images harm their perception of important qualities for a potential partner (such as thinking that physical attractiveness is most important when compatibility is what matters in the long run). Discuss how sexualized images increase aggressive behaviors against women.

- Suggest to your daughter that she dress for respect, comfort, and fun. Say what you don't like about a sexy item of clothing or outfit (you're afraid of what it says about her priorities or self-esteem).
- Encourage physical activity, which promotes positive mood, confidence, and ability to defend oneself from physical attack and abuse. Also help your kids get involved in other enjoyable organized activities that focus on things other than physical appearance, and help them develop skills and meet friends who don't emphasize sexiness.
- Make changes to media content and retail merchandising using social media and your pocketbook. Spread the word about products using sexualized images of women and girls and express outrage or boycott companies involved. Encourage girls to speak out also. One recent example of successful activism is the work of a group of thirteen- to sixteen-year-old girls who protested Abercrombie & Fitch T-shirts printed with the objectifying slogan, "Who needs a brain when you have these?" Support media and products with nonsexualized portrayals of males and females.
- Advocate for violence and dating violence prevention programs in schools and communities. See our resource section for ideas.

We also like another recommendation from the American Psychological Association's Task Force on the Sexualization of Girls: suggest that our kids redefine "hot" as confident and caring.

Hopefully, reading this chapter has helped you feel more equipped to deal with the issues of sexual and dating violence as well as sexualization, all unacceptably prevalent parts of childhood and emerging adulthood. We believe that together, parents and other caretakers can work to minimize them by expecting youth to treat people respectfully.

9

Drug and Alcohol Use That Heighten Chances of Violence

Instead of a criminal or a drug addict, I was looking at a boy—just a boy.

—Shannon Thompson, author of *Take Me Tomorrow*

Willy was a very talented, athletic high school junior with realistic plans to make it to professional football. He and his family were very proud that he already had a full-ride scholarship to play for a state university team. He was a good friend and classmates called him "the nicest guy." But Willy had an older brother who was a cocaine dealer. Despite his family's efforts, Willy had moved on from marijuana in ninth grade to cocaine by his senior year. His planned career path to professional football changed—he became a meth addict instead, already in and out of jail multiple times by the age of twenty.

After high school, Willy liked to call our seventeen-year-old son and harass him for some unknown reason. One day, we were about forty-five minutes away having lunch with friends when our son called from home saying that Willy had texted him. The message read, "I'm comin over there to kill you dude." Frightened, we told our son to leave the house immediately and were talking about calling the police. But our son decided to just lock the doors and see what happened since he'd never seen this kid act aggressively before and "he always said stupid stuff."

Although we didn't call the police, we definitely should have. That's because the threat constituted a crime and the public can't tell which threats are real and which are pranks. Also, young aggressive drug addicts are at risk for perpetrating violence and law enforcement needs to be informed of their activities to substantiate actions to protect the public. Happily, it was a false alarm. We feel very lucky.

This chapter will discuss how drug and alcohol use is linked to being victims and perpetrators of aggression and violence and how you can protect your kids. First, we'll give you some statistics. In the United States, drug use is highest among teenagers and young adults. Most people who abuse drugs take them for the first time during adolescence. According to the 2015 Monitoring the Future Survey, nearly half of US twelfth graders have either been drunk, used illegal drugs, or both, and about one-fifth have tried a drug other than marijuana. In 2013, more than one-fifth of eighteen- to twenty-five-year-olds reported using an illicit drug in the past month. Although we have made strides in reducing alcohol use in youth, binge drinking is still common.

Second, we want to point out that because of brain development, adolescents and young adults have higher risks for long-term changes in thoughts, emotions, and behaviors from exposure to substances, in addition to dependence and addiction. Being dependent on drugs or alcohol means experiencing uncomfortable withdrawal symptoms between doses or when weaning down the dose, such as aggression, irritation, anxiety, nervousness, depression, restlessness, or sleep problems. This commonly occurs with tolerance to a drug, which means more and more is needed to get high. Tolerance is a common component of addiction, which is compulsive drug seeking and use (being unable to stop) despite multiple detriments to lifestyle. Avoiding dependence and addiction is one good reason to work to prevent use by youth, and another reason is preventing danger.

Substance Use Is Linked to Danger for Young People

Although youth violence is a complex problem with many interrelated risk factors, drug or alcohol abuse in a youth—or his or her parent—means that the youth is at high risk for violent perpetration or victimization. When the CDC studies the effectiveness of parenting interventions to reduce teen violence, they look for reductions in delinquent behaviors and drug use because these are precursors.

We'll present evidence that substance use is highly related to aggression, violent crime, delinquency, and incarceration, as well as victimization including suicide. Let's begin by discussing overall use of substances before going on to specifics of the two most commonly used by adolescents and young adults—alcohol and marijuana—and ways to protect your kids.

Using Drugs or Alcohol Raises the Risk of Victimization

Research shows that using drugs or alcohol increases the risk of being a victim of violent crime. By how much, you wonder? Estimates vary, but one large study in the United States concluded that chronic drug users are 1.7 times more likely to be victims. About half of young adults who are treated medically after being assaulted were drinking or using drugs when they were attacked.

Many studies relating crime to substance use are done on college student populations because it's easier to collect the data. The US Bureau of Justice Statistics has reported that more than 40% of violent crimes and about 25% of robberies against college students are committed by a perpetrator believed to be using drugs. One of the most common types of violence in our society is intimate partner violence, affecting almost 30% of women and 23% of men. Alcohol and substance use raises the risk of being victimized.

There are many ways substances make people more vulnerable. According to the US Department of Justice, these include poor judgment, being less aware of surroundings, and passivity induced by the dulling effects of substances. Violent predators are thought to be more likely to take advantage of individuals who are drunk or high. Drug use and alcoholism also increase chances of being manipulated or taken advantage of by other users, employers, or gangs. Juvenile delinquents involved in drugs make attractive targets for victimization because they're more likely to carry cash or drugs and less likely to report being assaulted to police. Substance-using youth may also become alienated from peers and other support systems like parents, making them more vulnerable. Suicide victims are very likely to be intoxicated by substances. Approximately 70% of completed suicides occur while under the influence of alcohol or drugs.

The strongest predictor of being victimized is prior victimization, and victims of violence are likely to use substances as an escape from the trauma, which in turn heightens their risk of being victimized again. Having a parent with a substance abuse problem also greatly increases risks of victimization. The Drug Enforcement Administration reports that children of substance-abusing parents are three times more likely to be abused and four times more likely to be neglected. Another sobering statistic involves sexual abuse: child victims are almost four times more likely to develop drug addiction as a result of the trauma.

Substances Are Linked to Committing Crime and Juvenile Delinquency

There is overwhelming evidence that drug and alcohol use is highly related to committing violent crimes and incarceration in youth. A large US study showed that chronic drug users are 2.5 times more likely to be perpetrators. Alcohol use has consistently been shown to increase aggression and violence in youth and young adults, and is implicated in up to half of all violent crimes.

Some connections of drug use to criminal acts are fairly obvious, such as being arrested for possession of illegal substances, producing or selling drugs, and committing theft or assault to support drug activities. Lifestyles (such as involvement in gangs) and pharmacological effects of alcohol and drugs on personality make youth more susceptible to being perpetrators as well. Pharmacological effects include reducing inhibitions against doing socially unacceptable things, impairing anger control, and producing irrational, agitated behaviors.

The US Department of Justice's Office of Juvenile Justice and Delinquency Prevention confirms what research has shown over time: there is an undeniable link between substance abuse and delinquency. Being arrested for offenses like assault, theft, drug trafficking, prostitution, and even homicide are eventual consequences for many substance-abusing youth. Even when arrested on nondrug-related charges, those who use are much more likely to be arrested again.

Alcohol Use Is Linked to Aggression and Violence

We've already mentioned some general statistics regarding substance use, but now we'd like to give you more specific information about alcohol. Ads, movies, popular music, and TV shows make drinking look sexy, exciting, and normal for teens and emerging adults. Yet there is overwhelming evidence of a link between alcohol use and physical violence.

Young adults, more than any other age group, are likely to have been drinking prior to perpetrating or being victimized by violence. Encouragingly, according to the National Institute on Drug Abuse's 2015 report, alcohol use among adolescents remains at historically low levels. Despite this downward trend, about 10% of eighth graders, 22% of tenth graders, and 35% of twelfth graders reported drinking in the thirty days prior to the survey, and almost 20% of twelfth graders reported binge drinking (having five or more drinks in a row) in the prior two weeks. In 2010 it was estimated that 4% of twelve- to seventeen-year-olds needed treatment for alcohol use but didn't receive it. In addition, 45% of college students report binge drinking and 20% meet the criteria for alcohol abuse or dependence.

As with other substances, when alcohol use starts during adolescent brain remodeling, addiction is more likely to occur compared to when use starts in adulthood. Males and females are affected differently by alcohol. Because of physiological and anatomical differences, blood levels in females will be higher than males of similar weight after drinking the same amount, leading to greater impairment.

How Alcohol Makes Youth Vulnerable

Alcohol intoxication causes a loss of inhibition and awareness of surroundings. Being drunk or associating with people who drink excessively increases risk of being a victim of drug-facilitated sexual assault, robbery, or physical assault. Although most students who drink don't become victims, drinking alcohol is the number one risk factor for being sexually assaulted on college campuses. It's estimated that between one-half and three-quarters of sexual assaults in young adults involve alcohol consumption by perpetrators, victims, or both. It's crucially important to note, however, that a victim who happens to be drunk cannot in any way be blamed for being assaulted, and neither can a perpetrator blame violent actions on the fact that he or she was drunk.

As we said in chapter 3, suicides are often completed under the influence of alcohol. Kids who start drinking before age thirteen are more likely to attempt suicide at some point in their lives.

Alcohol's Link with Perpetration

Besides victimization, drinking excessive alcohol is also linked with violent behavior. One study revealed that adolescents who got drunk were three times more likely to commit violent offenses than those who didn't. Another study with eleven- to sixteen-year-olds showed a fourfold increased risk of being hit and a sixfold increased risk of hitting someone (and not as part of a mutual fight) with a history of drunkenness. The link between alcohol and physical aggression in adolescent boys is especially strong when those boys have a favorable attitude toward violence.

Alcohol intoxication is highly associated with committing violent crimes: estimates are that alcohol is involved in up to 50% of all violent crimes, including homicide and assault, and including those committed by youth. More than half of all domestic violence incidents involve alcohol. Drinking alcohol has been significantly linked to perpetrating intimate partner violence and increases the likelihood of adolescents engaging in dating aggression.

Why do drunken youth act violently more often? It's common knowledge that drinking alcohol makes people less inhibited and more likely to do things they wouldn't do when sober. Alcohol lowers one's ability to manage anger. It also reduces ability to reason, alters sense of reality, and exaggerates perceptions of threats, leading to aggressive responses. Uncontrolled anger can result in aggressive or violent behaviors. Young people are naturally more impulsive and quick to anger anyway, and alcohol further reduces their ability to make good decisions. When alcohol's influence is added, every bad decision can be magnified.

Because this is a parenting book, we must also mention the detrimental effects of alcohol on children exposed in utero. Alcohol can harm a developing baby when consumed by a mother anytime during pregnancy, even before she knows she is pregnant. In general, it is thought that continued exposure over time is worse. Children exposed to alcohol prenatally have increased risk of trouble with behavior, learning, reasoning, judgment, hyperactivity, and attention. Therefore, women who are pregnant or likely to become pregnant should not consume alcohol.

The dangers of driving drunk, including committing vehicular manslaughter and homicide, are well-known. In 2013, 17% of children killed in motor vehicle accidents were in alcohol-impaired-driving crashes.

Marijuana

He was a smart, funny boy who had it all—loving parents with financial means, top-notch education, good friends, health, faith, and tremendous opportunities. But he started smoking pot at age twelve, and a couple of years later was diagnosed with an anxiety disorder. Hanging out with new friends who used drugs, and failing classes by sixteen, his thinking had become dysfunctional, and he began acting aggressively. He dropped out of school, believing that he didn't need a degree and knew more than his teachers and parents. When he was seventeen, he became violent at home and spent a few days in jail before being sent for nine months to a residential treatment facility where he transformed into a happy, sober kid with aspirations. Not long after returning home, he rejoined his drug-using friend group and one night accidentally killed himself with an overdose of Oxy-Contin combined with marijuana. We were devastated by the loss of our beloved nephew.

While alcohol use has declined in youth, cannabis has gained popularity since the early 1990s. In 2015, about 12% of eighth graders, 25% of tenth graders, and 35% of twelfth graders used pot at least once during the previous year, and 1%, 3%, and 6% used it almost or actually every day (with the lowest number in eighth and highest in twelfth graders). Children with multiple serious behavior problems appear to have the highest rates of drug use, particularly marijuana.

Research also shows a substantial, continually increasing belief that pot isn't dangerous, although youth are typically unaware of its greatly increased potency due to selective breeding by growers. Potency is reflected by the concentration of the psychoactive chemical delta-9-tetrahydrocannabinol (THC), which produces the sensation of feeling high along with other psychological effects. In the 1970s, pot contained around 3% THC, but now can have up to 30%, with even higher amounts in concentrates like hash oil, budder, and shatter, the latter of which contains 90% or higher THC. Addiction can now occur, especially when use begins in adolescence.

Research shows that cannabis binds to cannabinoid receptors and disrupts proper adolescent brain remodeling. Studies have shown increased psychopathology linked to aggression and violence when use begins young, including anxiety, depression, psychosis, and schizophrenia, as compared with older adult onset. Studies have shown a two- to sixfold higher risk of psychotic symptoms and schizophrenia in adolescents who frequently use marijuana. Because brain development continues into early adulthood, exposure during one's midtwenties may prove to have similar effects.

Exposure to cannabis may be especially devastating for fetuses because of the extensive brain development that occurs during this period. Cannabis is the most frequently used illicit drug during pregnancy. The data on persistent behavioral (impulsiveness, inattentiveness, hyperactivity), cognitive (learning), and emotional (depression) problems in exposed children is alarming. Increased aggression in small children has also been found with prenatal exposure.

Marijuana Use and Being a Victim

As with alcohol, marijuana intoxication increases the risk of becoming a victim by making one less able to assess risks of surroundings and the people in them. Users are likely to hang out with other users or sellers and therefore are more likely to be drug trade-related assault victims. Cannabis is one of two substances most highly associated with being victimized by intimate partner violence (the other is opioids).

But there are also risks of violence against oneself: young marijuana users have an increased risk of depression and suicide, especially school-age, regular users. Evidence suggests that high doses, such as those found in cannabis-containing foods (called marijuana edibles), hashish, and other concentrates can cause short-term acute psychosis with hallucinations, delusions, and loss of the sense of personal identity, which could undoubtedly be frightening and lead people to do things they normally wouldn't.

Luke Goodman was a twenty-three-year-old who went on a ski vacation in Colorado with his cousin in 2015. They bought marijuana candies, and because Goodman didn't feel any effect from the recommended "dose," he ate more. Some time later, his cousin Caleb Fowler reported that Goodman became jittery and was talking incoherently. "He would make eye contact with us but didn't see us, didn't recognize our presence almost. . . . I had never seen him like this . . . it was almost like someone else was speaking through him," Fowler said. Once alone, Goodman took a handgun that he traveled with for protection and shot himself in the head. His mother insisted that her son had no suicidal tendencies, depression, or other risk factors for suicide.

In 2014, nineteen-year-old college student Levy Thamba, who had eaten a marijuana cookie, rambled incoherently and became very violent, smashing furniture in his Denver hotel room before jumping to his death from a balcony. Let your kids know that it can take hours to notice any effect from edibles and warn them about the high doses they may receive.

Marijuana and Delinquency, Aggression, and Violence

There is a common tendency to believe that because pot use can cause mellowness or calm sedation, users are less likely to be violent. But cannabis can produce altered perceptions of situations and trouble controlling emotions, resulting in panic attacks, confusion, hallucinations, suspiciousness, and paranoia that promote aggressive responses to being provoked. Withdrawal from the drug is often accompanied by anger and aggression.

A new, growing body of research shows that marijuana use can predispose some people to react violently or commit violent crimes. In one study, men reported that they were twice as likely to commit violent acts when high on marijuana compared to when they were intoxicated with alcohol. In a study of inner-city young adults, violent behaviors (attempted homicide reckless endangerment, weapons offenses, and assault) were more highly correlated to amount of teenage cannabis use than to cocaine or amphetamine use. Also, cannabis use was more highly correlated than alcohol to attempted homicide and weapons offenses.

A large review on cannabis and interpersonal violence concluded there's a strong link. Marijuana use is highly prevalent among men who abuse their intimate partners and is linked to increases in teen dating aggression, possibly due to impaired ability to inhibit inappropriate, premature responses to arguments. Not all studies show an increase in aggression with early adolescent cannabis use, but most do show an increase starting at about age eighteen.

There's also a strong link between juvenile delinquency and marijuana use, even when controlling for alcohol or serious psychological symptoms. Studies have shown that teenage cannabis users are significantly more likely than nonusers to use other drugs, and commit theft and other property crimes. About 80% of adolescents in the criminal justice system apparently diagnosed with a "conduct disorder" have been found to be dependent on cannabis. Some studies show no increase in violent crime with regular use, but show increased property and drug-related crimes.

Synthetic marijuana, commonly known as Spice or K2, contains chemicals similar to THC and was legally available until 2012. It's not a safer alternative to marijuana, as kids often believe, so it's good that use is dropping. In 2015, about 5% of high school seniors surveyed reported use in the previous year. Users often have anxiety, agitation, paranoia, and hallucinations.

Next to alcohol, marijuana is the most common substance found in impaired drivers. About 20% of teens and college students report driving after using pot, and even higher numbers ride with high drivers. Drugged driving accounts for an increasing proportion of traffic deaths and marijuana accounts for most of the increase. All drivers under the influence of cannabis are more likely to be involved in an accident, but habitual users (average of once-a-week use) are ten times more likely.

Link Between Other Substances and Crime

While we've made gains in reducing teen use of certain drugs (cocaine, narcotics, and alcohol), use of methamphetamine, heroin, and ecstasy remains steady. You need to know that adolescent cannabis use significantly increases the risk of using other illicit drugs, and conversely, using other illicit drugs is usually preceded by using pot.

Reasons underlying connections of alcohol and marijuana to victimization apply to other substances. These include loss of inhibition and awareness of surroundings, and vulnerability to crimes involving associates who use. Illicit drug use is also common in mental illness, another risk factor for victimization. But it's also important to know that victims often turn to drugs to cope. Being a victim of child abuse or witnessing violence in childhood increases the risk of later using cocaine, heroin, marijuana, and methamphetamine.

The association between illicit drugs and crime may seem obvious given that use, production, and sale of these illegal substances is, well, illegal. Links to violent behavior that we described previously for alcohol and cannabis also apply to other substances. These include being more likely to do things they wouldn't do when sober, lowered ability to manage anger and to use reason, altered sense of reality, and exaggerated perception of threats. Drug addicts also engage in violence to obtain the substance or the money needed to obtain it.

Now we'll briefly overview statistics on use of other substances that are also risk factors for aggression and violence when used.

Cocaine. It's fortunate that cocaine use has dropped in the last few years. Still, in a 2015 survey, nearly 1% of eighth graders and 2.5% of twelfth graders reported using it within the past year. Cocaine is strongly associated with increased aggressive and violent behavior, including perpetrating intimate partner violence.

Narcotics and heroin. Opioids include narcotics such as Vicodin, morphine, codeine, Percocet, and OxyContin, as well as heroin. Research suggests that aggression may be reduced during use but increased during withdrawal, and this may depend more on preexisting personality traits than the drug itself. Although youth narcotic use has dropped in the past ten years, in 2015, more than 8% of high school seniors reported using one to get high during their lifetime. At least once in the past year, more than 4% of seniors used Vicodin, and nearly 4% used the much stronger narcotic OxyContin, while only 0.5% used heroin. The typical heroin user is twenty-three years old on average, is Caucasian (90%), lives outside of urban areas, and started with prescription narcotics but switched to heroin because it's cheaper and more accessible.

Methamphetamine. The low amount of use in teens (less than 1%) hasn't changed much over the last few years, but meth is used by almost 3% of young adults. This is another drug that is strongly associated with aggression and violence as well as theft. In Los Angeles for instance, 35% of meth users aged eighteen to twenty-five have committed violent acts while under the influence.

Other amphetamines and stimulants. Amphetamines (Adderal, Dexadrine) and methylphenidate (Ritalin, Concerta) are stimulants youths use for nonmedical indications to feel high, be more alert, and to stay awake for late night cramming before tests. Almost 11% of twelfth graders report lifetime use of amphetamines for these non-medical reasons. High doses of stimulants are associated with anger and paranoia, and withdrawal in dependent users is associated with suicidal thoughts, anxiety, and irritability. Stimulants can be addictive and high doses can be lethal.

Club drugs. These include ecstasy (molly, MDMA), GHB, Rohypnol, ketamine (special K), and LSD. In 2015, about 6% of twelfth graders reported using ecstasy in their lifetime, and about one million Americans report using this drug, which is associated with being victims or perpetrators of crime. These hallucinogenic drugs are commonly used at "raves": all-night dances with techno music and laser lights. Raves are held anywhere from inner-city dance clubs to rural fields. Despite being advertised as safe and drug free, raves aren't places for young people. These venues often have rampant drug use and crime, with frequent drug overdoses. Besides getting high, club drugs are used to facilitate sexual assault, rape, and robbery.

Sniffed or inhaled substances. These contain hydrocarbons and include glue, paint, and aerosol fumes. They are also associated with violent and criminal behavior. Although rates of use among youth have dropped, nearly 5% of eighth graders, 3% of tenth graders, and 2% of twelfth graders reported use at least once in 2015.

Preventing Substance Use and Warning Signs of Use

According to Laurence Steinberg, distinguished professor of psychology at Temple University and author of *You and Your Adolescent*, "Parents are probably the most important influence on adolescent substance use and abuse." Research supports that parents are the most powerful influences on children's behavior, including substance use.

Societal stressors, peers, and media encourage our children to drink and use drugs, but we'll show you how you can work against these influences. Many parents find themselves either unconcerned about alcohol and drug use in their children (perhaps thinking that it's common and just a phase) or feeling helpless to stop it. Many adults have their own issues with alcohol and substances, which further impair their parenting skills: it's estimated that about 12% of children live with an adult who has an alcohol or drug abuse problem, or both. This increases the risk of growing up with a substance abuse problem.

Pearls of Prevention

Studies have shown which parenting measures guard against overall substance use. Be involved in your children's lives even when they're emerging as adults—they need you just as much as when they were little, but in different ways. Keep your relationships strong and avoid using harsh punishment or psychological control; this will help ensure they'll care about you and take your advice. Set clear rules on alcohol and drug use and enforce them even when your kids get angry or argue about them. Help build healthy self-esteem so your teens can better resist peer and media influences. Not knowing your children's friends, what they're doing, and where they're doing it is associated with higher rates of use.

Research on specifically avoiding the two most commonly used substances, alcohol and cannabis, is as follows. Parental monitoring and modeling of responsible alcohol use, as well as disapproving of underage drinking, works to reduce teen drinking. Even very low levels of nicotine dependence increase the risk of starting to use cannabis, so forbidding cigarette use helps. Enforcing a rule of no cannabis does work to reduce use among teens even when parents are users. When adolescents disapprove of pot use, or think their parents or close friends will disapprove, they're less likely to use.

Here's another crucial prevention tip: adolescents and young adults often use substances in an attempt to deal with stress and uncomfortable psychological symptoms such as depression or anxiety. You can help by teaching them coping skills. It's most important to encourage them to express their feelings, including fear, anger, worries, depressed thoughts, and anxiety. Then talk about their situations and offer support and get them professional help as needed. Support resilience to disappointments and adversity (see page 55).

Talk about the specific dangers of drug use starting in grade school and continue to do so over time, even when your kids say they already know. Tell them you'd like to teach them what you've learned and would like to learn from them too. Challenge inaccurate thoughts and beliefs they have about substances. Instead of angry confrontations, we suggest discussing the benefits youth might see (the pros) versus the risks of substance use (the cons). Have kids argue the cons like they are participating in a debate or trying to talk a friend out of using.

Point out that users may become dependent or addicted and willing to do anything—and lose everything—to keep using. Also, when others believe you have an alcohol or drug problem, get evaluated and treated for your sake and everyone else's. Here are other keys to helping kids avoid becoming victims or perpetrators due to substance abuse:

- Keep kids busy with home responsibilities and supervised activities to reduce boredom and isolation, two risk factors for substance use. Kids with too much time on their hands or lots of spending money tend to get into trouble. Studies have shown that youth who value religion and participate in those activities are less likely to drink, use drugs, or be depressed.
- Limit exposure to media that shows drug and alcohol use in positive ways, or coview and discuss. Exposure to popular music is linked to higher substance use.
- Talk about other ways people can feel high: hiking, being out in nature, stargazing, laughing with family and friends, exercising, playing sports, traveling, spiritual activities, performing on stage, or helping those in need.
- Keep kids away from drug users. Ask them, "How will you handle it if you find yourself where people are using drugs or drinking alcohol?" Praise any answer indicating nonuse and decide together which actions may work best.

Warning Signs of Substance Use

Signs of acute intoxication with alcohol or drugs include changes in eyes (redness, pupil size), odor of smoke or alcohol, imbalance, slurred speech, saying strange things, and being much more quiet or talkative than usual.

On the other hand, warning signs of chronic substance use are mostly gradual behavioral changes. These include strange changes in dressing style or activities, dropping grades, truancy, having more cash than they should, inability to account for how money is spent, repetitive lying, weight loss, strange phone calls, apathy, stating approval of substance use, and—the most important sign—having drug-related products or friends who use. Another warning sign is cash disappearing from your wallet. Other signs of substance use—strange behaviors and becoming increasingly secretive, withdrawn, aggressive, or moody— could also signal a serious emotional condition.

Here's a story from Brian's clinic to illustrate another warning sign: your kids come home from being out and don't want to see you. Kayla was an active teenager who would often lie to her parents by claiming that she had indeed notified them when she got home, but that they were sleeping and just didn't remember her checking in. Kayla's mother was suspicious. One night, Kayla came home two hours past curfew and was drunk. She quietly snuck into her bedroom. In Kayla's bed, she was surprised to find her mother awaiting her return! We recommend insisting that your kids spend a few minutes talking with you after being out so you can see whether they are moving and speaking normally, regardless of how late it is.

What to Do If You See These Warning Signs

Suspicion calls for action. Ask direct questions, such as, "Have you been taking or using something, son? I won't be mad, but it's my job to take care of you." Conduct surveillance of activities (including showing up unannounced where use might occur) and search for drugs and drug paraphernalia as needed. It's your right to know what's in your kids' pockets, vehicles, and rooms, and it's your responsibility to search them when you suspect drug use. Kids often use sneaky hiding places for drugs, such as under flooring, in light fixtures, behind electric socket and vent covers, and in secret linings to bags and clothes. It's best to search in their presence, but you don't need to forewarn them.

There are several ways to test for substances using urine, breath, oral saliva, and hair samples, and testing can be done using pharmacy and online kits or through doctor's offices. But check the accuracy of testing methods and make sure the sample could not have been substituted or altered before it's tested. Check the testing lab or product you use for ability to detect masking agents, such as added chemicals, and verify the validity of the test.

Positive drug tests or finding drugs or drug items (such as pipes, bongs, syringes, or cigarette papers) means your child is using or has used, even though they may falsely claim they are hiding items for a friend. Talking will do very little at this point, but action is essential. Start a rehab program or counseling, and take away everything the child needs to access the substance: drug-using friends, transportation, Internet, phone, cash, and credit cards. Enforce curfews and take away unsupervised time. Don't allow your child to work where he or she receives cash (such as in tips).

Remember, teens are big kids, not adults, so you can and should decide what's best. Say, "I'm doing this because I love you and want you to have a good life. I'll help you stop." Take away rights to privacy and privileges, gradually giving things back after your child has been sober for a while. Don't feel the need to convince them that your actions are necessary.

What to Try When Concerned
About a Caregiver's Substance Use

More than 10% of children live with a parent who abuses substances, which appears to be strongly linked to child abuse and neglect. Although estimates vary, the US Department of Health and Human Services found one-third to two-thirds of child maltreatment cases involved caregiver substance use. That's a good reason to intervene when you suspect someone caring for your children is using drugs or alcohol.

Finding the Words

Here are suggestions on how to approach a friend, relative, or coparent about his or her substance use: *I'm worried about you and the kids. If you drink alcohol (use pot or other drugs) before or while watching them, I'm worried that the side effects (pick something pertinent like memory trouble, slower responses, or altered perceptions) will make it much harder for you to watch the kids. It seems to make it harder on you to pay enough attention to be sure the kids are safe. How can I help you stop using? (or, I need your help to feel reassured).*

Be prepared for resistance, especially if the person is dependent or addicted. This may require multiple, gentle approaches and involving other people, but don't let it stop you from ensuring your children's safety, which may mean not allowing the caregiver to watch your kids.

Ideas for Approaching Drug or Alcohol Use in Other People's Kids

If your children hang around people who are using drugs or drinking, they'll most likely use too. See chapter 7 for advice on withdrawing your child from kids who are using and forging new friendships, and see page 17 for advice on talking to parents of friends who are using. Get to know those parents if you can, and if they also disapprove of substance use, try making a joint plan (oops, a bad pun) for keeping your kids off drugs.

Children today grow up with tremendous pressure to use drugs and abuse alcohol. Yet substance abuse is a leading cause of violence, crime, dangerous thinking, and shattered lives. Congratulate yourself on your efforts to help your children grow up free from their sinister spell. There is no shame in seeking help with substance use for ourselves or our children, but there is possible destruction and despair if we don't.

10

Home Gun Violence
and How to Guard Against It

An inquisitive two-year-old boy reached into the purse, unzipped the compartment, found the gun, and shot his mother in the head. . . . [She and her husband] carried [a gun] every day of their lives, and they shot extensively. . . . They loved it. Odd as it may sound, we are gun people.

—Terry Rutledge, father-in-law of Veronica, who was killed by her toddler in a Walmart in 2014

In 2014, Mary Barra, chief executive officer at General Motors (GM), testified before an outraged congressional committee about faulty ignition switches installed on GM model cars. At the time, GM had recalled millions of vehicles because the National Transportation Safety Administration linked thirteen deaths in the past decade to the switches. Thirteen deaths in ten years—that was enough to get Congress's attention and stir outrage. Ironically, that's about the same number of young people up to age twenty-four who are murdered in the United States *every day*—and 80% of them die from gunshot wounds. In 2014, firearm injuries caused the deaths of 444 children under age fifteen. Yet, firearm company executives haven't been called to testify before an outraged committee regarding their product's safety features to reduce this cause of death in youth, which is vastly more common than death from faulty ignition switches.

Gun ownership is a part of American culture and a right protected by the Second Amendment to the US Constitution. The United States has more guns than any other country in the world—almost three hundred million, or close to one gun for every man, woman, and child. Collectively we have about half of the guns in the world. In fact, there are more guns than cars on our streets. Approximately 60% are long guns, such as rifles or shotguns, and 40% are handguns, but handguns have recently been outselling long guns. About one-third of American adults own a gun and 40% of US households have a gun. Most households with guns have more than one, with 50% having at least four. It's estimated that about 4% of our citizens own 65% of the guns.

Despite firearm prevalence, discussions regarding ways to have them *and* promote their safety often turn into arguments about gun control. Whether you believe that guns kill people or people kill people, there is one fact that no one can deny: guns are designed to kill and people die. Gun involvement greatly increases the odds that a violent incident will result in a fatality. Physicians and public health specialists state that gun violence has reached epidemic proportions and represents a public health crisis. As you'll see from the data presented, gun violence disproportionately affects children and young adults.

This chapter will discuss current statistics related to gun violence and provide recommendations for parental action to protect children from it. We'll present evidence-based advice provided by professional organizations such as the American Academy of Pediatrics, the American Psychological Association (APA), and the National Rifle Association (NRA). We'll also discuss some implications of gun legislation and what parents can do. Recognizing that guns are not going away—they will be in our neighborhoods and communities for the rest of our lives—we present sensible gun safety practices and actions while respecting constitutional rights to own firearms.

Number of Shootings and Toll on America

Guns are used to commit up to 70% of all homicides. Guns are also used in many nonfatal violent crimes—almost 470,000 in 2011—such as robbery, aggravated assault, sexual assault, and rape. The total cost of gun-related violence in the United States is estimated at over $200 billion a year, much of it being picked up by taxpayers.

Although gun-related homicides in the United States have declined in recent years, US rates remain substantially higher than those of almost every other nation in the world, and are at least seven times higher than those in Australia, Canada, France, Germany, Italy, Japan, South Korea, Spain, Sweden, and the United Kingdom.

Guns, Injury, Assault, and Homicide in Youth

CDC data indicate that 3,800 young people under age twenty-five were murdered in 2014 by people using firearms. Of these victims, 1,450 were children or teens, and 220 were under age fifteen. In 2013 (the latest CDC injury data available), 11,600 children and teens were treated for firearm assaults, of which 665 were under age fifteen. Compared to older adults, homicide is a more common cause of death in children, teens, and young adults (most of their murderers used firearms), and murder is still one of the top three causes of death. Thus, gun violence disproportionately harms young people. It may surprise you that the National Gang Center estimates that only 13% of total homicides in the United States are gang-related, but percentages are higher in large cities.

More than three thousand children and teens are accidentally shot each year in the United States, usually by children around the same age, and more than one hundred of them die from their wounds. In Kentucky, a five-year-old boy who had been given a gun marketed for use by children (called "My First Rifle") accidentally shot and killed his two-year-old sister with a single shot to her chest. Of accidental shooting deaths of children, most occur in the victim's home or family vehicle when children are playing with loaded guns. In a recent review of gun deaths in twenty-six industrialized nations, 93% of fatalities in children and teens occurred in the United States. Again, where are the congressional hearings and demands for change?

To put the effect gun violence has on children into perspective, eighty-four American preschoolers (age five and younger) died of firearm wounds in 2013—more than the number of law enforcement officials killed in the line of duty that year. More than five thousand American children and teenagers died from gunshot wounds during 2012 and 2013—close to twice the number of people who perished in the 9/11 terrorist attacks and more than the 4,475 military personnel killed fighting during the entire Iraq War. More than thirty-five thousand children up to age nineteen were wounded by violence-related gunfire from 2011 to 2013, which is more than the total number of servicemen and servicewomen wounded during the Iraq War.

Guns Purchased for Home Safety

In 2013, the Pew Foundation reported that almost half of gun owners surveyed cited protection as their primary reason for gun ownership. So does owning a gun actually make us safer? Well, it depends on what you look at. Research shows that many resistance measures, both forceful and nonforceful, protect victims against property loss and overall injury during crimes such as robbery, property crimes, and assault. There is some evidence that resisting by using a weapon, including a gun, may protect against property loss better than other methods. However, there is little evidence that guns protect against property loss and injury more than other weapons. While most studies show no significant differences in injury rates with self-defensive gun use compared with other self-protection methods, guns don't appear to protect from being shot during an assault: one study actually found up to a fourfold increased risk of being shot when a victim was in possession of a firearm.

Also, multiple scientific studies of the National Crime Victimization Survey show that only about 1% of victims use guns for self-protection during personal-contact crimes such as assault or robbery. Privately conducted surveys have reported much higher self-defensive gun use, but most episodes described by respondents appear to involve using guns during escalating arguments rather than to thwart crimes. Adolescents are much more likely to be threatened with a gun than to use one in self-defense.

In contrast to findings on property loss and injury while being victimized by a crime, research shows a significantly higher risk of death for someone who has access to a gun, including in the home. In 2014, research using combined data from multiple studies to increase statistical power concluded that having access to a firearm doubles the risk of being a victim of homicide, regardless of gender. Most victims of homicide by firearm are killed by people they know, not strangers. As you'll read next, access to firearms appears particularly dangerous for women.

Higher Risk of Homicide for Females in Homes with Guns

Research shows that females (aged eighteen and older) living with a gun in the home are nearly three times more likely to be murdered than those with no gun in the home. Not only is purchasing a handgun not protective against murder for a female purchaser, but it increases her risk of being injured or murdered by her intimate partner or close relative. According to the American College of Obstetricians and Gynecologists, women are twice as likely to be shot and killed by intimate partners than to be killed by strangers using any method. A common victim of domestic violence is a female aged eighteen to twenty-four, and research shows that women in abusive relationships are at least five times more likely to be murdered by a current or former intimate partner when there is a gun in the home, and that gun is more likely to be used to kill her compared to all other methods combined.

In 2014, noting that women in domestic abuse situations were significantly more likely to be murdered when their abuser had access to firearms, the Supreme Court upheld a law preventing those convicted of domestic violence from purchasing or possessing a firearm. Research on restricted access to firearms in forty-six large US cities from 1979 to 2003 indicated that restricted access was associated with reduced intimate partner homicide by firearm.

Suicide Using Guns

At all ages, suicide is accomplished by firearm about half the time. Almost 2,450 young people up to age twenty-four killed themselves using a gun in 2014. More than twenty-one hundred teenagers committed suicide in 2014 and 41% of them used a gun.

Knowing someone who has committed suicide (especially a close family member) traumatizes children and is detrimental to their mental health, a risk factor for future violent behavior and victimization, including committing suicide. Access to a firearm increases the chance of being a victim of suicide threefold to fivefold, according to research. There is strong evidence that having firearms in the home substantially increases the risk of adolescent suicide—even in youth without a previous psychiatric diagnosis—and laws reducing child access to firearms appear to be associated with lower adolescent suicide rates.

Do guns cause people to commit suicide? Of course not. But guns are very good at doing what they were designed to do. About 85% of people who attempt suicide with a gun end up dying, compared to 60% of people who jump off high structures and only 2% of people who intentionally overdose. When people survive a serious attempt, only about 10% will complete suicide later, again showing increased survival for those who don't use guns in suicide attempts.

Family murder-suicide claims between one thousand and fifteen hundred lives per year in the United States, and more than 90% of these killings are accomplished by firearm. Most cases result in murder of a female partner, and many involve murder of one or more children or result in child survivor witnesses. These perpetrators are often depressed about finances or other matters and feel the family is also better off not living.

Handguns and Violence

While handguns represent about 40% of privately owned guns, they are used in up to 70% of homicides and most firearm-assisted suicides. Long guns are far more likely to be used for sport than the commission of crimes, partly because they are difficult to conceal. But strangely, since the early 1980s, handguns have become both smaller and larger: physically smaller as a transition from revolvers to pistols occurred, but larger in the caliber of bullets. In 1985, the most common handgun caliber bullet was the .22 (0.22 inch). By 1994, the average caliber for new handguns had increased to at least nine millimeters (0.35 inch).

Aubrey Peters was a vibrant sixteen-year-old who was considered a hero for once saving two little girls who fell through an ice-covered pond. On a frigid Indiana evening in December 2013, she was with a group of friends. One was twenty-year-old Jacob McDaniel. He showed the group two guns he had, a rifle and a handgun. He reportedly encouraged Aubrey to hold the handgun, but she declined. So he carefully removed the clip from the handgun and pointed it at Aubrey. Thinking the gun was empty, he pulled the trigger—a round still in the chamber fired. Aubrey clutched her chest and said, "What just happened?" She died shortly thereafter.

Thus, while deciding whether to place or keep guns in your home, consider that despite a possible protective benefit of weapons against property loss or injury during a crime, multiple research studies show that access to a gun doesn't protect against but clearly increases the risk of death, especially among women and youth. According to the American Psychological Association and the American Academy of Pediatrics, the presence of guns in the home predicts gun violence: a home gun is far more likely to be used to intimidate an intimate partner or family member, result in an accidental shooting or completed suicide, or kill someone known to the family than to defend the home by killing or injuring an intruder or criminal stranger.

What Parents Can Do to Reduce Gun Violence

So what can parents and other concerned adults do to reduce the risk of firearm violence in their homes and communities? There are no "silver bullet" solutions to reducing gun violence. It's going to take a multifaceted approach that won't be easy and it won't happen quickly. Most of our political leaders seem unwilling to address firearm violence. Because change is not coming from the top-down, it'll likely require grassroots efforts from concerned, reasonable citizens and community organizations working for sensible and respectful changes at the local, county, state, and national levels. Eventually, politicians will get involved.

This should not be an "us against them" conflict. Regardless of personal values and beliefs related to firearms, there is a need to reduce gun violence because it is a very common cause of harm to our youth. Most Americans, including gun owners and NRA members, believe that certain measures should be taken to promote gun safety. New 2015 data confirm widespread public support of gun safety policies and regulations, including from gun owners and non–gun owners, Democrats and Republicans, conservatives and liberals. Unfortunately, many surveys have posed dichotomous questions in which respondents must choose between support of Second Amendment rights and "gun control," leaving out the option of supporting both rights to own and ways to make guns safer (supporting gun safety). Yet, just as for automobiles, the right to own and operate a vehicle can be combined with safety measures to lower injuries and deaths. What follows are some ways parents and others can protect themselves and children from gun violence.

Have Conversations

Talk with family, friends, and neighbors about gun safety and storage. The American Academy of Pediatrics (AAP) recommends removing guns from the home to protect children. If you know the dangers but choose not to remove firearms from your home, follow the AAP's recommendations for safe gun storage: always keep guns unloaded and locked up, lock up ammunition separately, and hide keys and combinations to storage containers. Also, follow the NRA's best practices for safely handling a firearm and teach them to your children if they're allowed to use guns for target practice and hunting:

1. Always keep a gun pointed in a safe direction.
2. Always keep your finger off the trigger and the safety switch engaged until ready to shoot.

3. Always keep the firearm unloaded and ensure it's not loaded until ready to use (Aubrey's shooter mistakenly assumed the gun was unloaded with the clip removed).

Responsible gun owners are also informed about the laws in their communities and states. Lawful use of a firearm in one jurisdiction may be illegal in another. Legal fees associated with defending oneself for the unlawful use of a firearm can cost thousands of dollars.

Have conversations with other parents to protect your children from gun violence. In homes where you or your children visit, ask about the presence of firearms. If that seems hard to do, the APA suggests saying, "My child is very curious. Do you have guns or anything dangerous that he might get into?" If the homeowners have firearms, ask how they are stored. If satisfied with the answer, request that they send your kids home if guns will be handled. If you feel uncomfortable with the answer or situation, offer to have your home become a gun-free or gun-safe zone where your kids can play together. If homeowners refuse to answer your questions or honor your requests, it's telling you something about how much they value your relationship and your children's safety.

Here are conversations to have with your children about gun safety, whether you own guns or not:

- The NRA's Eddie Eagle rules for when children find guns are a good place to start: stop, don't touch, leave the area, and get an adult. Such lessons need to be repeated regularly. But children are inherently curious and don't always do what they're told (no kidding) and research shows they may be even more likely to handle accessible guns after receiving safety lessons because of curiosity. A 2006 study found that 73% of children aged ten and under knew where their parents kept their firearms and 36% admitted to handling weapons without adult supervision. These figures were substantially higher than what their parents thought.

- Discuss the three previously given gun safety measures. If you handle guns in front of your children, model these best practices.
- If you see irresponsible gun use in TV shows, movies, or news broadcasts, point it out and explain why it's bad to use a gun that way.
- Help your children develop a healthy respect for what guns are capable of doing, good and bad. Avoid glamorizing the destructive force of guns but emphasize the huge responsibility that having a gun requires.

There are also conversations you can have with businesses regarding gun safety. Whether you own guns or not, if you don't want guns carried by civilians in public places like coffee shops, stores, or places of worship, say something.

In the early 1970s, an effective public service campaign by the American Lung Association challenged the belief that it was rude to ask someone not to smoke. These commercials were often humorous but always ended with the same message—tell people that you mind very much if they smoke. Parents can start making their concerns about guns in their homes and communities known: "Yes, I do mind if you have a gun (in my home, place of worship, community center, and so forth)." So we can decide that just like there are places and times when one can't smoke, there are places and times when persons other than law enforcement personnel shouldn't carry guns.

If you feel uncomfortable eating in restaurants or being in places that permit patrons to carry firearms, let the managers or owners know. If they still want guns in their establishments, you have the choice not to be their customer. Hopefully, there will never be a day when restaurants have gun and no-gun sections!

Keep Firearms Locked Up

Illinois senator Richard Durbin noted, "It's a sad fact of life that some Americans are more concerned about locking up their silverware than their guns." Parents are responsible for the safety of all children in their homes. Both the NRA and the American Academy of Pediatrics recommend that any type of firearm and ammunition be inaccessible to unauthorized people, especially children. If one cannot afford a storage cabinet, trigger locks are important and a relatively inexpensive alternative, but both gun advocate and gun safety groups have expressed concerns about their unreliability. Best practice in firearm safety is to store ammunition in a different locked location. Keeping firearms locked up, unloaded, and separated from ammunition that is also locked up has been shown to reduce children's risk of injury.

Unfortunately, many gun owners improperly store their firearms: one study found that about one-third of handgun-owning households had a loaded and unlocked gun. In households with children, another study found 43% had unlocked firearms and 9% had loaded and unlocked firearms in the home. A study published in the *Archives of Pediatrics and Adolescent Medicine* found that 89% of unintentional shooting injuries of children occurred in homes, and most involved children playing with a loaded gun without adult supervision.

Warning Signs to Urgently Remove Access to Firearms

Even when locked up, here are warning signs that firearms must not be accessible—removing access can save lives:

1. Someone appears to be in crisis. According to the American Psychological Association, "One way an armed 'good guy' can become a 'bad guy' is to use a gun in a moment of temporary despondence or rage." Anyone can potentially reach this type of emotional state, regardless of mental illness history or lack of it. Research suggests that most homicides occur during interpersonal conflicts between relatives, friends, or acquaintances. An argument or misunderstanding, and emotions like fear, anger, and despair are more likely to become deadly when someone has a gun.

2. Deterioration of functioning or increased symptoms in a person with a serious mental illness, or someone who has dementia.

3. Prior to many high-profile shootings, family members and friends had noted concerning changes in the shooter's behavior. When you suspect something isn't right with a family member or friend, ask what is happening, get the person help, and offer to store the person's guns or take them away. Tell the person you are doing this out of love and concern for his or her safety. If the person lives too far away for you to personally check on him or her, or if you are afraid to do so, you can have local law enforcement conduct a "welfare check" on that person.

4. Someone is impaired by drugs or alcohol. Many accidental shootings occur when individuals are under the influence of drugs or alcohol. Alcohol misuse is associated with firearm ownership, and both are common and linked with perpetration of firearm violence against oneself and others. Alcohol-related firearm deaths equal those of alcohol-related motor vehicle crashes for men. Just as friends don't let friends drive drunk by taking car keys, friends or family can take away firearm access by taking the lockbox key or actual weapon. If that's not possible, they can remove an impaired person from the premises or remove themselves and their loved ones. A 2011 study found heavy alcohol use was most common among individuals who regularly carried a gun for protection and kept guns in their homes both loaded and unlocked. Evidence suggests that restricting access to firearms for persons with a documented history of alcohol misuse would be an effective violence prevention measure.

5. Someone displays warning signs for suicide (see page 78).

6. Someone displays warning signs of imminent violence toward others (see page 16).

7. Intimate partner abuse. As discussed, this is much more likely to turn lethal for victims when guns are present. If you or someone you care about is in a relationship characterized by aggression, violence, control, or emotional abuse, get professional help. At the very least, get the victim to develop a safety plan for what he or she can do when domestic violence escalates. This may include how to secure firearms and other weapons, escape

routes from various locations in the house, knowing where to go, and so on.

Attention to these warning signs won't always prevent a shooting. It can be difficult to know when someone is in a crisis or will be soon. But that does not mean we shouldn't try to intervene.

Remove Access for Minors and Support Child Access Prevention Laws

Child and adolescent brain development means that minors aren't equipped to make good decisions or control emotions yet (and remember that brain development continues into the midtwenties). Also, substance and alcohol use are common in youth and young adults. Even seemingly responsible, happy youths may be troubled and access to a weapon can turn a bad day into a horrific one. Besides the risk of accidental shootings, this is another reason that minors shouldn't have access to firearms.

It's important for owners to be aware of laws regulating the use of firearms in their communities. Some twenty-six states and the District of Columbia have enacted child access prevention (CAP) laws that hold gun owners legally liable if one of their weapons is used by an unauthorized person, including a child. These laws vary in terms of what unauthorized users do with their guns (simple possession or use during a crime), penalties for gun owners (fines to felonies), and how the gun needs to have been secured (some require the use of locked gun safes and others don't). Despite this variability, one study found that states enacting CAP laws had an overall 20% reduction in unintentional shooting deaths. In 2014, 50 children under the age of fifteen died of accidental firearm injuries and another 174 committed suicide using guns. CAP laws might have saved forty-four children's lives (20% of those who died). Given that thirteen ignition switch deaths over ten years caused congressional outrage, we think saving over forty children's lives in one year is worthy.

Despite the demonstrated benefits of CAP laws, the gun lobby has come out against them, stating that most responsible gun owners are already preventing access and we don't need laws requiring them to do so. If indeed there is a 20% reduction in unintentional shootings in CAP states, then the gun lobby appears to be suggesting that gun owners in the remaining twenty-four non-CAP states are more irresponsible. Irresponsible gun owners, not responsible ones, are most affected by the law. Just as for automobile safety, laws are often needed to encourage safe individual behavior to ensure public safety.

Demand That Guns Be Produced with Safety Devices

Smartphones are ubiquitous, but even though smart technology is available to support gun safety, for some reason we don't use it. Emerging technologies enable firearms to become "smart," where only authorized users wearing special devices (like a wristband or ring) can operate them. Other manufacturers are developing palm-print technologies so only users with authorized prints can fire guns. While still evolving, these technologies could greatly reduce gun-related injury and death without infringing upon Second Amendment rights—a sort of win-win for society.

Some manufacturers make their triggers so sensitive that a three-year-old has the grip strength to fire the gun, but it's possible to add mechanisms where the gun owner can increase the tension required to pull the trigger. This could further decrease the frequency of accidental shootings among children.

There are now even handguns that have safety devices that warn users when a bullet is in the chamber (even if the clip has been removed), or prevent the gun from firing when a bullet is in the chamber and the clip is removed. If either of these devices had been installed on the handgun shown to Aubrey Peters, her tragic death could have been prevented. The US General Accounting Office estimated that 23% of accidental firearm deaths could have been prevented by adding chamber-load indicators, and 8% more by adding safety locks.

As the Johns Hopkins Center for Gun Policy and Research noted in 2012, "Although unintentional or accidental shootings account for a small share of firearm related mortality and morbidity, these deaths and injuries are highly preventable through proper design of firearms."

In 2005, Congress passed the Child Safety Lock Act, which in part made it illegal for any licensed importer, manufacturer, or dealer to sell or transfer handguns without secure gun locking devices. This was a well-intentioned law, but the type of safety device required was not specified and gun owners were not obliged to use them once they got home. Furthermore, such devices are not required for firearms sold by private gun sellers.

Automobile manufacturers are mandated to install various safety devices (seat belts, air bags) in their cars for consumer protection. Based on findings that approximately two hundred deaths occur each year following people being backed over, back-up cameras will soon be mandated for all new cars. Gun manufacturers have few such mandates. In fact, the Federal Consumer Product Safety Act, which imposes health and safety standards on most consumer products, specifically exempts firearms and ammunitions from its requirements. The manufacture and distribution of products from toy guns to teddy bears have more product safety regulations than firearms. We can work to mandate that gun manufacturers incorporate safety devices into all new weapons sold.

Speak Out Against Production and Sale of Weapons That Have No Legitimate Sporting Purposes

The first 911 call from inside the Aurora theater came during the shooting. The call lasted twenty-seven seconds, and during that time, the caller's voice was drowned out by the sounds of people in distress and thirty distinct gunshots. James Holmes needed only twenty-seven seconds to dispense thirty rounds into a crowd of moviegoers. By the time his rampage was over, twelve people were dead and seventy wounded. Like the Columbine shooters before him and the Sandy Hook Elementary shooter after, Holmes used assault-style firearms that were legally purchased. He had the added advantage of a large capacity magazine holding one hundred rounds, but it jammed before he could empty it.

A review of 133 mass shootings committed between January 2009 and July 2015 found that attacks where assault-style weapons or large capacity ammunition magazines were used represented about 11% of the mass shootings (15 of 133), but resulted in 155% more victims and 47% more fatalities than when other types of weapons were used.

In contrast, armed with a shotgun, a knife, and multiple rounds of ammunition, Aaron Ybarra entered the Otto Miller Hall on the campus of Seattle Pacific University on June 5, 2014, and started shooting. Jon Meis, a student working as a building monitor, used pepper spray when Ybarra stopped to reload his gun. Meis then tackled him, and with the help of other students held Ybarra down until the authorities arrived. One student died and two others were hospitalized. Jon Meis's quick action when the shooter had to stop to reload his gun likely prevented many more injuries and deaths. Could he have saved so many lives if Ybarra had used an assault-style weapon or a magazine with one hundred rounds? Furthermore, if you need to hunt deer with a gun that shoots one hundred bullets in less than two minutes, you're a seriously lousy shot and have no business scaring away all the deer for real hunters.

Here are suggestions for supporting gun safety by limiting more dangerous weapons:

- If you don't want assault weapons sold in your community, inform the managers of stores selling them. Let them know that you'll no longer shop there as long as they continue to sell such weapons. If gun owners refused to buy such guns, or refused to buy magazines that hold one hundred bullets, these would eventually stop being produced.
- Promote child safety over gun industry profits. Irresponsible gun makers who market deadly weapons to young children should be boycotted. Just as "Joe Camel" came under fire in the 1990s

for appealing to children by glamorizing smoking, guns made in children's sizes and in pastel colors should come under fire too.

Push for Universal Background Checks

One way to reduce gun violence is to prevent at-risk persons from purchasing guns. On April 16, 2007, Virginia Tech gunman Seung-Hui Cho killed thirty-two innocent people and wounded seventeen others, and at least six more were injured jumping from windows. Cho reportedly had a very troubled childhood and his parents had sought mental health and spiritual treatment for him on multiple occasions. He clearly had warning signs of violent behavior. Two years prior to the shootings, a court ordered him to have outpatient psychiatric treatment for suicidal ideation. Under federal law, Cho should not have passed a firearm purchaser background check. Yet according to Virginia state law, he needed to have court-ordered inpatient treatment to be denied purchasing rights, so when only the Virginia database was checked, he was cleared to legally purchase the guns.

The Virginia Tech crimes demonstrate the problem with the current background check system. It is a patchwork of various local, state, and federal agencies checking various local, state, and federal databases. There really is no coordinated effort or database. The FBI handles federal background checks but there's no federal law requiring that these be performed.

According to the US Department of Justice, "Individuals prohibited by law from possessing guns can easily obtain them from private sellers and do so without any federal records produced by a background check." Private sellers include those at gun shows. States have the option of requiring licensed dealers to conduct background checks through state and local agencies. So depending upon where one lives and the type of seller, a background check may not be required at all to purchase a gun.

As of January 2015, seventeen states and the District of Columbia require background checks for all handgun sales, private and public. Compared to states that don't, these states have 46% fewer women killed by intimate partners, 48% fewer people using firearms to commit suicide, 17% fewer aggravated assaults with firearms, and 48% fewer law enforcement officials killed using handguns.

States are also encouraged, but not required, to enter certain types of information into the FBI database. Consequently, it's possible for someone to commit a felony on the East Coast and not be flagged by a background check conducted in the Midwest. Despite these limitations, the FBI's National Instant Criminal Background Check System denied more than 1.2 million gun purchases between November 1998 and May 2015.

Studies have found the following groups of people are at significantly higher risk for committing violent crimes, but none of these groups are currently prohibited by federal law from purchasing guns: (1) those convicted of misdemeanors where firearms or violence were involved, (2) those actively abusing alcohol or drugs, (3) those convicted of serious juvenile offenses, (4) those who engage in domestic violence against intimate partners but are not yet convicted, and (5) suspected terrorists here in the United States who are on the Terrorist Screening Center No Fly list. Currently, there are no restrictions on suspected terrorists amassing weapons bought in the United States either.

There is widespread public support for universal background checks. In June 2014, Quinnipiac University in Connecticut randomly polled 1,446 voters and asked, "Do you support or oppose requiring background checks for all gun buyers?" Ninety-two percent of respondents said yes, they supported them. Perhaps more surprising, current gun owners, including NRA members, also overwhelmingly supported background checks. Support was strong regardless of political affiliation as well. A year earlier, a Gallup Poll asked Americans a similar question and found a similarly high percentage of Americans supported background checks.

The intent of the background check exemption for private gun sales was to permit transactions like a grandfather selling or gifting a rifle to a grandchild. But this loophole also permits people to sell numerous guns to buyers at a gun show without conducting background checks. This has come to be known as the "gun show loophole." At gun shows, the major difference between a licensed dealer and an unlicensed dealer is that the licensed dealer will need to verify that you are eligible to purchase the gun. Guess which booth the guy who shouldn't have a gun will go to?

Finally, even with computers, a comprehensive background check can take a few days. Currently, state and local entities have three days to determine if someone can purchase a firearm. If they can't confirm the person's eligibility in that length of time, the sale is permitted to proceed by default. Dylann Roof, who shot and killed nine people in Charleston, reportedly purchased the gun he used illegally this way. According to the FBI, these "default-proceed sales" resulted in 3,722 prohibited purchases of guns in 2012. Expanding the length of time from three days to five days would have been sufficient to identify most of those prohibited purchasers.

Fight State's Efforts to Impose Gag Rules on Health Care Professionals

Several states have introduced legislation making it illegal for health care professionals to ask patients about gun ownership and safe storage practices. We know—it sounds crazy that proponents think it's OK for doctors to ask about seat belt use but not lethal weapons.

The American Academy of Pediatrics recommends that physicians ask questions of their patients and parents regarding the presence of firearms in homes and have a brief conversation about best practices for gun safety and storage. A 2003 study found that few family physicians were talking to patients about gun safety in their homes, but after they started to, patients followed more safety precautions.

When health care providers ask questions about the presence of guns in homes, it's because they're concerned for their patient's health and safety, just like they may talk about wearing helmets when riding a bike. Do we really want laws that prevent health care providers from doing their jobs and infringe on their First Amendment right of free speech?

Avoid Irrational Appeals to Fear

Most Americans cite safety concerns as their primary reason for purchasing and keeping guns in their homes. When guns were predominantly purchased for sport, bulky long guns were the best option. But as reasons for purchase moved toward safety, consumers wanted smaller, easier-to-handle weapons like handguns. Some also wanted assault-style rifles that are modeled after guns used in war. The nature of our safety concerns may have also changed. In the 1990s, guns were often bought to protect from home invaders and youth gangs. Starting in the early 2000s, the bad guys were terrorists. Today, some gun rights advocates feel that the bad guy is an out-of-control government.

Without purchasing a gun, there are multiple things that might increase the safety of your home. Most home invaders want to steal things, not hurt people. If they break into a home and hear someone is there, the vast majority will run out. Improved door and window locks, home security systems, motion detectors, long-range pepper spray, and dogs can all increase your home's safety. One gun expert suggested the purchase of a laser pen for individuals who don't want a gun in their home. In the unlikely event of a home intruder and the even more unlikely event of a home intruder staying despite knowing you're in the home, a laser pen can mimic the laser-guided targeting on some guns.

Become Politically Involved in Gun Safety

- If you're currently a member of an organization like the NRA, let your voice be heard. Speak out against its more extreme positions that infringe on your rights of gun safety. It's your organization too. If universal background checks are supported by the vast majority of NRA members, why isn't its leadership in sync? If the leadership won't listen, maybe it's time for new leadership.
- Consider joining other groups that are advocating for sensible gun measures. Here are some of them: The Law Center to Prevent Gun Violence, Parents Against Gun Violence, States United to Prevent Gun Violence, Mothers Against Senseless Killings,

or groups formed after specific shootings, such as Sandy Hook Promise, the Brady Center to Prevent Gun Violence, and Gabby Giffords's Americans for Responsible Solutions. Former New York Mayor and philanthropist Michael Bloomberg supports several groups: Mayors Against Illegal Guns, Moms Demand Action for Gun Sense in America, and Everytown for Gun Safety. None of these groups are calling for across-the-board gun bans—they are calling for dialogue and reasonable, responsible actions to curb gun violence and protect our children.

- Push Congress to reinstate funding for gun violence research. A 1993 study published in the *New England Journal of Medicine* reported that gun owners had a greater risk of being victims of homicide and suicide than non-gun owners. Remember this was during a time when Americans were buying guns for safety. The study received much media attention and because it was funded by the CDC's National Center for Injury Prevention and control, the gun lobby led an effort to eliminate funding for that center. While the center wasn't forced to dissolve, its 1997 budget came with strings attached. A clause in what was called the Dickey Amendment, named after congressman Jay Dickey, specified that "none of the funds made available for injury prevention and control at the CDC may be used to advocate or promote gun control."

Congress did not specifically ban research on gun violence with the Dickey Amendment to the 1997 Omnibus Consolidated Appropriations Act, but monies previously earmarked for gun violence research decreased from about $2.6 million to about $100,000 per year, and this restriction remains today. Because the Dickey Amendment isn't clear about what can and cannot be researched, federal employees are unwilling to risk their careers and agency funding. Consequently, federally funded research into gun violence essentially ceased.

In 2009, a study published in the *American Journal of Public Health* found a link between gun possession and gun assaults. This research was funded by the National Institutes of Health's (NIH) Institute on

Alcohol Abuse and Alcoholism. Guess what has happened? Language similar to the clause in the Dickey Amendment was added to the NIH's funding for 2012 and remains there today.

In 2014, there were nearly as many deaths from using firearms as there were from using motor vehicles. The federal government spends about $240 million each year on traffic safety research to prevent motor vehicle deaths—but it spends only about $100,000 on gun-related death prevention research. Ironically, in July 2012, former congressman Dickey coauthored an editorial for the *Washington Post* that called for repealing the Dickey Amendment and for increased funding for research on prevention of firearm injuries and deaths. As recently as July 2015, a House of Representatives committee refused to advance legislation that would have increased funding for gun violence research on to the full House for a vote.

If you choose to become politically active, you can write to your congressional representatives or send a letter to the editors of newspapers. You can blog, tweet, post, and twaxt (OK, we made up that last one, but maybe it'll be the next big thing). Let your elected officials know that reducing gun violence in your community is important to you and you vote for people who support sensible gun measures.

We have attempted to distinguish between the right to own guns and the incredible responsibility that accompanies gun ownership. Conversations on gun violence can be squelched when they degrade into debates about the right to own firearms, when that right is and will continue to be supported by our Constitution, leaving the problem of gun violence unresolved. Emotions can run high when groups have polarized, uncompromising opinions on what should or should not be done. With children caught in the crossfire, we believe that reasonable compromises can be made to protect our children by promoting gun safety, and by maintaining the right to own guns similar to how our laws and policies promote automobile safety. Reducing gun violence demands our collective efforts and cooperation to protect our children and ourselves.

11

Child Sexual Abuse
and How to Prevent Abduction

One missing child is one too many.

> —John Walsh, host of the TV series *America's Most Wanted*,
> whose six-year-old son was abducted and murdered

Parents have many common questions regarding safety of their children in public and with other people, including friends and caretakers. The risk of sexual abuse and abduction are two prominent concerns. In this chapter, we'll discuss warning signs and protective measures against child sexual abuse, strategies to prevent abduction, and tips on evaluating the safety of child care to prevent abuse. Sexual assault and rape prevention for adolescents and young adults outside of abduction situations was discussed in chapter 8. Let's begin by discussing abduction.

Child Abduction

There were about 460,000 reports of missing children in 2015. Based on the most comprehensive study of a past year, about 45% of children reported missing had run away or were thrown out or kept out of the home. A similar amount was missing for benign reasons and only about 10% were abducted. Nearly four-fifths were abducted by family members, and one-fifth by nonfamily members who were most likely acquaintances or otherwise known to the child. Only about 0.01% of missing children are victims of the most dreaded crimes: being abducted by strangers and held for long periods of time or murdered. Response systems have greatly improved: about 97% of missing children are now recovered.

Many abductions by family members occur in situations of contentious divorce, allegations of child abuse, or in opposition to anticipated or current legal custody agreements. About half of nonfamily abductions, most of which are of short duration, result in sexual assault of the child. Quick reporting of lost children to law enforcement allows for the best chance of recovery.

Children of all ages, including teenagers, need safety training; teenagers are abducted by strangers and slight acquaintances more often than young children are. It's best to gradually introduce safety ideas and then practice what you want your children to do or avoid doing. The world is basically a safe place, and you want to avoid using scare tactics to lead your children into believing that it isn't—long-lasting anxiety, a risk factor for victimization, can result. You might say that most people are good and want to help kids, but there are a few bad people who hurt kids and you want them to learn what to do to keep them safe.

The following recommendations were adapted from those made by law enforcement agencies, a program from the National Center for Missing and Exploited Children called KidSmartz, the National Crime Prevention Council, and Clint Van Zandt, a former FBI profiler. This information also is helpful to assist finding a lost child, and to prevent assault or theft.

Child Information to Have on Hand

As your children are able, they need to memorize and recite important contact information. For small children who can't yet remember, write their full name, address, phone number with area code, and a parent's or guardian's cell number and place of work on a card in their backpacks or pockets. But don't put their names or other data on the outside of these items because predators may take advantage of this information.

By age five (or before then if possible), children should know the following: when to call 911 and what to tell the dispatcher (their full names, addresses, and what is happening); their parents' names, home address(es), and phone number(s); where their parents are employed; and name and phone number of at least one close friend, relative, or neighbor. Teach them how to dial numbers on different types of phones with area code. Also ensure they know that it's harmful and against the law to call 911 as a joke.

Keep current photos of your children with you and at home. Generally, for children under two years of age, the photos should be very recent, ideally within the past three months. For children two to five years of age, the photos should be within the past six months, and for children six and above, within the past year. Know their height and weight. It's also helpful to make a mental note of what they're wearing before they leave the house, and if possible, to have samples of your children's fingerprints or DNA (baby teeth, plucked hair with follicle). Know your children's friends and their parents along with their phone numbers, addresses, and places of employment, or at least know how to easily obtain this information from someone other than your child. If your child has a cell phone, use one of the widely available tracking apps (such as those in our resource section).

Supervision Outside the Home

KidSmartz provides basic safety rules for children, which go something like this:

- Check first with your parent or the adult in charge before going anywhere, helping anyone, accepting anything, or getting into a car.
- Take a friend when going anywhere without trusted adults or when playing outside.
- Tell people no if they try to touch or hurt you. It's OK to stand up for yourself.
- Tell a trusted adult if anyone makes you feel sad, scared, confused, or uncomfortable.

A basic guideline is to know where your children are at all times. A child's age and developmental level figure into decisions about a child's safety outside the home and the level of supervision required. Ultimately, parents and other caretakers must be attentive to the situation and environment and use their best judgment. Also keep in mind that adolescents need help to stay safe no matter how trustworthy and smart they may seem. Here are some other general guidelines. Your local law enforcement agency may have useful web-based information pertaining to your community as well.

For small children younger than school age, know where they are and who's supervising them at all times. They generally shouldn't be out of a caretaker's sight when playing outdoors, including in yards. Grade school children also need supervision outdoors and it's best for them to play with others as well. Young children (elementary school age and younger) should never be left unattended in a public place or car.

When kids enter middle school, evaluate the environment's safety before allowing them to be in public places without supervision, and keep in mind that being with one or more friends increases safety. Statistically, children are far more likely to be abducted when they're alone. While in public places, preteen children should be in sight of a trusted adult, and adolescents are safer in groups when they aren't with trusted adults. Know generally where your teenagers are, what they're doing, and with whom. Have them inform you when they're leaving one location (like home) and what their plans are.

Staying Home Alone

Many experts say that you can consider letting children stay home alone at about age eleven or twelve, but only for a limited time such as one hour, with gradual increases in time as they age. Know your local laws—in some communities it is illegal to leave children under eighteen alone overnight. Kids who are home alone for long periods of time are more afraid and lonely, and parents can be charged with neglect in some states if left alone "for an unreasonable amount of time" when it affects a child's safety or welfare.

While making your decision, consider the safety of your neighborhood, how trustworthy and safety-savvy your children and their friends are, and how your kids feel about being home alone. Rules for activities and having friends over should be set and monitored. Kids should know how to keep their keys hidden and to lock the door and keep it locked after entering. They need to know how to handle emergencies and phone calls (instead of saying you aren't home, tell the caller that you, the parent or caretaker, can't come to the phone right now). They should never open the door when someone rings or knocks (even if you *are* home) unless you're right there with them or it's someone you have preapproved as a trusted adult, which we'll describe later in the chapter.

Regarding after-school safety, the American Academy of Pediatrics recommends that preteen children not return home to empty houses, even at age twelve, "unless they show unusual maturity for their age."

Walking to or from School or Elsewhere

High-risk times for abductions are going to and from school and into the early evenings. In terms of pedestrian safety, the National Center for Safe Routes to School recommends that children be supervised while walking before age ten. After that age, there is still safety in numbers against crime so it's best for children (even teens) to walk or bike together in groups. Kids should walk on sidewalks or several feet from the street.

If you take your children to school or other regularly scheduled activities, know your child's school pick-up policy and ask questions if necessary to make sure only people you authorize can pick up your kids. If your kids walk or bike, know the route they take and practice walking it with them. Tell your children not to go off that route (no shortcuts). Avoid routes with paths isolated from people, such as back roads, alleys, and parks. Use intersections with crossing guards whenever possible even if it takes a little longer. Designate safe places where children could go if they get scared, such as well-known neighbors, stores, libraries, and other public places.

When younger children take the bus, it's best to have them watched by a trusted adult while waiting at the bus stop. When coming home, have a trusted adult meet children at the stop and walk them home. When they're older, have them wait for buses and walk home in groups. Your child should stay away from cars parked near a bus stop and stay near the sidewalk. If a car approaches or follows, the child should run the other way, not the direction the car is going.

Teach Children What to Do If Lost

If small children get lost, tell them not to go looking for whoever they were with but to stay where they are unless in danger, and to make noise or do something to attract a lot of people's attention. Good people to tell about being lost are women with children, store clerks, security guards, people who work there, and uniformed police officers. If your children have phones on them, GPS personal locator services and apps may allow you to locate them (if turned on and still charged).

When going somewhere with older kids, designate a meeting spot if you get separated. Take young children to public bathrooms and have older ones go with other kids or a trusted adult. Also tell your kids that if they get lost, you'll look for them as long as it takes to find them.

If your child is missing, the first three hours are a crucial window for recovery, so it's very important to report it early to law enforcement.

Child Dos and Don'ts of Abduction Prevention

Stranger danger is no longer the best way to teach kids whom to avoid. That's because young children tend to think of a dangerous stranger as someone who looks and acts like a monster or cartoon villain, and you can't tell a pedophile or abductor by his or her looks. Children watch adults approach strangers without any problem all the time. Plus, kids need to approach strangers when lost or in trouble.

So instead of stranger danger, teach what to do and what not to do to stay safe. Safety involves knowing whom to trust rather than whom to avoid. Instead of trying to teach who a stranger is (which doesn't work well), teach your kids who trusted adults are. A trusted adult would be anyone well-known to the child and whom the child feels comfortable and safe around: a parent or close relative, teacher, or well-known parents of a friend. These are the people that you want your child to turn to if in danger and to tell about suspicious situations. Decide together and ask kids over time who their trusted adults are.

After talking about and giving an example for each of the items that follow, quiz your children by acting out situations and then asking them if they should or shouldn't do something to stay safe. Practice by using vehicles and things that abductors might use to lure, as described in the list that follows. First, here is a list of don'ts, or things your kids need to avoid doing. We present them as what to say to kids to help them understand. You won't want to say it all at once; just give little pieces of information and repeat them over time:

1. Don't go near a car or into a car when someone calls you over, even if the person knows you and you know him or her, because the person might want to take you away. Tricks people use to get kids into their cars are asking if you need a ride, offering candy, asking for help or directions (adults shouldn't be asking kids for help), offering money, and using an animal (offering it, looking for it, or showing it). Other tricks are saying that there's an emergency involving your mom or dad, saying that someone sent him or her to pick you up, or saying you're in trouble and need to come with him or her. The only other OK car to go to is a police car (marked, official).

2. Never go anywhere with anyone unless you have my (or our) permission.

3. Don't talk to an adult who comes up and wants to talk unless I'm there, or another trusted adult is there, even if the person gives you compliments or offer goodies or money for helping.

4. Don't go into someone else's home without my permission.

5. For high school kids, discuss who they may take rides from and tell them never to hitchhike.

Now for the dos, or what your kids need to do to stay safe:

1. Tell me if an adult asks you to keep a secret.
2. If a car is following you or comes near you, run the other way and tell me right away.
3. If an adult comes near you and wants to talk to you, tell me right away.
4. Tell me if your plans change for time outside the home.
5. Get permission to leave the house and go to someone else's house.
6. Tell me if you see an adult watching children play or sitting in a car near where kids play.
7. Tell me if someone makes you feel sad, uncomfortable, or scared.

If you or another parent aren't available, that's when children should tell these things to another trusted adult. When you need someone else to pick up your child from school or an event, you should tell the child directly who will be picking him or her up. Decide where and with whom children may play and when they need to be home. Know your child's friends and their parents.

Teaching Self-Defense Against Abduction

Start talking about self-defense against abduction as soon as kids are old enough to understand. Adapt these recommendations according to your child's age. For small kids, say, "All kids need to know what to do if a stranger tries to take them away and now you're big enough to learn!" For teens, say, "Just want to do a safety check with you. Got a few minutes?"

For small children, you'll want to just give them basics of what to do if someone tries to take them. These actions may be natural and reflexive, such as screaming, kicking, biting, and running. As kids get older, they should know more details of how to escape. But do *not* give details about what can happen to abducted children until your children are adolescents—that can cause unnecessary, harmful anxiety and won't help them stay safe.

The most important thing is that kids fight and try to get away and keep trying. Studies show that fighting to get away prevents abductions a majority of the time. All these protective actions go against how children are taught to behave, such as to be quiet and polite to adults. So make sure your kids know that you want them to be very bad to someone who tries to take them away.

These other recommendations are presented as what to say to your child to teach how to get away from an abductor:

- If someone grabs you, yell really loud (like you're trying to get someone's attention, not like screaming in a scary movie or on a roller coaster). Say, "Help, this isn't my dad (or mom)!" or "Help, call the police!" over and over. Make as much noise (pulling cans off a shelf in a store, breaking glass) and attract as much attention as possible.
- Run away if possible, still yelling, even if there's a gun or knife.
- If held, wriggle and twist out of it, or kick, punch, bite, or poke in the eyes.
- Or grab onto an object, such as a signpost, tree, mailbox, or the bike you were riding (an abductor can't get both a bike and a child into a vehicle).
- Never go with the person no matter what he or she says (the person might say that you won't get hurt if you go along quietly, or that your mom or dad will get hurt if you don't go).
- If you are put in the car, jump into the backseat and jump out the door. Or pull on the steering wheel or push on the gas to make the car crash. Pull out the keys and throw them out the window or in the backseat or between the seats. Honk the horn.
- Don't eat or drink anything given to you (because drugs may be added).
- If you are put into a trunk, find a latch to pull on. It might open the trunk or it may have wires inside to pull out. Pull on everything you find.
- If made to go into someone's house, make the lights go on and off at night, make noises, let the water run, or do anything else to attract attention from people outside.

- Tell your kids you'll look for as long as it takes to find them, so they should be telling everyone they can what their name is and that they've been kidnapped.

Practice saying no, yelling, and struggling to get away from you. Make it light and even laugh while you show each other what you'd do to someone who tried to take you. For adolescents and young adults, you can be more detailed about the need to fight hard to escape an abduction attempt.

In 2003, nine-year-old Jeannette Tamayo was abducted when walking home from school. During her captivity, she talked to her abductor and "treated him like a normal human being." She gained his trust, and told him about her plans for her future and the love she had for her family. After lying about needing asthma medication (that she would die without it), her captor released her.

If children are not able to escape abduction, some have been able to gain their captor's trust over time by talking with them and "being nice." This has allowed them to seize opportunities for escape or to engage their captor's sympathies, resulting in release. Perhaps this works by interfering with dehumanizing the victim, which is what murderers often do.

Helping Your Children Recognize and Follow Their Fear Instincts

Humans have the ability to recognize when something happening doesn't "feel right." This has been a good thing, because over the centuries it has enabled us to use the fight-or-flight response to survive. Young children often have difficulty recognizing this feeling—they are very trusting. As children progress through elementary school, they begin to recognize when something isn't right, but often have difficulty knowing what to do. By the time they enter middle school, kids usually recognize that when they feel uncomfortable about something, there are things they can do about it.

Finding the Words

. . . .

With the development of perspective taking, kids around age eight and up can begin to recognize how they might feel in dangerous situations, and you can help them practice by posing hypothetical ones. Say, *Let's talk about recognizing how we feel to help us recognize danger. For instance, how would you feel if a stranger came up to you and started saying how pretty you were and wouldn't leave you alone?* As your children learn to describe feelings of fear or anxiety, you can try to help anchor these feelings to specific physical sensations: *When you feel weird, afraid, or "creeped-out" about what's happening, where does your body feel icky or painful?* Most people feel fear in the stomach, chest, or head (they might say "my stomach hurts when I'm nervous"). You can then tie this sensation to action by saying, *When you feel this way, what kinds of things can you do to help yourself feel better (or protect yourself)?* Make suggestions if they aren't sure (such as going to tell a trusted adult) or have ideas that seem risky.

Talking about recognizing feelings also helps you identify things that worry your kids unnecessarily, so you can reassure them and alleviate anxiety. Praise them for telling you about concerning situations they encounter and working through them.

Evaluating Child Care Safety from Abuse

Many parents find choosing a child care arrangement difficult because of anxiety about their children's safety from abuse or abduction. You may want to ask a center if they do criminal background and registered sex offender checks on all their employees. However, these can be falsely reassuring—nine times out of ten, a person who sexually abuses children will have no record because most cases are not reported.

So you might want to also ask the following questions: how thoroughly they evaluate previous child care employment histories and references, if it's accredited by an organization, if it's licensed, what type of education their employees have, about their security measures, how they discipline children, and how long they've been in business. Also ask if children are always in groups supervised by two adults (in centers), or ensure that family members of a babysitter aren't left alone with children except in case of rare emergencies (for home day care settings).

Ask to talk to other parents who have used a day care facility for a while, particularly if it's a home day care setting. Visit a few times with your children before making your decision, and then visit often without letting the center know you are coming. You should always be allowed to see your child. Reevaluate the situation if you have uneasy feelings.

If your children are old enough, ask them what they do at day care or when a babysitter is watching them. Do they seem happy or unhappy after their day? You could gradually ask about which rooms they spend time in and with whom, if the adults are nice, if there are secrets, and what adults do when children are naughty.

Ask about a center's policy regarding picking children up. Make sure that no one else can pick up your child without your permission and ask to be contacted immediately if someone tries to.

Child Sexual Abuse

Sexual abuse is engaging a child in any sexual activity, and is perpetrated by touching or nontouching offenses or by exploitation (a perpetrator sexually using a youth for personal gain). It harms children in multiple, significant, and long-lasting ways. Many children develop PTSD, anxiety, depression, low self-esteem, and social phobias, and are more likely to be victims of sexual assault and intimate partner violence as adults. It's estimated that one in five girls and one in twenty boys in the United States are victims. It can happen at any age, but seven- to thirteen-year-olds are the most vulnerable.

Sexual abuse is a violent crime that most often happens to children at home or among family friends. Perpetrators are much more likely to be family members, caregivers, or acquaintances than strangers. So it's important to consider how well you know and trust the people you leave your children with, or how well babysitters have been screened or are known by family and friends. Men often seek out single moms to date in order to abuse their children. So it's very important to know a partner for a long time before leaving him alone with your kids. Also be aware that one-third of offenders are under the age of eighteen and may be an older sibling.

Preventing Sexual Abuse

Here are suggestions for teaching children sexual abuse prevention. Have frequent, short discussions with small children because they won't remember well and need reminders. Bringing it up may also help them disclose if something happened to them. First, talk about good touches (hugs, back rubs, pats on the back, stroking hair, kisses on the cheek), bad touches (private areas, hitting, or hurting), and secret touches (someone touches and then tells the child not to tell).

For young children, you might say, "I always want you to tell me about bad touches and secret touches. No one has a right to touch your private parts (covered by your bathing suit) without your permission. If someone touches your private parts or wants you to touch theirs, shout 'No!' or 'I don't want to be touched' and run away and tell me or a trusted adult no matter what the person says." For older children, use proper anatomical terms, such as genitals and breasts.

Out of the measures commonly taught in school programs, saying no or that they don't want to be touched has been shown by research to be the most effective way to prevent recurrent episodes of sexual abuse. Other successful measures in stopping the abuse are demanding to be left alone and crying.

Explain that people they know (even relatives like siblings) might want kids to do things with private parts and then not tell parents or anyone. Explain that abusers might claim that your child will get in big trouble or family members will get hurt if he or she tells. Say that no matter what, telling helps all of you stay safe. Tell teens that molesters may offer drugs or alcohol to increase vulnerability. Make sure they get enough positive, warm attention at home so they won't seek out or accept attention from someone who may want to molest them.

When Kids Go to Someone Else's House

Before letting your children go to someone else's house to play or hang out, meet the parents, preferably in their home, and keep their phone numbers. It's always safest when you know people well and have some kind of relationship with them. Ask what the kids might be doing and who will be watching or supervising them (if parents are leaving and older family members are babysitting, it probably isn't a good idea). Suggest that their child come to your house if you have any indication or feeling of uncertainty—follow your gut. Also, have your child call you if he or she feels uncomfortable for any reason.

Warning Signs That Someone May Be a Predator

Most child sexual abusers know their victim for an extended period of time, such as parents, family members, family friends, and supervisory adults in the child's life. It's also shockingly common for parents to know that someone else is abusing their child and yet not report it.

Here are some of the characteristics of adults that may indicate a risk for sexually abusing children, as shared by www.stopitnow.org and from research on perpetrators of child sexual abuse. Of course, these characteristics can be seen in people who are not sexual abusers, but they indicate suspicion:

- Insists on physical contact such as hugging, holding, kissing, tickling, and wrestling even though the child doesn't want it.

- Seeks emotional support or physical comfort from a child (tries to form an emotional bond).
- Frequently walks in while a child is dressing or into the bathroom when the child is using it.
- Frequently wants to be with the child alone, offering to baby-sit for free or have special outings, or is in frequent electronic contact.
- Gives a child gifts or money.
- Lavishes attention on a child.
- Gives drugs or alcohol to a child.
- Calls attention to sexual images in front of a child, tells dirty jokes, or talks about the child's body development.
- Previous criminal convictions, even of nonsexual offenses.

More obvious is the need to avoid contact with anyone known to have committed a sexual offense against a child. Many communities have databases of registered sex offenders available for review at the police department or on the web. Keep in mind that most sexual predators prefer to choose their victims in neighborhoods other than their own. The websites www.nsopw.gov and www.familywatchdog.us help parents locate registered sex offenders living in their communities.

Warning Signs of Child Sexual Abuse

The following is information adapted from the American Psychological Association, World Health Organization, Stop It Now!, and the American Academy of Pediatrics.

First, it's important to know normal behavior for children related to bodies and sexual interest. Interest in and knowledge of differences in gender anatomy is normal even for small children, who will show and touch their own genitals, and look at other people's. Beginning at about age six, experimentation may occur between kids the same age and same or opposite gender (such as playing doctor), which is not concerning as long as children appear to be having fun if and when you discover the activity. Children eight and older will often know sexual activity terms and have questions. Throughout childhood, masturbation is normal. But interest, knowledge, or activity outside the normal range along with other signs can be worrisome.

Here are warning signs of possible sexual abuse:

- Is afraid of or strongly avoids being with one particular person (especially alone or in a certain place) for no apparent reason.
- Is usually upset or quiet after being with someone.
- Resists removing clothing when it is required, such as bath time and bedtime.
- In adolescents, early pregnancy or running away from home.
- Premature knowledge of sex: knowing sexually explicit terms before age six or so, knowing about adult sexual acts before age eight or so, or portraying adultlike sexual activity before then.
- Uses new names for genitals or breasts.
- Draws or writes about things indicating inappropriate knowledge or frightening sexual themes.
- Hints at a new older friend (child or adult), and may have a secret about that person.
- Overreacts to questions about being touched inappropriately.
- Portrays sexual acts with parents, other children, or stuffed animals (the child may be trying to make what he or she experienced seem normal).
- Regression in behaviors, such as thumb sucking or clinginess.
- Physical signs of genital trauma, but these are unusual because physical force is rarely used: discomfort while walking or sitting; bleeding, bruising, or discharge from vaginal or anal areas; recurrent complaints of pain with urination or bowel movements.
- Other physical signs (that could be due to another problem instead) are bed-wetting and fecal soiling beyond the usual age, and headaches and stomachaches that aren't explainable medically.
- Other more general signs (that could be due to another problem instead) include increasing aggression, sleeping and eating problems, signs of depression and anxiety, self-injury, becoming

more obsessed with privacy, running away from home, and sudden and severe mood swings.

According to research, there are common ways that child sexual abusers try to keep children from telling anyone: giving children gifts or money, giving special rewards or privileges, and saying that they (the perpetrators) will have to go to jail or will get in trouble. Also, offenders have often tried to form an emotional bond and hope that children don't want to lose this affection by telling. Most offenders report that parents knew they were spending time alone with their children and many felt that parents liked them.

What to Do If You Notice Warning Signs

If you notice the physical signs just mentioned, take your child to see a doctor. A sexually transmitted infection in a preadolescent or early adolescent child below the age of being able to consent to sex strongly suggests sexual abuse and requires further investigation. Otherwise, the presence of one or more of the signs tells you that you need to investigate and make sure your child is safe. The more signs that are present, the more concern there is.

If your child tells you of events indicating abuse, it's crucially important that you believe and don't blame him or her. This and saying that you will protect the child from the abuser are the most important elements in the child's recovery. Take away access to the accused but don't confront this person yourself. Notify the police, especially when your child is young because they may be able to make sure that evidence is collected properly. Your child will also need professional counseling. Contact a child advocacy center in your area for support. Be aware that parents who don't report sexual abuse because it involves a family member or partner are at risk of having their child taken away from them, because courts may deem failure to report to be child endangerment.

Some parents may find topics in this chapter disturbing and may be frightened to talk to their kids about them. But addressing dangers like abduction and sexual abuse helps us alleviate fear in the end, knowing that we've acted to keep our children safe. Remember to gradually introduce ideas, talk, and practice scenarios again over time, and normalize learning about safety as part of growing up. Above all, reassure your kids that knowing what to do will help keep them safe and that you'll always take care of and love them.

We hope that you'll find this book's information and tools useful as you help your children grow into emotionally strong adults equipped with shields that will protect them against violence and aggression and defend their freedom to enjoy the good things in life. We recognize that at times the content may have been difficult to read—this is scary stuff. But we believe that informed parents are in the best positions to make meaningful changes within their families and communities that can reduce the frequency of violence and aggression in all our lives. United by power and passion, we can work together to strengthen our nation by protecting youth from becoming victims and perpetrators.

Acknowledgments

There are so many people we want to thank for their contributions to this writing project. Foremost, we are grateful to Chicago Review Press for supporting our goal of helping to reduce violence and aggression in children's lives by taking a chance on us and publishing this book. We also feel greatly indebted to our editor, Lisa Reardon, for her invaluable guidance to shape, focus, and transform our drafts into this much improved final form, and appreciate the contributions of our project editor, Lindsey Schauer, and the book's copyeditor and proofreader. In addition, we sincerely thank our agent, Don Fehr of Trident Media Group, for believing in and facilitating this endeavor.

We also want to express our gratitude to colleagues who reviewed and provided excellent, insightful feedback and advice on portions of our manuscript: Dorothy Wright, PhD, Stephen Wright, PhD, Jennifer Murdock-Bishop, PhD, and Amie Cieminski, PhD. Heartfelt thanks are also due to our dear friend, educator, and editor Marguerite Spencer, MA, who has provided consistent support for our writing projects, and to Sergeant Brad Lenderink of the Denver Police Department's Investigative Support Division/Intelligence Unit. In addition, many psychology graduate students at the University of Northern Colorado helped us gather hundreds of statistics and references used from news and institutional websites and scientific literature. Their assistance made our job significantly easier.

Hundreds of personal stories and clinical cases of violence and aggression have taught us so much about the difficulties and dangers facing children and their parents today. Youth, parents, counselors, nurses, physicians, educators, and other professionals whom we've had the pleasure of working with or who have attended our seminars have generously shared these with us. We also feel very fortunate that extended family members, patients, and counseling clients shared their experiences and thank them all for greatly contributing to our ability to write this book.

Finally, we are especially grateful for the love and support of our young adult children and our parents. Their stories, experiences, and insights into the difficulties of growing up safe and strong today were crucial to our work.

Resources

Bullying

Bystander Revolution
www.bystanderrevolution.org
Source of peer-to-peer advice on bullying backed by experts

Cartoon Network: Stop Bullying—Speak Up Campaign
www.cartoonnetwork.com/promos/stopbullying/index.html
Videos and other antibullying resources

Cyberbullying Research Center
http://cyberbullying.us
Cyberbullying information and resources for parents and adults working with youth

Gay, Lesbian & Straight Education Network
www.glsen.org
Advocacy group for ensuring safe education for all students

National Crime Prevention Council
www.ncpc.org/topics/bullying
Resources for kids, parents, and educators

NoBullying.com
Bullying and cyberbullying information, programs, and resources

PACER's National Bullying Prevention Center
www.pacer.org/bullying
A wide range of resources for kids, teens, parents, and schools, including:

Teens Against Bullying
www.pacerteensagainstbullying.org

Kids Against Bullying
www.pacerkidsagainstbullying.org

Safe Supportive Learning: Training for School Bus Drivers
http://safesupportivelearning.ed.gov/creating-safe-and-respectful
-environment-our-nations-school-buses-training-toolkit
Training toolkit for bus drivers to support safe climates for students
on buses

Sesame Street: Bully Prevention
www.sesamestreet.org/parents/topicsandactivities/topics/bullying
Bullying scenario videos with discussion guides

US Department of Health and Human Services: Stop Bullying
www.stopbullying.gov
Information, advice, and prevention training resources on bullying,
including cyberbullying

Child Abuse and Neglect

American Humane Association
www.americanhumane.org/children
Child abuse and neglect information and prevention programs

Child Welfare Information Gateway
www.childwelfare.gov/topics/preventing/programs
Child abuse and neglect prevention programs

Childhelp
www.childhelp.org
Child abuse help and prevention, intervention, and treatment programs

National Child Abuse Hotline
(1-800) 4-A-CHILD (422-4453)
Counseling for parenting crises and adult survivors of abuse, parenting
help referrals, and how to report child maltreatment

Community Resources to Reduce Youth Violence

4–H Clubs
www.4-h.org
Mentoring and programs to grow confident, capable, and caring kids

Big Brothers Big Sisters of America
www.bbbs.org
Large, successful, national mentoring organization

Blueprints for Healthy Youth Development
www.blueprintsprograms.com
Identifies programs effective at reducing antisocial behaviors and promoting healthy youth development

Boys & Girls Clubs of America
www.bgca.org
Character and life-skill development and support for at-risk youth

Education Development Center (EDC): 3 Bold Steps for School
Community Change
http://3boldsteps.promoteprevent.org

Model for building partnerships between schools and communities to prevent bullying and substance use, and promote mental health and early childhood social-emotional learning

Interagency Working Group on Youth Programs (IWGYP): Program Directory
http://youth.gov/evidence-innovation/program-directory
Searchable directory of evidence-based programs that prevent and/or reduce delinquency or other problem behaviors in youth

MENTOR: The National Mentoring Partnership
www.mentoring.org
Searchable registry of area mentoring programs and tools and support for mentoring organizations

Office of Justice Programs, Office for Victims of Crime
www.ovc.gov/help/index.html
Resources for victims of crimes

Office of Juvenile Justice and Delinquency Prevention's Model Programs Guide
www.ojjdp.gov/mpg
Information about evidence-based juvenile justice and youth prevention, intervention, and reentry programs

STRYVE (Striving to Reduce Youth Violence Everywhere)
http://vetoviolence.cdc.gov/apps/stryve
Community youth violence prevention initiative from the CDC

Dating Violence
Dating Matters: Understanding Teen Dating Violence Prevention
http://vetoviolence.cdc.gov/apps/datingmatters
Free online training for educators and youth leaders to improve teen health

Loveisrespect
www.loveisrespect.org
Organization educating and empowering young people to prevent and
end abusive relationships

Domestic Violence

Loveisrespect
www.loveisrespect.org
Although designed for dating violence, website information and
support may aid domestic violence victims

National Coalition Against Domestic Violence (NCADV)
www.ncadv.org
Education, assistance, and advocacy resource center

National Domestic Violence Hotline
www.thehotline.org
(1-800) 799-SAFE (7233)
TTY: (1-800) 787-3224
Call for anonymous, confidential help

Drug and Alcohol Abuse

National Council on Alcoholism and Drug Dependence (NCADD)
http://ncadd.org
Help for parents, youth, and others concerned about someone's alcohol
or drug dependence

National Crime Prevention Council
www.ncpc.org/topics/drug-abuse
Information on substances of abuse and strategies for prevention of
drug abuse

SAMHSA's National Helpline
www.samhsa.gov/find-help/national-helpline
(1-800) 662-HELP (4357)
TTY: (1-800) 487-4889
Treatment referral and information about substance use and mental health disorders

SAMHSA's National Registry of Evidence-Based Programs and Practices (NREPP)
http://nrepp.samhsa.gov
A searchable registry of evidence-based substance abuse and mental health interventions

Substance Abuse and Mental Health Services Administration (SAMHSA)
https://findtreatment.samhsa.gov
Search engine for behavioral health (substance abuse) treatment centers

Gangs

Gang Resistance Education and Training (G.R.E.A.T.)
www.great-online.org
School-based gang and violence prevention program from the Office of Juvenile Justice and Delinquency Prevention

National Crime Prevention Council
www.ncpc.org/training/training-topics/gang-violence-prevention
Gang violence training, tools, and resources for kids, parents, and community officials

National Gang Center
www.nationalgangcenter.gov/Content/Documents/Parents-Guide-to-Gangs.pdf
Information for parents and communities about gangs and prevention programs from the Office of Juvenile Justice and Delinquency Prevention

Office of Juvenile Justice and Delinquency Prevention Strategic Planning Tool

www.nationalgangcenter.gov/spt

List of programs for community delinquency and gang involvement prevention and intervention

Gay, Lesbian, Bisexual, and Transgender Youth Support

Gay, Lesbian & Straight Education Network

www.glsen.org

Advocacy group for ensuring safe education for all students

The Trevor Project

www.thetrevorproject.org

(1-866) 488-7386

Crisis intervention and suicide prevention for LGBTQ youth

Gun Safety

Moms Demand Action for Gun Sense in America

http://momsdemandaction.org

Nonpartisan grassroots organization that advocates for stronger gun laws and reduction of gun violence

National Crime Prevention Council

www.ncpc.org/topics/safe-firearms-storage

Safe firearm storage information and campaign products

Project Childsafe

www.projectchildsafe.org

Safe gun storage by a shooting sport organization

Media: Entertainment, Internet, and Cell Phone Safety

American Academy of Pediatrics

www.healthychildren.org/english/family-life/media/pages/default.aspx

Advice on various forms of electronic media

Center for Media Literacy
www.medialit.org
Educational tools for teachers and youth leaders

Common Sense Media
www.commonsensemedia.org
Help for making smart family and student media choices, media literacy education resources, and advocacy

Facebook Family Safety Center
www.facebook.com/safety
Internet safety and cyberbullying prevention information

Federal Bureau of Investigations
www.fbi.gov/stats-services/publications/parent-guide
A parent's guide to Internet safety

Media Education Foundation
www.mediaed.org
Documentary films about media, culture, and society for the classroom or home

My Mobile Watchdog
www.mymobilewatchdog.com
Parental control software for smartphones, including tracking

National Crime Prevention Council Cell Phone Safety Guide
www.ncpc.org/topics/internet-safety
Internet safety information and lessons

National Crime Prevention Council
www.ncpc.org/topics/cell-phone-safety-1

NetSmartz411
www.netsmartz411.org
Searchable online resource for answering questions on Internet
safety

Parents Television Council
http://w2.parentstv.org
Education and advocacy for responsible entertainment, includes campaigns

Parents Television Council: Female Sexualization
http://w2.parentstv.org/main/campaigns/fs.aspx
Campaigns fighting female sexualization

TeenSafe
www.teensafe.com
Monitors social media, tracks phones, provides guide to teaching tech
savvy

Mental Health

American Academy of Child and Adolescent Psychiatry
www.aacap.org/AACAP/Families_and_Youth/Facts_for_Families
/Home.aspx
Facts for families, an alphabetized topical list of mental health topics

American Psychological Association Psychology Help Center
www.apa.org/helpcenter/index.aspx
Information and support for psychological and emotional issues

American Psychological Association Society of Clinical Child and
Adolescent Psychology
www.effectivechildtherapy.org
A searchable website providing educational videos about childhood disorders, help finding a therapist, and evidence-based treatment options

American Psychological Association Society of Clinical Psychology
www.div12.org/psychological-treatments
A searchable registry of empirically supported mental health treatments
for adults and children

Mental Health First Aid USA
www.mentalhealthfirstaid.org/cs
Often free in-person training that teaches you how to help people
developing a mental illness or in a crisis

National Association of School Psychologists (NASP)
www.nasponline.org/resources-and-publications/resources/school
-safety-and-crisis/addressing-grief
Tips on helping children deal with grief

National Institute of Mental Health
www.nimh.nih.gov/health/index.shtml
Mental health disorder information and resources

SAMHSA's National Registry of Evidence-based Programs and
Practices (NREPP)
http://nrepp.samhsa.gov
Searchable registry of evidence-based mental health and substance
abuse interventions

Substance Abuse and Mental Health Services Administration
(SAMHSA)
https://findtreatment.samhsa.gov
Search engine for behavioral and mental health treatment centers
SAMHSA's National Helpline
(1-800) 662-HELP (4357)
TTY: (1-800) 487-4889
www.samhsa.gov/find-help/national-helpline
Treatment referral and information about mental and substance use
disorders

Parenting: General Topics and Support

American Academy of Child and Adolescent Psychiatry
www.aacap.org/AACAP/Families_and_Youth/Facts_for_Families
/Home.aspx
Alphabetized topical list of advice on parenting and mental health topics

Boys Town
www.boystown.org/parenting/guides
Topical advice on raising boys and girls and common concerns

Centers for Disease Control and Prevention (CDC)
www.cdc.gov/parents
Articles and videos on parenting by child age and topic

Child Welfare Information Gateway
www.childwelfare.gov/topics/preventing/promoting/parenting/general
Parenting tips, resources, and programs

Safety of Children and Neighborhoods (also see Media)

National Center for Missing & Exploited Children
www.missingkids.com/safety
Information on safety to prevent abduction, including their Kidsmartz
program
www.missingkids.com/Hotline
(1-800) THE-LOST ((1-800) 843-5678)
Also known as the CyberTipline; call to report information about
missing children or suspected child sexual exploitation

National Crime Prevention Council
www.ncpc.org/topics/home-and-neighborhood-safety
Home and neighborhood crime prevention
www.ncpc.org/programs/mcgruff-club
McGruff Club safety and crime prevention program for kids aged
six to ten

www.ncpc.org/topics/hate-crime
Hate crime information and prevention strategies

National Runaway Hotline
www.1800runaway.org
(1-800) RUN-AWAY ((1-800) 786-2929)
Support for youth in crisis

US Government Safety and Crime Prevention for Parents
www.usa.gov/topics/parents-safety.shtml
Wide variety of safety and parenting topics

School Safety

Council of Educational Facilities Planners International
www.nassp.org/knowledge-center/topics-of-interest/school-climatesafety
Safe schools: A best practices guide, from the National Association
of Secondary School Principals website

National Association of School Resource Officers
https://nasro.org/cms/wp-content/uploads/2013/11/NASRO-To
-Protect-and-Educate-nosecurity.pdf
A publication explaining the role of school resource officers

SAMHSA's Safe Schools/Healthy Students Initiative
http://sshs.samhsa.gov
A federal grant-making program designed to prevent violence and
substance abuse among youth, schools, and communities

School Safety and Security Toolkit
www.ncpc.org/resources/files/pdf/school-safety/11964-School%20
Safety%20Toolkit%20final.pdf
A guide for parents, schools, and communities by the National Crime
Prevention Council
www.ncpc.org/programs/be-safe-and-sound-campaign

Be Safe and Sound program for school safety and security by the National Crime Prevention Council

US Secret Service and US Department of Education
www2.ed.gov/admins/lead/safety/threatassessmentguide.pdf
Threat Assessment in Schools: A Guide to Managing Threatening Situations and to Creating Safe School Climates

Self-Esteem in Girls

American Psychological Association
www.apa.org/pi/women/programs/girls
Resources for parents and girls to fight sexualization of girls

Dove Self-Esteem Project
selfesteem.dove.us
Articles and workshops for building female body confidence

Sexual Violence

Dru Sjodin National Sex Offender Public Website
www.nsopw.gov/en
Searchable sex offender database

Rape, Abuse, and Incest National Network (RAINN)
https://rainn.org
The nation's largest anti–sexual assault organization with information, assistance, and activism
National Sexual Assault Hotline
(1-800) 656-HOPE ((1-800) 656-4673)
Confidential support and referral service for survivors of sexual assault

Suicide

National Institute of Mental Health
www.nimh.nih.gov/health/topics/suicide-prevention/index.shtml
Suicide risk factors, statistics, and prevention strategies

National Suicide Prevention Lifeline
www.suicidepreventionlifeline.org
(1-800) 273-TALK ((1-800) 273-8255)
Intervention for people at risk for suicide and gateway for helping reduce the problem

References and Suggested Reading

Here are some of the available resources for readers desiring more information on topics related to youth victimization and perpetration of violence and aggression, as well as child-rearing. We have used many of these books as references for our work. Please see our website, www.warningsignsforparents.com, for additional extensive references from the research literature, national professional organizations, news media, and other sources used to write this book, as well as sources for quotations and links to parenting tools.

Beck, Aaron T. *Prisoners of Hate: The Cognitive Basis of Anger, Hostility, and Violence.* New York: Harper Collins, 1999.

Berdahl, Laurie, and Brian D. Johnson. *7 Skills for Parenting Success.* Greeley, CO: JB Family Publishing, 2009.

Borba, Michele. *Building Moral Intelligence: The Seven Essential Virtues That Teach Kids to Do the Right Thing.* San Francisco: Josey-Bass, 2001.

Cohen-Sandler, Roni, and Michelle Silver. *I'm Not Mad, I Just Hate You!: A New Understanding of Mother-Daughter Conflict.* New York: Viking, 1999.

Coloroso, Barbara. *The Bully, the Bullied, and the Bystander: From Preschool to High School: How Parents and Teachers Can Help Break the Cycle of Violence.* New York: Harper Resource, 2003.

Edgette, Janet Sasson. *Stop Negotiating with Your Teen: Strategies for Parenting Your Angry, Manipulative, Moody, or Depressed Adolescent.* New York: Perigee, 2002.

Garbarino, James. *Lost Boys: Why Our Sons Turn Violent and How We Can Save Them.* New York: Free Press, 1999.

Gottman, John, and Joan DeClaire. *Raising an Emotionally Intelligent Child: The Heart of Parenting.* New York: Simon & Schuster, 1998.

Greene, Ross W. *The Explosive Child: A New Approach for Understanding and Parenting Easily Frustrated, Chronically Inflexible Children.* New York: HarperCollins, 1998.

Grossman, Dave, and Gloria DeGaetano. *Stop Teaching Our Kids to Kill: A Call to Action against TV, Movie & Video Game Violence.* New York: Crown Publishers, 1999.

Hyland, Terry L., and Jerry Davis. *Angry Kids, Frustrated Parents: Practical Ways to Prevent and Reduce Aggression in Your Children.* Boys Town, NE: Boys Town Press, 1999.

Kimmel, Michael. *Guyland: The Perilous World Where Boys Become Men.* New York: HarperCollins, 2009.

Kurcinka, Mary Sheedy. *Raising Your Spirited Child: A Guide for Parents Whose Child Is More Intense, Sensitive, Perceptive, Persistent, and Energetic.* 3rd edition. New York: HarperCollins, 2015.

Lickona, Thomas. *Character Matters: How to Help Our Children Develop Good Judgment, Integrity, and Other Essential Virtues.* New York: Simon & Schuster, 2004.

Safe Havens International Inc., Michael Dorn, Sonayia Shepherd, Steve Satterly, and Chris Dorn. *Staying Alive: How to Act Fast and Survive Deadly Encounters.* Hauppauge, NY: Barron's Educational Series, 2014.

Severe, Sal. *How to Behave So Your Children Will, Too!* New York: Viking, 2000.

Simmons, Rachel. *Odd Girl Out: The Hidden Culture of Aggression in Girls.* New York: Harcourt, 2002.

Simon, George K. *Character Disturbance: The Phenomenon of Our Age.* Little Rock, AR: Parkhurst Brothers, 2011.

Solomon, Andrew. *Far from the Tree: Parents, Children, and the Search for Identity.* New York: Scribner, 2012.

Steinberg, Laurence. *You and Your Adolescent, New and Revised Edition: The Essential Guide for Ages 10–25.* New York: Simon & Schuster, 2011.

Swearer, Susan M., Dorothy L. Espelage, and Scott A. Napolitano. *Bullying Prevention and Intervention: Realistic Strategies for Schools.* New York: Guilford Press, 2009.

Szalavitz, Maia, and Bruce D. Perry. *Born for Love: Why Empathy Is Essential—and Endangered.* New York: William Morrow, 2010.

Walsh, David, and Nat Bennett. *Why Do They Act That Way?: A Survival Guide to the Adolescent Brain for You and Your Teen.* New York: Free Press, 2004.

Index